ESPECIALLY FOR

....

FROM

....

DATE

....

daily wisdom for women

2024
Devotional Collection

BARBOUR
PUBLISHING

WELCOME TO
DAILY WISDOM FOR WOMEN 2024

*"In me you may have peace. In this world you will have trouble.
But take heart! I have overcome the world."*

John 16:33 niv

Jesus makes clear that we should expect trouble in this life—but He also offers us peace in Him, commanding us to "take heart" no matter what challenge we face because He is the ultimate victor over all. This is the theme of encouragement you will find as you read through this 2024 edition of *Daily Wisdom for Women*.

Although "take heart!" may feel like an antiquated phrase, it's filled with power. In these words, Jesus is telling us to be courageous, steadfast in faith and patience. He's reminding us to turn our hearts toward the good, the right, the light, and the just around us. To love others unselfishly and fully. To enrich our hearts with hope and assurance. To root ourselves in the truth that we're already victorious because God has made it so—and will continue to make it so—until Jesus returns to redeem us and make everything whole again.

Four women have authored these 365 inspirational writings, each day's devotion corresponding to a particular day's reading based on Barbour's Read through the Bible in a Year plan found at the back of this book. As you read your way through the wisdom that follows, may God give you the power and desire to *take heart*, knowing your doing so is what will glorify God.

GOD CAN MANAGE IT ALL

So now you see how the Creator swept into being the
spangled heavens, the earth, and all their hosts in six
days. On the seventh day—with the canvas of the cosmos
completed—God paused from His labor and rested.

GENESIS 2:1–2 VOICE*

If God is able to create heaven and earth and everything in between in six days, rest assured He can manage whatever hardships happen in your life. Be it relationship troubles, financial struggles, health challenges, or an overwhelming feeling of fear, you're safe with God. You don't have to start the new year anxious, because the Lord is fully capable to care for you. As a believer, you need not be wrapped up in worry. Instead, you can stand strong in your faith, knowing He's with you always.

So friend, take heart! The one who created something magnificent from a bunch of nothingness is completely invested in you and your life. He loves you without condition. And His wonders are still evident today. This year, press into the Lord when life feels too big. He is willing and able to bring you through to victory!

. . . .

Lord, my mind cannot comprehend all You're able to do. I cannot
even begin to understand Your unlimited capabilities. Yet I am
grateful that Your awesomeness covers my awkwardness. Thank
You for being bigger and better than anyone or anything else.

*A Bible reading plan that corresponds with each day's scripture can be found at the back of the book.

THE JOY OF JESUS

When they saw the star, they were filled with joy! They entered
the house and saw the child with his mother, Mary, and they
bowed down and worshiped him. Then they opened their treasure
chests and gave him gifts of gold, frankincense, and myrrh.

MATTHEW 2:10–11 NLT

It's Jesus who brought true joy to the world. The scriptures tell us joy happened by just seeing the star in the sky and knowing what it signified. The world was ready for His grand entrance, as many had been hoping and waiting for the Messiah to come. And when the wise men saw baby Jesus, they bowed and blessed. They worshipped Him.

Just as Jesus brought joy into the world at His birth, that joy is still here today. As a believer, you can access it through faith. And you can let it be what strengthens you, settling your spirit as you trust the Lord in your circumstances. Be courageous! Let joy be what keeps your heart tender and your mind focused on God's goodness. There are lots of distractions and discouragements designed to bring us down, but you have the power to choose to allow the joy of Jesus to reign in you today and always!

. . . .

Lord, You are why I can be joyous when the circumstances surrounding
my life aren't. You are why I can remove every burden then smile.
Thank You for joy. Now help me grab hold of it every day.

YOU ARE HIS

After his baptism, as Jesus came up out of the water, the heavens were opened and he saw the Spirit of God descending like a dove and settling on him. And a voice from heaven said, "This is my dearly loved Son, who brings me great joy."
MATTHEW 3:16–17 NLT

What an amazing image of parental love. Anytime we see a father or mother show such pride in his or her child, it warms our heart. To see them gush about their kid makes us long for the same. Maybe you grew up with this kind of attention, but many didn't. There was a lack that left deep wounds and feelings of unworthiness.

Let today's verses help you remember that you are God's child too. You've been adopted into His family, and His love for you is unmatched. The Lord chose you to be His and extends blessings and promises because of it. God enthused over Jesus, so make it a certainty in your mind that He does the same over you. Yes, you are His dearly loved daughter who brings great joy. Hold your head high in confidence today.

Lord, thank You that I have a solid place in Your family. Because I am a believer and have chosen to follow You, I'm now called a child of God. I belong. And that's a good feeling for me. I love You, Father!

HE WILL MEET YOU THERE

When I call, give me answers. God, take my side!
Once, in a tight place, you gave me room;
now I'm in trouble again: grace me! hear me!
PSALM 4:1 MSG

The brutal truth is that life is hard. There are seasons where we aren't sure we're going to come through victorious. There are moments so overwhelming we struggle to hold on to hope and peace. There are people so difficult to love, ones who take every bit of patience we can muster. And when we extend our best effort to straighten the crooked path, we're often left to feel defeated and discouraged.

Let's remember God will meet us in those times. We weren't created to handle life alone, trying in our own strength to make right what's gone wrong. Each prayer for help reaches God's ear. Every tear is collected. All details are known. And in His great love for you, your Father is ready and able to work things out for your good and His glory.

So, in your vulnerability, cry out for help and healing. Don't hesitate to ask God to make sense of your situation. Be quick to invite Him into the chaos of your circumstances. As His daughter, you have access to the throne room of grace. And the Lord is there, waiting.

Lord, hear me today and intervene.
I need the kind of help only You can give.

WHEN IT'S TIME TO MOVE

*Without any hesitation, Abram went. He did exactly as
the Eternal One asked him to do. Abram was 75 years
old when he left Haran. He took with him his wife Sarai,
his brother's son Lot, all of their possessions, and all of the
persons they had acquired for their household while in
Haran; and they all set off toward the land of Canaan.*

GENESIS 12:4–5 VOICE

Was Abram just a bold man by nature? Or was he sold-out for God
and full of faith? Regardless, whatever the Lord asked of Abram, he
followed to a tee. He never hesitated in obeying God's request to
pick up his life, collect his belongings, saddle up his family, and go.
His faith emboldened his desire to do as God asked. And without
wavering, he stepped out of his comfort zone and into an adventure.

Let Abram's willingness to do new things encourage you.
Sometimes it's easier to just stay put and hope for the best. But faith
is active, and it's designed to challenge believers to new journeys with
God. What has He put on your heart lately? Do you feel a stirring
to try something unfamiliar? Is God leading you to new places? Be
courageous! Go when God calls you.

* *

*Lord, give me courage and confidence to go where
You lead me. I want to follow without hesitation!*

LOVING THE UNLOVABLE

You have heard that it was said, You shall love your
neighbor and hate your enemy; but I tell you, Love your
enemies and pray for those who persecute you.
MATTHEW 5:43–44 AMPC

Love is something we long for but often struggle to give. The reality is we want others to love us without condition. We don't want our shortcomings exposed or our flaws considered. Instead, we want to be fully loved while having the freedom to be selective about who we will love in turn.

But that's not God's plan! In His economy, we're to love the unlovable. . .*unconditionally*. He wants us to be kind and generous to those who aren't. It's not that we're to be a doormat for others to stomp on, but rather His hands and feet. And regardless of how nasty others were (are) to us, anger and hate are to have no place in our hearts. Ask God to help you see the seemingly unlovable the way He does.

The Lord will help you extend grace and forgiveness. He'll give you the heart to help in appropriate ways. And in His graciousness, God will change your attitude so you can pray for the unlovable, asking God to bring them blessing and healing.

. . . .

Lord, help me not be so quick to judge and expose the sins of others,
especially because You've been so merciful to cover mine. You loved
me when I was unlovable. Give me courage to do the same!

NOTHING IS IMPOSSIBLE

"I will bless her and will surely give you a son by her. I will bless her so that she will be the mother of nations; kings of peoples will come from her." Abraham fell facedown; he laughed and said to himself, "Will a son be born to a man a hundred years old? Will Sarah bear a child at the age of ninety?"

GENESIS 17:16–17 NIV

In a typical order of things, it would make sense to laugh at the idea of an elderly couple bearing children at their age and in their condition. But in that moment, Abraham and Sarah forgot the divine nature of God. They forgot He was the one to create the heavens and the earth. In their humanity, they forgot the beautiful truth that nothing is impossible with God.

What about you? Where have you lost your way, certain you are facing a dead end? What circumstances look too overwhelming to be overturned? Where are you hopeless?

Well, chin up, buttercup! God not only knows every detail of what you're facing, but He is also working everything out for your good and His glory. Take heart! Everything is possible when God is involved. The disease can disappear. Finances can flourish. Relationships can rebound. Your job can jazz you up once again. And fear can fly the coop.

Lord, what a blessing to know all things are possible with You!

YOU ARE A PRIORITY

But You placed the son of man just beneath God and honored him like royalty, crowning him with glory and honor. You ordained him to govern the works of Your hands, to nurture the offspring of Your divine imagination; You placed everything on earth beneath his feet.
PSALM 8:5–6 VOICE

Everything is going to be okay. It may not feel that way right now, but you and your circumstances haven't escaped the gaze of God. This is when your faith needs to be steadfast as you trust for divine intervention. So take heart, for you will find peace and experience comfort. You will be hopeful once again. There will be healing and restoration in the deep places of your heart. For you are His priority today and always.

How can you be so confident God will take care of you? Because He ordained Jesus to nurture *the offspring of His divine imagination.* Jesus has been tasked with *governing the works of God's hand*s. And because you are His divine creation, that means He's responsible for being intricately involved in the details of your life.

So, stand strong in faith as you wait for Him to reveal His handiwork. The Lord is ready to make all things whole again.

Lord, what a privilege to be in the hands of Jesus.
Help me trust in You every day and in every way.

OBEDIENCE IN ALL THINGS

"Do not lay a hand on the boy," he said. "Do not do anything to him. Now I know that you fear God, because you have not withheld from me your son, your only son." Abraham looked up and there in a thicket he saw a ram caught by its horns. He went over and took the ram and sacrificed it as a burnt offering instead of his son.

GENESIS 22:12–13 NIV

Can you imagine what Abraham was thinking as he prepared to obey? God asked him to sacrifice something so very important—something he possibly loved above all else in the world. And because of his great faith, Abraham was resolved to follow God's leading and kill his promised son, no matter what.

The Lord is holy and wants us to live holy lives—lives of obedience in all things. And while we may not always understand why He asks what He does, we don't have to. Our job is to remember that God is good all the time and we can trust His ways. Always.

In the end, Abraham's son Isaac lived. God provided a ram as a sacrifice instead of the boy. But had He not, Abraham was prepared to obey and follow through. His heart was turned toward the Lord. And he knew if God asked this of him, it would be followed by a blessing.

Lord, where You lead, I will follow.
Give me the courage to do so! Always.

ALWAYS AND THROUGH ANYTHING

*For the Eternal will be a shelter for those who know
misery, a refuge during troubling times. Those who know
Your name will rely on You, for You, O Eternal One,
have not abandoned those who search for You.*

PSALM 9:9–10 VOICE

When life hits hard, where do you go for help? Maybe you lean on your husband or kids. Maybe you call your mom, favorite aunt, or best friend. Maybe you find solace in a habit that numbs the pain for a bit. Or maybe you hide away in bed and binge your go-to chick flicks. There are no shortages of worldly options, but none of them bring peace for long.

God has made it clear that He is with you always and through anything. If you will let Him, God will be a shelter for your heart and heal the misery that's weighing you down. He will be a refuge where you can feel protected. And the Lord will be your reliable ally, sticking by you through every storm.

Don't wait another day to run to God. No matter what you're battling, He promises to be in it with you. You aren't alone. So take heart, knowing there is hope.

. . . .

*Lord, it calms my heart to know You are with me. Let me feel
Your sweet presence today. Strengthen me with hopefulness.*

IN THE MESS AND MAYHEM

*And behold, a leper came up to Him and, prostrating himself,
worshiped Him, saying, Lord, if You are willing, You are able
to cleanse me by curing me. And He reached out His hand
and touched him, saying, I am willing; be cleansed by being
cured. And instantly his leprosy was cured and cleansed.*
MATTHEW 8:2–3 AMPC

Be strong knowing your God isn't only able, He is also willing. Too often, we go through life feeling ashamed about who we are. We feel guilt for what we've done. And because we feel so unworthy of God's healing touch, we choose to stay stuck. Maybe we're worried our choices have disqualified us. We fear our current season of sinning has ruined our chances of being rescued. And being so aware of our imperfection makes it difficult to feel we can relate to a perfect God.

With all due respect, stop it. If Jesus took time to touch a leper, nothing will stop Him from touching your flawed life. The Lord never asks us to clean ourselves up before we approach the throne. Instead, He promises to meet us right in the mess and mayhem. There are no prerequisites necessary to encounter the healing touch of God. You are safe with Him.

. . . .

*Lord, what a relief to know You are always approachable.
Thank You for loving me enough to accept me as I am.*

THE WHIPPING WAVES OF LIFE

He replied, "You of little faith, why are you so afraid?"
Then he got up and rebuked the winds and the waves, and it
was completely calm. The men were amazed and asked, "What
kind of man is this? Even the winds and the waves obey him!"
MATTHEW 8:26–27 NIV

If Jesus can calm a storm that rumbles through the sea, He can most certainly calm the storm wreaking havoc on your life. There is nothing you're going through that the Lord cannot manage. There's nothing too tangled or too messy. God can't be confused by our circumstances and unable to determine a solution. He's not wringing His hands with worry. In His perfect timing, God will simply rebuke the chaos, and peace will be the result.

Choose to rest in His comfort today. When the waves of life start whipping, cry out for help before you find yourself in fear like the disciples. Exercise your faith, trusting God will do what only God can do. Be honest about your concerns. Tell Him the reasons why your anxiety is high. Unpack the details surrounding your apprehension. And then watch and be amazed. You're going to be okay. He will ensure it.

Lord, I trust You to calm the whipping waves of life for me.
Embolden my faith so I can confidently wait for You to move.

GOD REMAINS

But the Eternal has not moved; He remains in His holy
temple. He sits squarely on His heavenly throne. He observes
the sons of Adam and daughters of Eve, examining us
within and without, exploring every fiber of our beings.

<small>PSALM 11:4 VOICE</small>

Sometimes we feel distant from God. We feel a disconnect, especially when we really need Him. We decide our prayers are bouncing off the ceiling because nothing is happening. So, we get frustrated. We find ourselves questioning God about why He's ignoring us. We feel rejected and abandoned in our time of need. And we're left deeply disappointed and discouraged.

But here's the honest truth. Your Father *remains in His holy temple.* He hasn't moved. So when you feel cut off, look at where you are. Chances are you're the one who has taken a step in the opposite direction. You turned your back on the Lord. Or you're living in ways He simply cannot bless. If God *remains*, then we need to see if we have.

Talk to your Father today and reconnect. Repent. Worship. Be courageous to open your heart back up as you recommit to righteous living. God promises to never leave you, and He's unable to break a vow.

* * *

Lord, forgive me for turning from You and not owning the distance
it caused. Be with me as I recommit myself to living Your way.

THE DESIRE FOR COMMUNITY

*Help me, O Eternal One, for I can't find anyone who follows You.
The faithful have fallen out of sight. Everyone tells lies through
sweet-talking lips and speaks from a hollow and deceptive heart.*

PSALM 12:1–2 VOICE

You were built for community. You were made to find a group of
family and friends to walk out the adventure of faith together. Even
more, it's vital you do. Why? Because we all need a support system
to navigate the ups and downs of this crazy world. Life is not easy,
relationships are challenging, finances are stressful, and health can be
a roller coaster. So without sweet community, it will be hard to thrive
and flourish in our faith.

If you're struggling to find your people, ask God for help. His
desire is for you to find those who will love you well! This has been
His plan all along. So let your wishes be known and ask for what
you need. Ask for faith-filled friends. Ask for honest, loyal, and
trustworthy confidants. Take heart and be brave! And know that
God is listening when you pray. He wants the very best for you today
and always.

. . . .

*Lord, hear my cry for community. See my desperation
for people to do life with. Please bless me with friends
and family who are like-minded and faith-filled.*

YOU'RE WORTH MORE

"Are not two sparrows sold for a penny? Yet not one of them will fall to the ground outside your Father's care. And even the very hairs of your head are all numbered. So don't be afraid; you are worth more than many sparrows."

MATTHEW 10:29–31 NIV

God sees you. You're known to the Creator. He understands the complexity of your life and recognizes the stress you are facing because of it. God fully grasps your emotional state. He has compassion for your feelings. And He appreciates the mess you find yourself in right now as you try to move forward in faith. Remember, to the Lord, you are worth more than the sparrow He loves.

Let God remove the fear you're facing today. He will do it. So, make space and spend time in prayer, unpacking it all with Him. Whatever is weighing on you, share it. Those places that stir up fear and anxiety, talk about it. Know that you're not alone and that He isn't asking or expecting you to navigate this without Him. Get it fixed in your heart and mind that your Father is crazy about you, even knowing the number of hairs on your head. Because you matter so greatly to God, you need not fear anything.

. . . .

Lord, thank You for seeing my worth even in my imperfection. Let me cling to that beautiful truth when I feel overwhelmed by life.

FROM SELF-FOCUSED TO CHRIST-FOCUSED

"If you don't go all the way with me, through thick and thin,
you don't deserve me. If your first concern is to look after
yourself, you'll never find yourself. But if you forget about
yourself and look to me, you'll find both yourself and me."

MATTHEW 10:38–39 MSG

Let today's scripture be what encourages you to stick through the dark valleys and mountaintop moments with God. We need Him desperately in both places but often don't stay close and lean on Him for help and guidance. Rather, we sometimes set the Lord on the shelf and try to manage life alone. We go into self-preservation mode and turn inward, focused only on ourselves and our abilities. And our relationship with the Lord suffers.

What if we looked to God first? What if we replaced our default button of self-centeredness with one that pointed to being Christ-centered instead? If we're going to be women of faith, then let's be women of faith. Amen? Because when we choose to live for the Lord and trust Him above all else, scripture says we'll find Him. And we'll also find ourselves—our identity as a child of God.

Let's have the courage and compassion to love God more so we'll be able to reap the benefits and blessings that come from doing so.

· ·

Lord, turn my eyes toward You. Help me love You more.

THE DAYS YOU DON'T ALWAYS FEEL STRONG

Who may worship in your sanctuary, LORD? Who may enter your presence on your holy hill? Those who lead blameless lives and do what is right, speaking the truth from sincere hearts.

PSALM 15:1–2 NLT

Choose today to live boldly for the Lord. Let your faith be loud at the right times and strong when needed. Let the promises of God—the ones drizzled throughout His Word—be what keeps you upright in hard times and always expectant for His goodness to break through. Wake each morning with the determination to lead a blameless life so He is glorified. And at every opportunity, be confident to speak the truth with compassion and courage. This is bold living.

Yet there will be days you don't feel strong. There will be times you just want to tuck yourself away and regroup. Be careful this pursuit to live boldly for God doesn't become performance based with unrealistic expectations. There is always God's grace and mercy for our human limits.

Spend times of weakness or shyness with the Lord and let Him restore your boldness. Let Him reignite your passion and purpose. And watch as you find your footing once again.

Lord, what a relief to know You don't expect perfection. Thank You for loving me through the ebbs and flow of my faith. You are simply the best.

THE CONSISTENCY OF GOD

*The wise counsel GOD gives when I'm awake is confirmed
by my sleeping heart. Day and night I'll stick with GOD;
I've got a good thing going and I'm not letting go.*
PSALM 16:7–8 MSG

What a huge blessing to realize God is always the same. The wisdom He gives one day is the same wisdom the next. It's because there's no way to improve it that it remains consistent. It stands flawless. And in a world that changes its mind with the wind, what a comfort to know God never does. We can count on His consistency. We can believe in His unfailing dependability. When you cling to the Lord and follow His will and ways, your foundation may shake but it will never break.

So put that smile back on your face. You have a Father who won't ever let you down. He's trend-proof. He is trustworthy in every way. Who He was with Eve and Sarah and Mary is the same God He is with you, today. God won't change! And that means He'll be the one to steady your heart when you're faced with people or circumstances that are full of unpredictability.

Stick with God and hold on as you navigate your one and only life here. Let Him be your anchor.

*Lord, what a blessing to know You are
always dependable and unchanging.*

GOD'S WILL BE DONE

*The LORD was with Joseph so that he prospered, and he lived
in the house of his Egyptian master. When his master saw
that the LORD was with him and that the LORD gave him
success in everything he did, Joseph found favor in his eyes
and became his attendant. Potiphar put him in charge of his
household, and he entrusted to his care everything he owned.*

GENESIS 39:2–4 NIV

The gold nugget from today's reading is understanding that God's
favor matters. His will will be done. And no matter how badly we
fail or flounder, His plan will come to pass. The truth is that He is
able to elevate the unlikely person as well as bring down the one who
seems like the natural fit. And that should keep us from taking credit
for what happens in our life.

Of course, our obedience matters. Our pursuit of righteous living
matters. Our faith matters. Following God's lead and walking the
path carved out for us matters. But let it be a comfort knowing He
is in control and His plans for us are good. The Lord will give us
success in the right things and at the right time. God will open and
close the right doors. So, let's take a deep and confident breath and
let the Father lead.

Lord, bless me as I follow Your path for my life.

A PRIVATE AUDIENCE

A hostile world! I call to GOD, I cry to God to help me.
From his palace he hears my call; my cry brings me
right into his presence—a private audience!
PSALM 18:6 MSG

Have you ever considered that when you cry out for God's help, it results in a private audience? Let that beautiful truth sink in for a moment or two. With all the people in the world, He is able to be one-on-one with you—His beloved. With the massive number of prayers coming His way at any given time, He can focus His attention fully on you.

The Bible tells us God is omnipresent, which explains why He can be completely present with you and everyone else at the same time. In His supernaturalness, the Lord has a way of making each person feel seen and heard. In other words, you don't have to wait your turn for time with God. It's immediate.

In that moment, right when you need Him, the Lord is wholly with you. God has made a way for you to have a private audience in His presence, anytime you need it. Let that bless you today.

. . . .

Lord, it's a privilege to be Your child. Thank You
for always making me feel like a priority.

SURPRISED

But me he caught—reached all the way from sky to sea; he pulled me out of that ocean of hate, that enemy chaos, the void in which I was drowning. They hit me when I was down, but GOD stuck by me. He stood me up on a wide-open field; I stood there saved—surprised to be loved!
PSALM 18:16–19 MSG

Have you ever been surprised to know you are loved? Or maybe surprised when you saw the way others cared for you? Maybe you were caught off guard by the person who went to bat for you or jumped to your defense. Or maybe you were flabbergasted to hear the ways someone complimented your work or ideas.

As a believer, being loved by God shouldn't be a surprise. He thoughtfully created you and determined every detail with care. He gave His one and only Son to save you. And when you find yourself in a predicament, God is ready and able to come to your rescue. You are His and He deeply loves you.

Today, be confident and assured about your worth in the eyes of the Lord. And be encouraged knowing there's no *ocean of hate* or *enemy chaos* to stop Him from saving you. There's nothing too high or too deep or too wide to keep God from His beloved.

Lord, thank You for loving me with such fervor. Help me believe it!

THE GIFT OF PERSPECTIVE

*Then Joseph said to his brothers, "Come close to me." When
they had done so, he said, "I am your brother Joseph, the one
you sold into Egypt! And now, do not be distressed and do
not be angry with yourselves for selling me here, because
it was to save lives that God sent me ahead of you."*

GENESIS 45:4–5 NIV

Sometimes the sweetest gift we can receive is perspective. The problem
is we often get so focused on seeing the situation from our van-
tage point, we become overwhelmed and discouraged. Because we're
only looking at it one way, we may feel slighted or abandoned or feel
like a victim. But let's be women who look for silver linings because
doing so is a sure way to encourage our heart!

Joseph didn't ruminate on all that went wrong in his life. Instead,
he took a thirty-thousand-foot view and trusted God to decode
the details in due time. Doing so allowed him to see God had been
planning a rescue mission.

Why not take a step back to get a different perspective on the
circumstances of your life? Ask the Lord to reveal what is yours to
know. Let Him bring truth into focus.

*Lord, help me trust that You are
working all things together for good.*

A PRIVILEGE TO LOVE

May the words that come out of my mouth and the
musings of my heart meet with Your gracious approval,
O Eternal, my Rock, O Eternal, my Redeemer.
PSALM 19:14 VOICE

It's a privilege to love the Lord, our God. Once we finally surrender our life and turn our heart toward Him, faith takes over in miraculous ways. We begin to pursue righteous living that benefits us and blesses God. We don't do it perfectly, but we purpose to show compassion to others unselfishly. We try to love them fully, without joy-draining rules and regulations. And we ask God to tame our tongue so we may bring life with our words.

Choose to be the kind of woman who is usable by God. Let the way you live point to Him. Let the things you say bless His name. Be mindful that pleasing the Lord is important—not perfectly, but with purposeful intentions.

And every day, spend time in the Word. Let prayer be a daily conversation. Worship God with your life. And be full of hope and assurance, always encouraged by His promises.

Lord, help me live in ways that bring You glory. I want my days
to spotlight Your goodness so others are emboldened to trust
You in theirs. In every way, may I be a bright spot in Your day.

HOPES AND DREAMS

May He grant the dreams of your heart and see your plans
through to the end. When you win, we will not be silent!
We will shout and raise high our banners in the great name
of our God! May the Eternal say yes to all your requests.

PSALM 20:4–5 VOICE

Whatever it is your heart desires, it matters to God. The things you dream and hope for are important to Him. And while not everything you long for is in your best interest, the Lord gave you a mind for hope and vision. He gave you creativity and ambition. So don't ever discount those crazy, passionate ideas for your life.

Maybe you are thinking of selling your possessions and starting over to simplify your life. Maybe you're considering leaving your high-paying job behind and becoming a missionary in a third world country. Maybe you want to go back to school for a different degree. Maybe you want to homeschool your kids. Maybe you want to retire early. Or maybe you desire a drastic change from how you've always lived your life.

Be courageous! Watch as God opens and closes doors. Spend time in prayer, asking for guidance. Enjoy the process of dreaming. And stay close to God, following His leading on this new adventure!

* * *

Lord, my heart is stirring and I'm becoming restless.
Help me discover what's next for me!

WALKING ABOVE IT ALL

"Yes, come," Jesus said. So Peter went over the side of the boat and walked on the water toward Jesus. But when he saw the strong wind and the waves, he was terrified and began to sink. "Save me, Lord!" he shouted. Jesus immediately reached out and grabbed him. "You have so little faith," Jesus said. "Why did you doubt me?"

MATTHEW 14:29–31 NLT

Chances are we'd all love the opportunity to flex our faith the way Peter did. Who wouldn't want to defy gravity and walk on water, especially when it led to Jesus! But in a moment of humanity, Peter took his eyes off the one who made this feat possible and reality set in. Peter saw what was happening in the natural and it trumped what was happening because of faith.

Can't you relate? We can get knocked to our knees by difficult circumstances yet have peace that makes no sense to the world. It may be a nasty divorce or the loss of a job or another negative pregnancy test. And because we've chosen to place our trust in God's will and timing, we're able to walk on water. But the moment we focus on fear, sadness, or worry, our hope begins to sink.

You can take heart knowing peace is always possible, no matter what you're facing. Let your faith elevate you above the heartache as you walk toward the Savior.

. . . .

Lord, I'm keeping my eyes on You.

WHEN THE IMPOSSIBLE HAPPENS

Then Pharaoh's daughter went down to the Nile to bathe, and
her attendants were walking along the riverbank. She saw
the basket among the reeds and sent her female slave to get it.
She opened it and saw the baby. He was crying, and she felt
sorry for him. "This is one of the Hebrew babies," she said.

EXODUS 2:5–6 NIV

We all love a story where something impossible happens. It's that
hope in us that craves good to come from difficulties. We want to
see the underdog rise from the ashes and prevail. And we cheer with
passion as someone wins, especially when coming from behind. So,
when we read about a slave's baby being rescued by Egyptian royalty,
it catches our attention.

Be encouraged by Moses' story. Let it bolster your faith that
impossible things are always possible when God is in the mix. If it's
His will, you can rest assured it will come to pass, even when the
odds are stacked against you. Nothing can stop what God ordains!

So today, choose to live in that victory mindset. Rather than let
your situation determine your mood, decide that God's good and
perfect plan will pan out. Resolve to trust the outcome either way
because you can trust the playmaker!

Lord, thank You for Your loving and complete control of
my life as Your will always prevails in miraculous ways.

GOD WILL EQUIP YOU

Moses said to the LORD, "Pardon your servant, Lord. I have never been eloquent, neither in the past nor since you have spoken to your servant. I am slow of speech and tongue." The LORD said to him, "Who gave human beings their mouths? Who makes them deaf or mute? Who gives them sight or makes them blind? Is it not I, the LORD? Now go; I will help you speak and will teach you what to say."
EXODUS 4:10–12 NIV

Knowing Moses dealt with insecurities somehow makes us feel better that we do too. This pillar of faith battled his nerves. He felt unqualified. He questioned God's plan. And he was afraid to step out of his comfort zone. Thank You, Lord, for including these details in Your Word!

God purposefully shared Moses' story to encourage us. It's there by design. So, what truths does it speak into your life? How does it increase your faith? How does it bolster your courage to step out and trust God?

The Lord listened to Moses' concerns with compassion and eventually reminded him of His Godship. As He spoke with Moses, He called out unbelief. He revealed a lack of trust. And God reminded him of who He is and what would be done to help Moses walk out the task. Dear one, He will do the same for you!

Lord, thank You for promising to equip me for the call on my life.

EVEN IN THE DARK MOMENTS

Even in the unending shadows of death's darkness, I am not overcome by fear. Because You are with me in those dark moments, near with Your protection and guidance, I am comforted.

PSALM 23:4 VOICE

There is something supernatural about the presence of God. His power is unmatched by anything in the heavens or earth. His presence can calm any nerve, illuminate any darkness, free any captive, strengthen any weakness, reveal anything hidden, and restore anything broken. It's the mightiest force for good the world has ever and will ever know. Even more, He is always available to the believer.

Take heart, for you are not alone! Scripture confirms that God's presence is with us always. That means right now, in your valley of darkness, the Lord is there. He is keeping you close, protecting and guiding you through this season. And when you surrender every fear into His capable hands, you're blessed with peace.

It may seem impossible to imagine, but you can find comfort even in the darkest moments. Next time one comes along, pray. Ask for an awareness of God's presence. Ask for His truth to trump the lies. Then let the Lord's comfort wash over you, knowing you're not alone.

· ·

Lord, what a blessing to know Your presence is a constant in my life. Let that bring me comfort and peace, no matter what.

GOD OWNS IT

The earth and all that's upon it belong to the Eternal.
The world is His, with every living creature on it.
With seas as foundations and rivers as boundaries,
He shaped the continents, fashioned the earth.

PSALM 24:1–2 VOICE

There is comfort in knowing the earth belongs to God. It's His possession. It's in His control. The Lord owns the planet we live on—that and every living creature on it. God determined borders of land and sea. He formed and framed the world. It's His.

Let that news be consoling, especially as we look at the craziness of this place. To truly believe nothing happens unless God allows it brings relief to a weary heart. It reassures us that He sees the chaos and calamity and will use it for our good and His glory. His ownership of the world lets us release a collective exhale together, trusting His perfect plan and textbook timing are in place this very moment. We can be confident in these truths today.

So be brave. Don't let the ups and downs of humanity steal your joy. Follow the path of peace because God is there. And when it all feels overwhelming, remember He's got the whole world in His hands.

Lord, it's a relief to realize You are in charge. Help me cling to that truth when things feel out of control.

ENOUGH FAITH?

*"You don't have enough faith," Jesus told them. "I tell you
the truth, if you had faith even as small as a mustard seed,
you could say to this mountain, 'Move from here to there,'
and it would move. Nothing would be impossible."*

MATTHEW 17:20 NLT

Scripture is clear that we don't need an Everest-sized faith to see God's
goodness. Instead, it tells us even faith the size of a mustard seed has
power. But too often, we're told our faith isn't strong enough. We're
shamed for not believing hard enough. Not only is that unscriptural
and inaccurate, but it's also downright mean to imply to someone
who is hurting.

Only God can judge the heart of another. He's the only one who
can look at someone's faith to determine if it's authentic. So let's let
the Lord handle it.

What should we do? God tells us over and over again to love
those around us. And love isn't judgmental. It's not condescending.
It doesn't keep measurements, nor is it all-knowing. So, let's choose
to be faith-filled women who help others find courage and confidence in God. Let's share the times He's moved mountains in our
own life, giving Him the glory rather than anything we did. Let's
love others well so they see the way to God because of us.

*Lord, help me be a lover and not a judger.
Let me always point others to You!*

FROM SLAVE OWNERS TO GIFT GIVERS

The Israelites did as Moses instructed and asked the Egyptians for articles of silver and gold and for clothing. The Lord had made the Egyptians favorably disposed toward the people, and they gave them what they asked for; so they plundered the Egyptians.

EXODUS 12:35–36 NIV

What an amazing turn of events, all because God moved hearts. He took the slave owners and made them into gift givers. He created in them a generous heart to bless those they had mistreated the day before. His chosen people didn't walk out of slavery empty-handed. They left Egypt with all they asked for and beyond. God is so amazing!

The truth is God owns all things anyway, and for Him to do a little wealth redistribution was a way to remind the Israelites of that fact. He is our provider. And because God did it once, He can do it again.

If you're struggling financially, take heart! The Lord not only sees the challenges facing you, but He also has plans to meet your needs. Your job is to follow God's lead and wait on His timing. If you're pressing into faith, He won't let you fail. And when the time is right, the Lord will bring you exactly what you need. He'll never abandon those who genuinely pursue His help.

. . . .

Lord, give me confidence to know You see me and are working all things for my good and Your glory. Help me trust You!

STAY. WAIT. TRUST.

*I'm sure now I'll see God's goodness in the
exuberant earth. Stay with GOD! Take heart.
Don't quit. I'll say it again: Stay with GOD.*
PSALM 27:13–14 MSG

David had a lot to worry about. He had every reason to be afraid.
He was at war with powerful armies. . .and his enemies were
approaching. He was in a stressful position to say the least. No one
would have blamed David had he panicked and run for his life. Nor
would it have been any surprise had he chosen to run blindly into
battle. It's difficult to stay cool, calm, and collected under pressure.

But David had *the one thing* that grounded him—the one thing
that could keep him focused and clearheaded. And that one thing
was complete trust in the goodness of God. David knew, without
a doubt, that waiting on God was the very best solution for a bad
situation. Why? . . . Because God has everything under control, and
He will always show us the way to go (Deuteronomy 31:8). He will
reveal the very best solution to our problems.

When your world is crumbling. . . No matter how bad things get
. . . Take heart! Stay. Wait. Trust. God has it all in His hands.

*Heavenly Father, sometimes life is hard and scary,
and I can't face it alone. I need You! And so, I will
stay. I will wait. I will trust You, Lord. Amen.*

WIND-BLOWING, WATER-PARTING POWER

Then Moses and the people of Israel sang this song to the LORD:
"I will sing to the LORD, for he has triumphed gloriously;
he has hurled both horse and rider into the sea.
The LORD is my strength and my song; he has given me victory.
This is my God, and I will praise him—
my father's God, and I will exalt him!"

EXODUS 15:1–2 NLT

God had a plan to deliver Israel from the Egyptians. And this song of Moses and the Israelites celebrates His victory. More than just a victory chant, this song celebrates God's awesome power and strength . . .it tells of His ability to control nature in ways that are common, yet also strange. (He made the winds blow and the waters divide.) "But you blew with your breath, and the sea covered them. They sank like lead in the mighty waters" (Exodus 15:10 NLT). The Egyptians were no match against God's power! If God has this kind of power over nature, does *any* enemy stand a chance against Him?

What kind of victories has God given you? Have you experienced healing? Has a broken relationship been mended? Have you overcome a financial hardship? Whatever triumph the heavenly Father has led you through, praise Him! Thank Him for His blessing and His wonder-working power!

Miracle-working God, I praise You for every victory. You are powerful.
You are good. When there appears to be no way, You make a way.

DIFFICULT, BUT POSSIBLE

Jesus said. . . , "Truly, I say to you, only with difficulty will a rich person enter the kingdom of heaven. Again I tell you, it is easier for a camel to go through the eye of a needle than for a rich person to enter the kingdom of God." When the disciples heard this, they were greatly astonished, saying, "Who then can be saved?" But Jesus looked at them and said, "With man this is impossible, but with God all things are possible."
MATTHEW 19:23–26 ESV

When Jesus told His disciples it's easier for a camel to fit through a needle's eye than a rich person to enter heaven, they were amazed. Was Jesus saying rich people couldn't get into heaven? A camel won't fit through the eye of a needle, after all. . .no matter how talented or determined the seamstress.

And so, the disciples asked Jesus, "Who then can be saved?" . . .

Notice that Jesus didn't use the word *impossible* when He referred to the odds of a rich person entering heaven. He merely emphasized the difficulty. It's not easy. . .but it's certainly possible—because our living God offers His saving grace! Thankfully, salvation is not the work of human beings, but it *is* the work of the living God!

"With God all things are possible." Do you believe it?

. . . .

God of grace and possibilities, I am thankful that I don't have to do life alone—I'll always have You!

MORNING JOY

Sing the praises of the Lord, you his faithful people;
praise his holy name. For his anger lasts only a moment,
but his favor lasts a lifetime; weeping may stay for
the night, but rejoicing comes in the morning.

PSALM 30:4–5 NIV

During our hardest trials, the nights are long. When we toss and turn and can't sleep. . . When we can't stop the tears from falling. . . When our minds race with negative thoughts. . . When we don't have the words or even the energy to pray. . . When it seems like our world will never be made right again. . . There is hope because God's Word promises that morning will come! And with the new morning comes hope! And hope will always come because of Jesus.

Although we may not have a smooth and easy road ahead, our loving heavenly Father is beside us every step of the way. And, if we stick close to Him, He offers us His favor. He promises that joy will come again—despite the pain and sorrow we're experiencing in the moment.

So, like the psalmist, offer your sincerest praise. Thank the heavenly Father for His love. Thank Him for His promises. Thank Him for new mornings of rejoicing after long, sleepless nights.

* * *

Lord, thank You for Your favor. You are so good to
me. Although You don't promise me a life free from
hardship and pain, You do promise hope and joy.

HEART-VISION

*As they were leaving Jericho, a huge crowd followed. Suddenly
they came upon two blind men sitting alongside the road.
When they heard it was Jesus passing, they cried out, "Master,
have mercy on us! Mercy, Son of David!" The crowd tried
to hush them up, but they got all the louder, crying, "Master,
have mercy on us! Mercy, Son of David!" . . . They said, "Master,
we want our eyes opened. We want to see!" Deeply moved, Jesus
touched their eyes. They had their sight back that very instant.*

MATTHEW 20:29–31, 33–34 MSG

In this fascinating account from the Gospel of Matthew, two blind
men call out to Jesus—and they're persistent. Repeatedly they say,
"Master! . . . Son of David!" They beg Jesus for healing; and, being
deeply moved, He obliges.

Jesus performed many miracles during His time on earth, and
this particular story of healing might not seem special in comparison,
except that it brings to light this fact: the *blind* men "saw" Jesus;
while the *seeing* men—like the Pharisees, Sadducees, and scribes—
did not. What a contrast between those with faith and those without!
The blind men saw with their hearts what their eyes could not!

How is your "sight"? If it needs correcting, go to the Lord in
prayer. Ask. . .and He will restore your heart-vision!

*Lord, help me to stretch and grow my faith. If my
heart-vision is failing, I trust You to restore it.*

RESCUED

But I trust in you, O Lord; I say, "You are my God."
My times are in your hand; rescue me from the hand of
my enemies and from my persecutors! Make your face
shine on your servant; save me in your steadfast love!

PSALM 31:14–16 ESV

David was going through a challenging time in his life. He was lonely, distressed, sick, weak, hated, and afraid. And if that wasn't enough, he had no support system—no family and friends to walk beside him and show him he was loved and cared for (Psalm 31:9–13). What a sad, depressing, miserable situation. And yet, there's beauty that comes from David's suffering.

Although he didn't trust in people, there's no mistaking that David had unwavering trust in his heavenly Father. He believed with every ounce of his being that God would rescue him. He knew God would save him from his enemies. God would take care of him, no matter how bad things got. And David made sure to express his confidence to the Lord: "But I trust in you, O Lord. . . . Save me in your steadfast love!"

What about you? Are you struggling? Lonely? Afraid? Weak? . . . Look to David's example and take heart. With the Rescuer by your side, you're *never* alone. He is your strength. He is your hope. He is all you'll ever need!

God, I trust You'll bring beauty from the
difficult situations in my life. Rescue me!

WONDERS OF HIS LOVE

Praise be to the LORD, for he showed me the wonders of his love when I was in a city under siege. In my alarm I said, "I am cut off from your sight!" Yet you heard my cry for mercy when I called to you for help.

PSALM 31:21–22 NIV

Dictionary.com defines *wonder* as: "something strange and surprising; a cause of surprise, astonishment, or admiration." Here in Psalm 31, David was praising God because God had shown him the *wonders* of His love. David was awestruck with the unexpected love His heavenly Father had shown to him—especially during challenging times.

It's difficult to comprehend the overwhelming, unchanging, never-ending love of God with our finite human brains. For we're conditioned to expect love with limits. Human love is conditional after all. It's imperfect. It's inconsistent. It fails more often than we'd like to admit. But. . .God's love is big. It's generous. It never changes. It runs so deep that it's hard for us to fathom. God's love is quite astonishing!

When you find yourself disappointed by love—the love of a friend, family member, or fellow churchgoer—think on Psalm 31. Remember, there is one who loves you without limits. Praise Him!

Lord of love, I praise You! Although I can't fully comprehend the depths to which You love me, I am so grateful. When human love fails, remind me to look to You—the one who loves me fully and without limits.

A COMMANDMENT OF THE HEART

One of [the Pharisees], an expert in religious law, tried to trap him with this question: "Teacher, which is the most important commandment in the law of Moses?" Jesus replied, "'You must love the LORD your God with all your heart, all your soul, and all your mind.' This is the first and greatest commandment. A second is equally important: 'Love your neighbor as yourself.'"

MATTHEW 22:35–39 NLT

Jesus didn't mince words when the Pharisees asked Him about the most important commandment. He didn't hesitate before responding. And He didn't tell them He needed to think about it awhile.

Love God.

Love others.

Jesus said these rules were of *equal* importance!

Human nature says, "Seriously, Jesus? Are You kidding me? I understand loving God is super important. . .but loving others can't be *equally* important. People are the worst sometimes!" God is fully good. People? Not so much. God is fully love. People? Not a chance!

While loving people is probably one of the hardest things to do, God places it as a top priority for a reason. If we don't love others, how will we stand apart from the world? How will we reach others with His love? Without love, we won't. When loving others is a struggle, pray. Ask the heavenly Father to pass His supernatural kind of love on to you. He can—and He will!

. . . .

This "loving others" thing is hard for me, Lord. I need Your help please!

NO SPIT-AND-POLISH FAITH

[Jesus said,] "The religion scholars and Pharisees are competent teachers in God's Law. You won't go wrong in following their teachings on Moses. But be careful about following them. They talk a good line, but they don't live it. They don't take it into their hearts and live it out in their behavior. It's all spit-and-polish veneer."

MATTHEW 23:1–3 MSG

A good "spit-and-polish" is all about appearance. While something may look bright and shiny after a quick spot cleaning, any flaws beneath the surface remain. It's nothing even close to a true, deep clean.

The religious scholars and Pharisees were a "spit-and-polish" sort of lot. Though they knew God's law inside and out, they didn't allow it to seep deep into their hearts. They didn't walk the talk—their head knowledge didn't become true heart knowledge. And when God's Word doesn't make it all the way to our hearts, nothing about us changes much—we can't be truly transformed.

Scripture says: "Anyone who belongs to Christ has become a new person. The old life is gone; a new life has begun!" (2 Corinthians 5:17 NLT). You can't have a spit-and-polish kind of faith and experience this new life mentioned in the Bible. Take God's Word to heart today. Let it sink deep. Ask God what He would have you do, and then do it!

. . . .

No spit-and-polish faith for me, Lord. I want a true, life-transforming relationship with You.

THE HOPEFUL WAIT

We wait in hope for the LORD; he is our help and our shield.
In him our hearts rejoice, for we trust in his holy name. May your
unfailing love be with us, LORD, even as we put our hope in you.
PSALM 33:20–22 NIV

So often our waiting times are full of stress and anxiety. We wait and worry. . .we worry and wait. And the waiting is made even more difficult when our minds are overflowing with irritating, anxiety-inducing what-if thoughts like

What if I lose my job?
What if my friend won't forgive me?
What if I end up alone?
What if my future doesn't go as planned?

Waiting doesn't often feel hopeful, does it? . . . Is there even such a thing as "hopeful waiting"? . . . The answer, according to God's Word, is *yes*!

Whatever you're waiting for, God is a constant hope. You can trust Him because He's got everything under control. He sees all. He hears all. He knows all. And if that's not enough to ease your worried mind, He is our shield of protection. . .and His love is unfailing!

So, dear one, rejoice! Receive His protection. Welcome His love. In the most difficult waiting season, He will come to your rescue!

. . . .

Father God, I will take heart as I wait. Thank You
for rescuing me, even in the most difficult seasons
of life. I will put my hope and trust in You alone!

INVITED TO THE PRAISE PARTY

*I will bless the LORD at all times; his praise shall continually
be in my mouth. My soul makes its boast in the LORD;
let the humble hear and be glad. Oh, magnify the LORD
with me, and let us exalt his name together!*

PSALM 34:1–3 ESV

Psalm 34 opens with praise—from David to the Lord. David had been hiding out in Philistine territory. He was being hunted down by King Saul. And David certainly felt threatened and afraid. In his frustration and mounting fear, David could have walked away from God altogether—it wouldn't have been a shock.

But instead, David chose to focus on the goodness of God in the middle of his mess. David said the Lord's praise would "continually" flow from his mouth. What courageous faith! David set a stellar example for us to follow—in good times and bad.

While we can choose to praise alongside David, how much better would it be if we were to invite others to our praise party? "Oh, magnify the LORD with me, and let us exalt his name together!" said David. Welcome others in as you praise the Lord. Help them to continually recognize and then acknowledge God's goodness. Help them to hope in the Lord alongside you!

. . . .

*Lord, You are so, so good! In the middle of my mess,
I will praise You! Help me to invite others into my
praise. I want to shine my light for You always!*

FULLY CONTENTED— HEART, MIND, AND SOUL

Open your mouth and taste, open your eyes and see—how good God is. Blessed are you who run to him. Worship GOD if you want the best; worship opens doors to all his goodness.
PSALM 34:8–9 MSG

When you get a taste of what the world has to offer, it always leaves you hungry for more. More money. More stuff. More "likes" on social media...Just *more*. Add all the "mores" of the world together, and you'll still end up with a negative number when it comes to contentment! Strangely enough, the world *never* satisfies today—and it never will.

But thankfully, there's one thing that always leads to true contentment—it's the never-ending goodness of God. He's *way* better than anything the world has to offer. And He offers blessings too many to count. He freely gives of His love, His kindness, His rescue...and He offers eternal life (if we only say yes to His gift of salvation).

Each of God's many blessings leads to real, lasting contentment. It's true! Just take a taste and see for yourself. You'll never long for a taste of the world again! Your heart, your soul, your mind will be fully satisfied—and that's a promise you can count on!

God, thank You for providing all I need to experience true contentment here on earth. You are so much better than anything the world offers. You are my everything. You're all I need.

WELL DONE!

"The man who had received five bags of gold brought the other five. 'Master,' he said, 'you entrusted me with five bags of gold. See, I have gained five more.' His master replied, 'Well done, good and faithful servant! You have been faithful with a few things; I will put you in charge of many things. Come and share your master's happiness!'"

MATTHEW 25:20–21 NIV

Read the parable of the talents in Matthew 25:14–30. Perhaps you cheered for the servants who doubled their master's money and were rewarded for their wisdom. And no doubt, you cringed a little when you read about the final servant who hid his talent and was cast "into the outer darkness" (Matthew 25:30 ESV) upon his master's return.

We'd certainly rather follow in the footsteps of the faithful servant, yes? . . .

And so, we must make use of the giftedness God gave us— whatever it may be, whether a little or a lot. It looks different for each of us. But we all have something to give, something to share with the world. God has a purpose for our gifts, and we're not to squander them away.

Remember that using our gifts is an act of service to the gift-giver. And whatever we use, He promises to multiply. What a wonderful blessing!

* *

Gift-giver, You are so faithful. Help me to be faithful to You too. I want to use my time, talents, and treasures for You. Show me how.

BEAUTIFUL BEGGAR

"I was hungry and you gave me something to eat, I was thirsty
and you gave me something to drink, I was a stranger and you
invited me in, I needed clothes and you clothed me, I was sick and
you looked after me, I was in prison and you came to visit me. . . .
Whatever you did for one of the least of these. . .you did for me."
MATTHEW 25:35–36, 40 NIV

Brilliant blue jays flitting at the bird feeder. Chubby squirrels playing a game of tag. A graceful deer grazing in a country field. We all ooh and aah at the wonders of God's creation in nature, don't we? We even go out of our way to care for them. . . .

Feed the deer? Check. Overflow the bird feeder? Check. Buy a bag of peanuts for the squirrels? Check.

But. . . Give money or food to a beggar in the streets? . . . *No way am I doing that, God!*

If you find that Judgmental Judy is extinguishing your loving generosity, consider this: Just as we notice the heavenly Creator's exquisite fingerprint in nature, we should just as easily recognize His beauty in the face of a filthy beggar. When we serve others, including the downtrodden, the down-and-out, we serve Christ! It doesn't get any better than that!

. . . .

Creator, help me to recognize You in every part of Your
creation. With Your help, I can love others fully and well.

THE BETTER THING

When Jesus was. . .a guest of Simon the Leper, a woman. . .anointed him with a bottle of very expensive perfume. . . . The disciples. . . were furious. . . . [Jesus] intervened. "Why are you giving this woman a hard time? She has just done something wonderfully significant for me. . . . When she poured this perfume on my body, what she really did was anoint me for burial. You can be sure that . . .what she has just done is going to be remembered and admired."
MATTHEW 26:6–8, 10, 12–13 MSG

The woman mentioned in Matthew 26 anointed Jesus with a jar of very pricey perfume. The disciples immediately criticized her for her actions; but rather than remaining silent or nodding in agreement, Jesus came to her defense.

Where the disciples saw only waste, Jesus saw significance. Beyond the pouring out of the perfume, He saw a beautiful act of love worthy of being remembered. And He said so!

How do you want to be remembered? As a successful career woman? A fabulous cook? A wonderful wife and mother? . . . While nothing is wrong with these things, perhaps the better thing would be to be remembered for our love. When we do everything in love, the Lord will take notice. He'll speak up in our favor!

. . . .

When I am criticized for any action that comes from a place of love, Father, I am so thankful You always have my back.

GLORIOUS HOPE

Your unfailing love, O Lord, is as vast as the heavens;
your faithfulness reaches beyond the clouds. Your righteousness
is like the mighty mountains, your justice like the ocean
depths. You care for people and animals alike, O Lord.

PSALM 36:5–6 NLT

In verses 1 through 4 of Psalm 36, the psalmist doesn't mince words. He doesn't try to soften the truth. He says that the wicked have no fear of God. They can't even see how horrible they really are! They say terrible things. They turn their noses up at anything wise or good. They make evil plans.

But. . .in the lines that follow (verses 5–6), the psalmist's focus shifts to God's unfailing love and justice—all grounds for hope. God is all things good. His righteousness is like the mighty mountains. His justice is as deep as the oceans. There are no limits to His love—and it extends to everyone. He even cares for the animals!

The psalmist didn't wrap up this portion of his writing with the woes of human wickedness. No! Instead of leaving us in despair, he offers glorious hope for our me-first, no-one-else-matters-not-even-God culture. So, take heart! Grab hold of the precious promise Christ offers. Envelop your beautiful heart and soul in the never-ending love of our good, good Father!

God, Your love knows no limits. Just as You care for me,
You care for all creatures. Thank You for Your faithfulness,
righteousness, and justice. I love You, Lord!

STEADFAST

How precious is your steadfast love, O God! The children of mankind take refuge in the shadow of your wings. They feast on the abundance of your house, and you give them drink from the river of your delights. For with you is the fountain of life.

PSALM 36:7–9 ESV

God's love is steadfast—it's constant and unmoving, firmly fixed in place. A steadfast love won't fade. It won't change. It won't fail.

These verses from Psalm 36 celebrate all the blessings Christ-followers receive because of God's steadfast love: gifts of His protection, His provision, His life, His light. . . When we accept Christ into our hearts and make Him Lord of our lives, we enter a relationship with Him. And when we walk closely with Him, our life is like a continual feast where only the best food and drink is offered. Where we're always satisfied. Always safe. Where we never lack a single thing.

If you've accepted Christ as your Lord and Savior, enjoy the feast! If you haven't, take the step toward a fulfilling life today. Pray this prayer right now. . .

. . . .

Heavenly Father, thank You for Your steadfast love. I claim all the blessings a life with You has to offer. Please forgive my sins. Thank You for sending Jesus to take my punishment—the punishment I deserved. I accept Your gift of eternal life. I want to change my life starting right now. I want to walk with You all my days.

CHOOSE TO TRUST

Trust in the LORD and do good. Then you will live safely in the land and prosper. Take delight in the LORD, and he will give you your heart's desires. Commit everything you do to the LORD. Trust him, and he will help you. He will make your innocence radiate like the dawn, and the justice of your cause will shine like the noonday sun.

PSALM 37:3–6 NLT

It's easy to celebrate the successes of those who work hard, are generous, love Jesus, and love their neighbors. But, on the flip side, it's difficult to be happy for, or even accept, that some absolutely awful people have easy lives, with one success after another. You know *those* people. . . . They're rude and disrespectful. They steamroll anyone they think is in their way. They lie, cheat, and steal. And yet—they get the promotion, the big raise, the new house, new car, new boat, and they take the best vacations.

Psalm 37 offers great encouragement when you feel discouraged by the unfairness of life. All these promises are *yours* when you choose to fully trust God: safety, prosperity, your heart's desires, God's help, and justice.

When you compare the fleeting, here-today-gone-tomorrow stuff of the world with the eternal promises of God, only *one* stands out as the very best blessing. Claim His promises today. Choose Him! Trust Him!

. . . .

*Father, I wouldn't trade the promise of
Your blessings for anything. I choose You!*

SEEN

GOD keeps track of the decent folk; what they do won't soon be forgotten. In hard times, they'll hold their heads high; when the shelves are bare, they'll be full.
PSALM 37:18–19 MSG

If you've spent time on any social media platform, you've seen people do some questionable things to get attention. The lengths some people will go for a meaningless, virtual thumbs-up is unbelievable—and quite sad. Yet, if we're not careful, we can get drawn into culture's way of thinking. . .and soon find ourselves longing for the "likes," wanting to be noticed.

Instead, we try our best to follow God's lead. To be kind and speak loving words. To serve others well and be generous. Yet *none* of it's recognized. It feels like doing the right thing is pointless when no one seems to notice. Someone should, at the very least, say thanks! Shouldn't doing the right thing get us recognized in some way?

Take heart! Because although our fellow humans don't seem to notice or care, the heavenly Father does. In fact, He "keeps track" of all the good we're doing. And He will bless us for our kingdom work.

So, hold your head high. The only one who matters sees you! He knows. He cares!

- -

*Lord, I confess I want people to notice all the good
I'm doing. Remind me that I don't need the approval
of humans to have value in the world. I have value
because I'm Yours! Thank You for seeing me!*

HE LIVES!

Mary Magdalene and the other Mary came to keep vigil at the tomb. Suddenly the earth reeled and rocked. . .as God's angel came down from heaven. . .right up to where they were standing. He rolled back the stone and then sat on it. . . . The angel spoke to the women: "There is nothing to fear here. I know you're looking for Jesus. . . . He is not here. He was raised, just as he said."
MATTHEW 28:1–2, 5–6 MSG

Two women grieving the death of Jesus came to visit His tomb. We can assume they intended to sit awhile and cry together. . .perhaps share some memories of their beloved Jesus. But instead of having a quiet time of grieving, they were greeted by a surprise visitor straight from heaven!

God's angel didn't come quietly. He arrived with the force of an earthquake! After rolling back the stone that sealed the tomb, he was quick to tell the women to not be afraid. And then. . .he shared miraculous news: *Jesus is alive!* Imagine the women's fear-turned-to-overwhelming-joy.

We too can experience this same kind of inexplainable hope. . . this deep and lasting joy. Why? . . . Because *He lives!* Our Savior gave His life so we can live forever. He triumphed over sin and death—for eternity!

*No matter what, Lord, I have hope.
I have lasting joy. Because You gave all on
the cross, I get to spend eternity with You!*

GOD'S PLAN

For in You, O Lord, do I hope;
You will answer, O Lord my God.
PSALM 38:15 AMPC

Say the words of this psalm out loud. Do you have this kind of unwavering hope? Do you *really* believe God hears and will answer?

If you've ever put your hope in a human relationship, odds are you were let down at some point. You were disappointed by a broken promise. Or things just didn't go quite like you had planned. The problem is that, just as in our human relationships, we often put our very limited human expectations on God. And then, when He does things His way (and not ours), we feel let down. We're disappointed. *We had a plan, after all, and God didn't stick to it! . . .*

The difference is that humans are imperfect. They're selfish. And they don't always look out for our well-being. But we can trust that when God doesn't do things our way, it's for good reason. Because He knows what's truly best for us. So, we can always hope in His plan. We can wholeheartedly trust that He will answer at the right time. And whatever His plan, it's perfect!

"For I know the plans I have for you," says the LORD.
"They are plans for good. . .to give you a future and a hope."
JEREMIAH 29:11 NLT

God, I'm sorry for all the times I've put my limited human expectations on You. You are my hope, and I trust You!

JESUS, HELP!

*Simon's mother-in-law was in bed with a fever,
and they immediately told Jesus about her. So he went
to her, took her hand and helped her up. The fever left her.*

MARK 1:30–31 NIV

Simon's mother-in-law was sick, and what did the disciples do? . . .
The Bible doesn't describe hours of pacing the floor, worrying and
waiting to see if her condition would improve or decline. The men
didn't stand around discussing the options and possible outcomes. No.
They *immediately* told Jesus! The disciples *knew*—they had complete
faith—that Jesus was the one who could heal her. And He did! Jesus
showed up, grabbed her by the hand, and made her well.

How much stronger would our faith be if we acted like these
disciples? Whatever the situation, what if, instead of worrying ourselves
to death. . .instead of trying to handle it on our own. . .we'd say,
without hesitation, "Jesus, help!" We'd save ourselves a lot of stomach
lining, that's for sure!

Jesus will *always* show up in the middle of our mess. He is
trustworthy. He is reliable. He is powerful. He is love. And so, why
would we ever rely on anyone else?

Call on His name. Don't hesitate! Watch how quickly He shows
up! You'll discover that, with Jesus, you're never alone—you're never
without hope! Praise Him!

. . . .

*Heavenly healer, I'm in the middle of a mess, and I need
Your help! I put all my trust and hope in You today.*

UNCEASING WONDERS

*Many, L*ORD *my God, are the wonders you have done, the things you planned for us. None can compare with you; were I to speak and tell of your deeds, they would be too many to declare.*

PSALM 40:5 NIV

Think about all the amazing people you know and the wonderful impact they've had on the world. Certainly, you know women who have selflessly cared for the sick and dying. You probably know a handful of men and women who have donated thousands of dollars to charity. Perhaps you're acquainted with someone whose invention has improved the world. All are fantastic contributions, for sure. . .but when you think of the wonders of God, can anything really compare?

The honest answer is no—because there is no end to His wonders. Creation. Miracles. Salvation. Blessings. His love. His grace. His glory. His omnipotence. His omniscience. His power. His compassion. It's not even possible to name them all. . .because His wonders continue, even now! But sadly, our human tendency is to ooh and aah over the accomplishments and generosity of men and women, while we often overlook the limitless love and power of our heavenly Father.

Take a moment right now to increase your joy by thinking on the wonders of our God. And then spend time in quiet conversation with the one who loves you most.

God of unceasing wonders, forgive me for all the times I've failed to recognize Your greatness. Nothing compares to You!

GOOD ENOUGH?

[Jesus said,] "Healthy people don't need a doctor—sick people do. I have come to call not those who think they are righteous, but those who know they are sinners."

MARK 2:17 NLT

You've probably never heard someone say, "Don't call the doctor; I'm too sick." When people are sick, that's when they most need the help and expertise of a trained physician.

Just like a doctor cares for sick people, Jesus cares for sinners. In fact, He came specifically *for* sinners. But, if we're being completely honest, we've probably thought that some people aren't quite "good enough" for our Jesus. And over time, we become proud of our Christian status, wearing it like a crown. After all, we're "better than" those terrible sinners, aren't we? We're not *that* bad. And "For shame, for shame..." some people just can't get their act together, can they? . . .

Thieves. Rapists. Murderers. The "worst" kinds of people. Are they good enough for *your* Jesus? No matter the sinner, no matter the sin, when a lost soul repents and turns to Jesus, He says, "Yes!" Luke 15:7 (NLT) says: "There is more joy in heaven over one lost sinner who repents and returns to God than over ninety-nine others who are righteous and haven't strayed away!"

Take this verse from Luke to heart. There's room for *all* people in Christ's flock. Even a sinner like you. Even a sinner like me.

Jesus, thank You for coming to save a sinner like me!

ABUNDANTLY BLESSED

Dignify those who are down on their luck; you'll feel good—that's what GOD does. GOD looks after us all, makes us robust with life.

PSALM 41:1–2 MSG

Have you ever avoided someone in need? We've all passed by someone "down on their luck" at one time or another. We make excuses. . . "I'm too busy." "I don't have extra cash to spare right now." "I have enough problems of my own." The truth is every time we say no to an opportunity to serve another human being, we're also turning down a blessing from God. We're also missing the bigger opportunity to share the love of Jesus through our actions. We, Christ's followers on earth, are to act as His hands and feet to the world. And every time we choose to ignore a need, we miss a chance to change the world with His message of love and hope.

Now imagine a Jesus who ignores us—who's too busy to help, to care, to listen, to love. . . How might our life be different with a Jesus like that? We likely wouldn't want to find out! Life with a loving, selfless Jesus is simply better—it's the *best* life.

Choose the better life. Choose to serve others. Choose Jesus.

God, I am so sorry for looking the other way when I just don't feel like lending a hand. I want to do better. Place new opportunities in my path to serve. I promise to say yes!

LORD OF ALL

A huge storm came up. Waves poured into the boat, threatening to sink it. And Jesus was. . .sleeping! [The disciples] roused him, saying, "Teacher, is it nothing to you that we're going down?" Awake. . . he told the wind to pipe down and said to the sea, "Quiet! Settle down!" The wind ran out of breath; the sea became smooth as glass.

MARK 4:37–39 MSG

Turn on the news and you'll hear about the next disastrous tornado, earthquake, flood, tsunami, ice storm. . . It's one thing to view live camera footage from the safety of your living room, and another thing altogether when you experience the calamity for yourself. It's a scary thing to look wild, uncontrollable nature dead in the eye.

And yet, we have it on good authority that someone has everything under control—and His name is Jesus. In fact, this account from Mark 4 is where it's established that, in addition to the power Jesus holds over humanity, He also holds power over all of nature. In the middle of a raging storm, Jesus' disciples were terrified they'd drown at sea. And with nothing more than a few words from Jesus' lips—"Quiet! Settle down!"—the raging sea became smooth like glass.

When all of life seems out of control, remember Jesus' calming of the storm. He truly is Lord of all.

When life rages with storms beyond my control, show me You are near, Lord. Calm the storms. Ease my troubled soul.

VERY CAPABLE JESUS

Why am I discouraged? Why is my heart so sad?
I will put my hope in God! I will praise him
again—my Savior and my God!
PSALM 42:5–6 NLT

Anger. Sadness. Depression. Anxiety. Hopelessness. Despair. All are running rampant in our world today. Ask anyone, and it seems the consensus is this: life is hard, and it's getting harder by the minute. Fewer people are capable of coping with the stress of it all. They can't do it alone. They need help. They need hope. *They need Jesus.*

God never promised life would be easy (John 16:33). The Christian life doesn't come with a magic wand that protects us from all things horrible or hard. There's no hocus-pocus prayer to eradicate the world's problems. Life is sometimes difficult, and there's no way around it.

But there is hope! . . . Because when we accept Jesus as the Lord of our lives, what we *do* have is a very capable Jesus. When we *can't*, He *can*! The Bible is overflowing with promises of His power, His love, His salvation, His faithfulness. . . Hope in Jesus today. The future looks bright when your gaze is fixed on Him!

. . . .

I am discouraged and depressed. I need Your help coping,
Father. I can't do it on my own. You are big enough to handle
all my problems and the world's problems too. And so, I will
place every worry and fear in Your perfectly capable hands.

CONFUSION TO CONFIDENCE

Why do You sleep, O Lord? Arouse Yourself, cast us not off forever! Why do You hide Your face and forget our affliction and our oppression? For our lives are bowed down to the dust. . . .Come to our help, and deliver us for Your mercy's sake and because of Your steadfast love!

PSALM 44:23–26 AMPC

Have you ever witnessed wonderful Christian people experience unbearable, undeserved pain and suffering? It's confusing and unfair, isn't it? Such was the feeling of the Israelites whose relationship with God was based on His promise that if they followed His instruction, they'd be blessed. But their enemies were winning—and it seemed like God had turned His back and left them defenseless.

According to the psalmist, Israel had done nothing wrong: they had not strayed from God, nor had they been unfaithful to Him (verses 17 and 18). Despite their confusion, the Israelites still believed God would act on their behalf. They knew that, no matter what, His love was unfailing. The Israelites could have turned sour on God. They could have said, "Looks like we're on our own!" But they *knew* God. They trusted Him.

And so should we. When it seems like God is far away, tell Him you need Him. Tell Him you are confident in His protection and love. Then wait for Him to show up. Because He will!

*God, I need You. Though I am confused,
I trust You will show up!*

WHOLLY HIS

"You must faithfully keep all my commands by putting them into practice. . . . Do not bring shame on my holy name. . . . It was I who rescued you. . .that I might be your God. I am the LORD."

LEVITICUS 22:31–33 NLT

Many rules are given in the Old Testament book of Leviticus. And here, in chapter 22, the Lord explains the "why" behind the rules and the importance of following them. God didn't create a willy-nilly rule book to make people miserable. No. His rules were intended to set His people apart. Following His rules is one way Christ-followers stand out from the rest of the world.

As Christians, if we take no notice of God's rules. . .if we are careless with our thoughts, words, and actions. . .if we go about our day-to-day lives living however *we* want to live, we'll make *zero* impact for Christ. We'll blend in with the rest of the world. This is not how God intended for us to live. But when we choose to follow His teaching, we bring positive attention—not shame—to His name. When we choose right living, we honor God. We show He is holy and perfect. And *this* is how we change the world and impact God's eternal kingdom!

* * *

God, I am wholly Yours. I want to show others that You are holy and perfect. I can do that by following Your rules.

THE FOREVER-REIGNING KING

My heart is bursting with a new song; lyrics to my king erupt
like a spring for my king, to my king; my tongue is the
pen of a poet, ready and willing. Better by far are you
than all others, my king; gracious words flow from
your lips; indeed, God has blessed you forever.
PSALM 45:1–2 VOICE

Earthly kings are fallible. The mistakes King Saul made prompted God to tell priest and prophet Samuel to anoint a better man to wear the crown. This better man was David who, although the apple of God's eye, also made mistakes, with one sin (committing adultery with Bathsheba) leading to another (the killing of her husband, Uriah). Later, David's son Solomon, an ardent follower of God at the beginning of his reign, eventually drifted away from the Lord when his marriages to foreign women led him to worshipping their gods.

Although good earthly leaders are hard to come by, we need not lose heart. For we have a King who never missteps. The goodness of Jesus, our eternal King, makes our hearts burst with love and affection. He makes us better women than we'd ever imagined we'd be. The words that drop from His lips are precious, poignant, and powerful. Today, write some lines of praise to the King who implores you to take heart.

. . . .

Lord, my heart bursts with love for You.
Hear my song of praise ring out!

CALM AMID THE STORM

Jesus was quick to comfort them: "Courage! It's me. Don't be afraid." As soon as he climbed into the boat, the wind died down. They were stunned, shaking their heads, wondering what was going on. They didn't understand what he had done at the supper. None of this had yet penetrated their hearts.

MARK 6:50–52 MSG

After feeding and sending home the crowd of five thousand plus, Jesus insisted His disciples row to Bethsaida. He Himself went into the hills, to pray.

As the night fell, Jesus sighted the boat far out in the sea, His followers straining at the oars, struggling against the wind. So Jesus walked toward them. On the water.

When the disciples saw Him, they panicked, thinking He was a ghost. The first words out of Jesus' mouth were "Courage! It's me. Don't be afraid." As He climbed into the boat, the wind calmed. Yet the truth of who Jesus was and what that meant had not yet sunk into His followers' hearts.

The same may be true of today's woman. She may not yet fathom all Jesus is, what His presence in her life truly means. But there's one thing of which she may be certain: when trouble threatens, Jesus will fly to her rescue, streaming words of comfort and encouragement into her ears, giving her calm amid the storm.

Thank You for the calm of Your presence, Jesus, for the encouragement of Your words. May all You are penetrate my heart.

BE OPENED!

*Then, looking up to heaven, He sighed deeply and
said to him, "Ephphatha!" (that is, "Be opened!").
Immediately his ears were opened, his speech difficulty
was removed, and he began to speak clearly.*

MARK 7:34–35 HCSB

The noise of this world and the voices of the people within it can at times be deafening. Jesus knows this. He understands what you're going through. And He offers you a solution: a pathway from this world into the next, from the tumult to the tame, from the chaos to the calm. But the only way you can access that world, His world, His kingdom, is to allow Him to take you away from the crowd. There, in those private moments with Him, He will find a very personal and intimate way to connect with you. Your only task is to obey His command to open yourself to His Word, His touch, His love.

When you do so, when you open yourself up to Jesus' ministrations, all the difficulties plaguing you in this world will fall away from your shoulders. And you will find yourself saying, "Everything he does is wonderful" (Mark 7:37 NLT).

*Lord, I come to You today, out of this world and into Your
presence. I open my entire self—my heart, mind, body, spirit,
and soul—to You, Your Word, Your touch, Your love, Your peace.*

FIX YOUR EYES

[Jesus said,] Don't you see yet? Don't you understand?
You have eyes—why don't you see? You have ears—
why don't you hear? Are you so hard-hearted? . . .
Jesus touched [the blind man's] eyes again; and when
the man looked up, he could see everything clearly.
MARK 8:17, 25 VOICE

Sometimes we just don't get it. We just don't understand that Jesus wants us to be focused and reliant not on our own selves but on Him alone. It's as if we're blind and deaf to how He wants us to live.

When Jesus was walking on the earth in bodily form, His own disciples had trouble processing what He was trying to teach them. Perhaps that was because Jesus' ideas sometimes go against our very human nature.

Yet Jesus would implore us not to be discouraged. After all, we're women of God in training. To grow in Jesus, we must simply look up. "Come, gaze, fix your eyes on what the Eternal can do. . . . 'Be still, be calm, see, and understand'. . . . The Eternal, the Commander of heavenly armies, surrounds us and protects us" (Psalm 46:8, 10–11 VOICE).

. . . .

Lord, help me to get a better focus on You, to keep my eyes on
what You can do, to be still, calm, and understand that You are
surrounding me in the moment, my protector and Creator. Amen.

AT THE CENTER

GOD spoke to Moses and Aaron. He said, "The People of Israel are to set up camp circling the Tent of Meeting and facing it."
NUMBERS 2:1–2 MSG

God doesn't want you living as an outlier, someone existing on the edges of faith. He wants you to have Him as the center of your life, your plans, and your dreams.

In those times when you feel distant from God, take a look around you. What have you made the center of your life? Perhaps it's the almighty dollar. Maybe it's the dreams you have never realized. Maybe your plans have taken precedence over God's. Or perhaps responsibilities of family and work have put some space between you and the Lord to the point where you no longer feel His presence.

Today, take some time to determine the role God is playing—or not playing—in your life. If He's no longer center stage, take heart. God is eager for you to find your way back to Him. What steps may you need to take to recenter your life in Him?

* *

Lord, forgive me for straying from Your presence.
Help me to rearrange my priorities so that You are
once again taking center stage in my life, my plans,
my dreams, and my heart. In Jesus' name I pray, amen.

SHE WHO BELIEVES

*Jesus said, [You say to Me], If You can do anything? [Why,]
all things can be (are possible) to him who believes! At once the
father of the boy gave [an eager, piercing, inarticulate] cry with tears,
and he said, Lord, I believe! [Constantly] help my weakness of faith!*
MARK 9:23–24 AMPC

Sometimes, like this father, you may find that your faith only goes far enough to ask God for help. After that request, you're not sure anything else that needs to be done is possible.

Jesus wants to nip that mindset in the bud! He wants you to know, to remember, to live with the assurance that if you have faith, if you believe Jesus can do anything—even something beyond which you could ever hope or imagine—anything and everything is possible! Why? Because you're a daughter of God, a supernatural being who is all-powerful and all-knowing. You're a sister of Christ, the one whom death and darkness could not overcome. You're a believer led by the Spirit who protects you from danger, calms your chaos, and fills you with hope.

A woman who believes Jesus can do anything, a woman who trusts Him to meet her needs will find not only peace of mind but a plethora of possibilities, an overabundance of opportunities. Be a she who believes!

*Lord, continually remind me that with You
in my life and heart, nothing is impossible!*

YOUR FOREVER LOVE AND GUIDE

We have meditated upon Your loyal love, O God,
within Your holy temple. . . . For so is God, our True God,
forever and ever; He will be our guide till the end.
PSALM 48:9, 14 VOICE

This life we live is full of uncertainty. We can, if we so choose, allow a plethora of what-ifs to fill us with stress and anxiety. *What if I lose my job? What if my country goes to war? What if I can't earn enough money to feed my family? What if I never realize my dreams?*

Whenever you find yourself drowning in a sea of uncertainty, drown out the what-ifs by meditating on God's love. Remember how, no matter what happens, He will be walking with you. He will not let you fall.

When you fail to see a solution, when you cannot find your way out of doubts, remember that not only does God make everything possible (Numbers 4:49), but He will help you find your pathway. He will give you clear direction, holding your hand, leading you step by step. He will never leave nor forsake you but be your guiding light through life and death—and beyond!

Lord, my light, love, and guide, help me to trust You more
and more every day, to meditate upon Your love, to know
that no matter where I land, You will be with me. Amen.

TAKE COURAGE

Many severely censured and reproved him. . .but he kept on shouting out all the more, You Son of David, have pity and mercy on me [now]! And Jesus stopped and said, Call him. And they called the blind man, telling him, Take courage! Get up! He is calling you. And throwing off his outer garment, he leaped up and came to Jesus.

MARK 10:48–50 AMPC

The story of Bartimaeus, a blind beggar who heard Jesus was walking by, is at first heart wrenching. For all this man has to his name is a cloak and perhaps some coins he earned from begging. But suddenly a break comes his way when he hears Jesus is walking by.

Through the darkness of his world, he shouts for Jesus to have mercy upon him. Then, when others tell him to stop shouting, he yells all the louder. Finally, Jesus tells His disciples to call Bartimaeus over. They obey by telling the beggar, "Take courage and get over here. Jesus is calling you." In response, Bartimaeus throws away his entire world and runs to Jesus.

When Jesus asks what he wants, Bartimaeus asks for his sight. And Jesus grants his plea and prayer.

When all seems against you, when darkness surrounds you, when people try to discourage you, throw all aside and take up your courage, calling out for Jesus all the more. He will respond. He will answer your prayer.

Jesus, may nothing discourage me from reaching out to You!

MOTIVE AND MIRACLES

Have faith in God [constantly]. Truly I tell you, whoever says to this mountain, Be lifted up and thrown into the sea! and does not doubt at all in his heart but believes that what he says will take place, it will be done for him. For this reason I am telling you, whatever you ask for in prayer, believe (trust and be confident) that it is granted to you, and you will [get it].

<small>MARK 11:22–24 AMPC</small>

In today's verses, Jesus makes an amazing statement! He tells His followers that as long as they have faith in God and His abilities, as long as they believe that what they ask will take place, whatever they request of God will be done for them! All they have to do is pray in faith and voilà! God will answer just as they ask.

Yet there is a piece missing from this prayer formula. And that is the idea that although God does love to give His people good things when they ask for them (Matthew 7:11), they will only receive their requests if they are rightly motivated and aligned with God's will (James 4:3; 1 John 5:14). In other words, the miracle of prayer exists if your motives are pure.

. . . .

*Lord, thank You for the miracle of faith and prayer.
I pray You would align my will and desires
with Your own. In Jesus' name, amen.*

HEARTFELT THANKFULNESS

*"Set out a sacrifice I can accept: your thankfulness. Be true to
your word to the Most High. When you are in trouble, call for
Me. I will come and rescue you, and you will honor Me."*

Psalm 50:14–15 voice

There is nothing God needs from you. All of this world—the hills,
mountains, forests, animals, and birds—is already His. He needs no
sacrifice of a bull, lamb, or goat. For He does not hunger. All God
wants from you is your heart.

What God doesn't want are empty promises. He doesn't want you
to pray the Lord's Prayer out of habit, to the point where your brain
and heart are not cognizant of the words you are saying, mentally
or aloud. Yet God could use a thank-you. And for you to be true to
whatever you say to Him.

Today, look deep within your inmost being. Consider the words
you're praying to the Lord. Speak to Him with your whole heart, letting
Him know how much you appreciate all He has done for you, from
the rising of the sun to the birth of your child to the food on your
table. Simply thank Him for all the big and little blessings in your life.

Then rest in the knowledge that God will not only accept your
thanks but will answer your call, will rescue you whenever trouble
comes your way.

Hear, Lord, my heartfelt prayer of thanksgiving to You. . . .

FOLLOW THE LIGHT

*Whether it was a couple of days or just a month or even longer,
however long the cloud covered the tent, the Israelites stayed put;
but when it lifted, off they went again. So it was that the Israelites
obeyed God's command. When the Eternal One indicated that they
stop, they stopped; when He directed them to move, they moved.
They served Him exactly as God commanded them through Moses.*

NUMBERS 9:22–23 VOICE

Back in the day, the Israelites were blessed with the actual visible
presence of the Lord. When the cloud of God hovered over the tent
of meeting, the Israelites stayed where they were. When it lifted, they
pulled up stakes and moved on. They faithfully followed their Lord,
stopping when He stopped, moving when He moved.

We too should always be ready to stay put or move on as God
commands. How are we to know what to do and when? Simply follow
Jesus, the one who told us: "I am the light that shines through the
cosmos; if you walk with Me, you will thrive in the nourishing light
that gives life and will not know darkness" (John 8:12 VOICE).

Take heart. You have not been left to fend for yourself, to walk
alone, directionless. Simply follow the Light of Life and you will
find your way.

. . . .

*Lord of life and light, please show me the way. Tell me
when to move on, when to stay put, each passing day.*

DON'T LOSE HEART

*You will hear of wars, or that war is coming, but don't lose heart.
These things will have to happen, although it won't mean the
end yet. Tribe will rise up against tribe, nation against nation,
and there will be earthquakes in place after place and famines.*
MARK 13:7–8 VOICE

It can be hard to stay calm these days. Between shutdowns and
shootouts, pandemics and politics, inflation and insurrections, climate
change and conflict, we may be finding it difficult to keep our chins
and our courage up.

Thankfully, Jesus has some words we can sink our mind into. Over
two thousand years ago, Jesus told His followers that although we
may find ourselves stressed out, heartbroken, and fearful, we need not
lose our heads. Instead, we're to take heart. For no matter what we're
going through, Jesus promises to walk with us through it. Although
the world appears as if it is coming to an end, Jesus reminds us not
to lose heart. Instead, we're to pluck up and continue to proclaim His
good news to whoever we meet.

Today, rest in Jesus' presence. Remember that no matter what's
going on around you, "if you're faithful until the end, you will be
rescued" (Mark 13:13 VOICE).

*Thank You, Jesus, for reminding me that I need not lose my
courage or wallow in despair during these days. For no matter
what happens or when, You will always be by my side. Amen.*

CORRECTIVE VISION

We are not able to go up against the people [of Canaan],
for they are stronger than we are. . . . There we saw the Nephilim
[or giants], the sons of Anak, who come from the giants; and we
were in our own sight as grasshoppers, and so we were in their sight.
NUMBERS 13:31, 33 AMPC

Moses sent twelve spies into the Promised Land. Ten came back saying that even though the land did indeed flow with milk and honey, just as God promised, the Israelites could never overcome the giants that lived there.

Only two of the spies, Joshua and Caleb, had the right perspective. Because God was on their side, they knew they were "well able to conquer it" (Numbers 13:30 AMPC). Unfortunately, the myopic ten got all the other Israelites riled up, telling them they were as grasshoppers next to these giants. So God proclaimed the Israelites would wander for forty years in the wilderness, until they all died off. None but Joshua and Caleb would live to see the Promised Land.

What's your vision like these days? Are you allowing the problems of this world to stress you out, to overwhelm you? If so, it may be time to correct your vision of God in relation to the obstacles before you.

Lord, help me to see that You're greater and mightier than
whatever challenges stand before me. With You in my
life, I'm well able to conquer any giants in my path!

SELF-FULFILLING PROPHECY

"As I live, I will make sure that what you're complaining about really does happen—you'll die out here in the desert. . . . Not a single one of that group will have the privilege of entering the land I made an oath to give to you. Only Caleb (Jephunneh's son) and Joshua (Nun's son) will enter."

NUMBERS 14:28–30 VOICE

God's children have two choices: they can either take heart because they believe in God, His plans, and His promises or they can complain because they do not trust Him. At all.

Even though the Israelites had witnessed many of God's seemingly impossible miracles, they still had no confidence in Him (Numbers 14:11). And because of their mistrust, they refused to enter the land He had promised them. Not only that, but they were so frightened and angry that they made a move to stone Joshua and Caleb, the only two spies faithful to God and the vision for His people.

So God swept into the tent of meeting, ready to kill each naysayer. After Moses talked Him out of it, God came up with the idea of allowing all the Israelites' complaints to become their reality!

Don't allow your grumblings to become your self-fulfilling prophecy. Instead, put all your faith and confidence in God.

You, Lord, do as You promise. It's You alone I will trust. No matter what comes my way, I will praise Your name for You promise me nothing but good!

SIGNALS OF REMEMBRANCE

"When you look at these tassels you'll remember and keep all the commandments of GOD, and not get distracted by everything you feel or see that seduces you into infidelities. The tassels will signal remembrance and observance of all my commandments, to live a holy life to GOD. I am your GOD who rescued you from the land of Egypt to be your personal God. Yes, I am GOD, your God."
NUMBERS 15:39–40 MSG

Where has your focus been lately? Perhaps it's the electric car that has turned your head. Maybe it's that job that will require you to spend less time with the family but will certainly earn you more prestige and money.

If your focus is more on the world than the Word, it may be time for some readjustment. But take heart: God will help you find a way to keep your eyes fixed on Him so that you will not be tempted to follow your own heart and eyes and, in so doing, step out of His will and way.

. . . .

Help me, Lord, to every day find a way to keep You and Your commandments fresh in my mind and heart. For my aim is to continue to walk with You and not away from You. Amen.

A VALIANT SUPPORTER

The truth is, these strangers are rallying against me; cold-blooded men seek to slay me; they have no respect for You. [pause] But see now! God comes to rescue me; the Lord is my valiant supporter. . . . God has pulled me out from every one of the troubles that encompass me, and I have seen what it means to stand over my enemies in triumph.

PSALM 54:3–4, 7 VOICE

The chief priests turned Jesus over to the Roman governor Pilate. When Pilate asked Jesus if He was the king of the Jews, Jesus simply responded with "You have said so" (Mark 15:2 VOICE). "The chief priests went on to accuse Jesus of many things, but Jesus simply stood quietly" (Mark 15:3 VOICE).

Jesus remained silent as the day went on. While being whipped, forced to wear a purple robe, crowned with a circlet of thorns, mocked, beat with a reed, spat on, stripped, re-dressed, and nailed to the cross, Jesus said nothing.

How did He remain so strong and stoic? Jesus knew our Father, our valiant supporter, would rescue Him. He knew God would pull Him out of trouble by raising Him from the dead, giving Him triumph over His enemies!

God is your valiant supporter. Remember that no matter how bad things may seem, in God you will always triumph!

Thank You, Lord, for always coming to my rescue, for being my valiant supporter!

TAKING COURAGE

Joseph, he of Arimathea, noble and honorable in rank
and a respected member of the council (Sanhedrin)...
daring the consequences, took courage and ventured
to go to Pilate and asked for the body of Jesus.

MARK 15:43 AMPC

How wonderful that Joseph of Arimathea asked for and obtained Jesus' body, then helped prepare it for burial and put Him in his own tomb!

Joseph is mentioned in only two other places in the Bible. In Matthew 27:57, he's described as a disciple of Jesus, and in Luke 23:50–51 (VOICE) he's called a "good and fair man" who had "objected to the plans and actions of the council" and was "seeking the kingdom of God."

We might wonder what finally gave Joseph the courage to come out and say he was a follower of Jesus. Perhaps he went to God, on his knees in prayer, and asked for his Lord's corpse. Perhaps he dared the consequences because he'd found, trusted, and followed the words of Psalm 55:22 (AMPC): "Cast your burden on the Lord [releasing the weight of it] and He will sustain you; He will never allow the [consistently] righteous to be moved (made to slip, fall, or fail)."

May you do the same.

. . . .

Today, Lord, I cast my load of problems, challenges, and sorrows
upon You, knowing that as I do so, You will sustain me and
help me to take courage no matter what comes against me.

LET GO AND LET GOD

When struck by fear, I let go, depending securely upon
You alone. In God—whose word I praise—in God
I place my trust. I shall not let fear come in.
PSALM 56:3–4 VOICE

Jesus had told His followers—men and women alike—that He would rise from the dead. Yet it seems their finite minds had trouble keeping His words in their heart. For when the women went to the tomb to anoint Jesus' body, saw the stone rolled away from the entrance, and then saw an angel sitting inside the tomb, they were startled to the point that the "man in white" (Mark 16:6 VOICE) told them not to be afraid. He reminded them Jesus had already risen. He instructed them to tell Peter and the rest of the disciples that Jesus had gone before them into Galilee.

Even then the women, as they turned from the tomb and hurried off to spread the good news to others, were trembling and struck with terror. Yet it was just as Jesus and the man in white had said it would be.

Psalm 56:3–4 holds good advice for all of God's followers. When you are struck by fear, depend on and trust in God, relying on His Word. With truth as your guide and guard, your fear will fade, and courage will cover you!

- -

Lord, when I am struck by fear, I will depend
on and trust You and Your Word alone.

STILLING DOUBTS

When Zechariah saw him, he was startled and overcome
with fear. But the angel said to him: Do not be afraid,
Zechariah, because your prayer has been heard. Your wife
Elizabeth will bear you a son. . . . There will be joy and
delight for you, and many will rejoice at his birth.

LUKE 1:12–14 HCSB

Zechariah and Elizabeth were an elderly, childless couple "righteous in God's eyes, careful to obey all of the Lord's commandments and regulations" (Luke 1:6 NLT). Like any faithful followers, they had over the years sent many petitions up to God.

As a priest with regular duties in the temple, Zechariah was going through his usual routine of burning incense in the sanctuary when the angel Gabriel appeared before him. This unusual visitor not only startled Zechariah but shook him with fear. But, as angels usually do, Gabriel began reassuring him, telling him not to be afraid. His prayers had been heard and would soon be answered.

Zechariah's response of disbelief prompted Gabriel to tell him, "You will become silent and unable to speak until the day these things take place, because you did not believe my words, which will be fulfilled in their proper time" (Luke 1:20 HCSB). A muted Zechariah would prevent any additional doubts to come from his lips.

Would that an angel would still any thoughts of doubt that crop up in our own minds!

Lord, mute my doubts. Help me believe the seemingly impossible!

BLESSED IN BELIEVING

When Elizabeth heard Mary's greeting, the baby leaped in her womb, and Elizabeth was filled with and controlled by the Holy Spirit. And she cried out with a loud cry. . . . And blessed (happy, to be envied) is she who believed that there would be a fulfillment of the things that were spoken to her from the Lord.

LUKE 1:41–42, 45 AMPC

Both Zechariah and Mary were alarmed and afraid when the angel Gabriel came to call. So the heavenly emissary reassured both to not be afraid. But while the elderly, childless, temple priest Zechariah responded to Gabriel's words with disbelief, Mary—a young virgin girl—asked for no signs of its truth. She simply asked how it would be accomplished. After Gabriel explained the details, Mary responded simply, "Here I am, the Lord's humble servant. As you have said, let it be done to me" (Luke 1:38 VOICE).

When we take God and His angels at their word, bowing to the belief that the impossible will become our reality, when we do not fear the plans and procedures God puts in place, we are overwhelmed with blessings and joy and, like Mary, cannot help but praise the Lord!

So take heart, woman of God. Fear nothing. Just believe and you too will be blessed.

. . . .

I am Your humble servant, Lord. May everything You have promised me, everything You have spoken about me come true! To Your praise and glory! Amen.

HEART TO HEART

Because of and through the heart of tender mercy and loving-kindness of our God, a Light from on high will dawn upon us and visit [us] to shine upon and give light to those who sit in darkness and in the shadow of death, to direct and guide our feet in a straight line into the way of peace.

LUKE 1:78–79 AMPC

It was God's love for you, His tender heart full of mercy and kindness, that prompted Him to send His only Son to earth to shine His light upon those who sit in darkness.

That can be a lot for a woman of God to take in. The fact that such a sacrifice would be made for her. That a love so great would move God to move in this world, to break up the darkness, to direct her feet so that she could and would walk the path of peace.

Everything comes down to God's love and light. To the idea, the fact, the truth that His heart seeks and speaks to your own. Today, meditate on God's love, on His desire to put your fears to rest. Allow His heart to open and enter your own.

. . . .

I come to You today, Lord, so that Your heart may speak to my own. Put my fears and doubts to rest as I meditate and open myself to Your everlasting love.

IN TOUCH

[Simeon] was a just and pious man, anticipating the liberation of Israel from her troubles. He was a man in touch with the Holy Spirit. The Holy Spirit had revealed to Simeon that he would not die before he had seen the Lord's Anointed One. The Spirit had led him to the temple that day, and there he saw the child Jesus.

LUKE 2:25–27 VOICE

It's one thing to be in touch with the Holy Spirit. It's another to be so in tune with Him that your eyes are open to His revelation *and* you actually follow where He leads. That's what Simeon did.

Simeon opened himself up to God's Spirit, witnessing His revelation, then going where it led him—to the temple. There Simeon met the one who would free Israel. He saw Mary and Joseph bringing Jesus the deliverer and took Him up in his arms. Then he began praising God for keeping His promise, for allowing him to witness His salvation, this child that would become the light to Gentiles and the glory of His people.

When you elected to believe Jesus was the Son of God, you too were gifted with the Spirit. In Him you can take heart and realize God's promises if you choose to connect to that Spirit and follow His leading.

. . . .

Spirit of the Lord, my eyes and ears are open to Your leading. What would You have me do and say, where would You have me go today?

DESCRIPTORS

*You have been to me a defense (a fortress and a high tower)
and a refuge in the day of my distress. Unto You, O my Strength,
I will sing praises; for God is my Defense, my Fortress, and High
Tower, the God Who shows me mercy and steadfast love.*

Psalm 59:16–17 ampc

When doubts begin to assail you, when you feel weak, powerless, hopeless, vulnerable, it's time to change up your thinking, to get yourself back on God's page. To do so, turn to the Psalms.

Psalm 59 is a record of David's thoughts when King Saul sent men to watch David's house, hoping and looking for an opportunity to kill him. The psalm begins with David's plea to God for deliverance. He then explains the situation he's in to God, letting Him know all the harrowing details. He even offers God a few suggestions about how to handle things. But the real value is David's praise for what God is going to do, as well as his descriptors of who God is to him.

Just as God was to David, He is to you. When fear strikes, when trouble abounds, go to God. Tell Him what's happening. Relate to Him all the gory details so you can get them off your chest. Then praise Him, calling Him your Strength, Defense, Fortress, High Tower, the one who is merciful and loving. And your heart will rise up to meet His!

. . . .

My Strength, Fortress, High Tower, come to my rescue!

A HEART CHANGED

Bear fruits that are deserving and consistent with [your]
repentance [that is, conduct worthy of a heart changed,
a heart abhorring sin]. . . . And the multitudes asked him,
Then what shall we do? And he replied to them, He who
has two tunics (undergarments), let him share with him who
has none; and he who has food, let him do it the same way.

Luke 3:8, 10–11 ampc

To take heart in Jesus we must have a change of heart. That means
we must make a way for Jesus' message and words to enter into our
inmost being. We must pull down wrong thinking and erroneous
ways and bring them in line with what Christ would have us do. We
must examine our own individual souls and remove anything that
might hinder us from going where He would have us go.

A changed heart for Christ means sharing ourselves and our goods
with others. It means not trying to find a way to rule but to serve.
It means being honest in our endeavors and our speech. It means
pouring out love, not spewing hate; pursuing peace, not creating chaos.

How wonderful this world would be if we opened our arms
instead of closing our fists.

. . . .

Lord, show me where my heart needs to be changed. Lead me
to serve, speak truth, radiate love, and promote peace.

DELIVERED BY THE SPIRIT

The Spirit of the Lord [is] upon Me, because He has anointed Me [the Anointed One, the Messiah] to preach the good news (the Gospel) to the poor; He has sent Me to announce release to the captives and recovery of sight to the blind, to send forth as delivered those who are oppressed [who are downtrodden, bruised, crushed, and broken down by calamity].

LUKE 4:18 AMPC

It was the Spirit that Jesus was full of and controlled by. It was the Spirit that led Jesus into the wilderness where He conquered the lies of the devil with the truth from the Word of God.

From that battle, Jesus teaches His followers that bread alone won't sustain us but the Word of God will; that it is God alone we are to worship; that God has sent angels to guard, guide, and watch over us.

Jesus came to preach the good news, free captives, give sight to the blind, and deliver those whose hearts and spirits may be crushed, beaten, and broken down by troubles.

You have the Spirit within you to lead you. You have the Word to fend off deceitful thoughts. You have a God who cares for you more than you could ever know or imagine. You are not alone. You are not deserted. God your Savior goes with you.

*In You, Lord, I find the truth, light,
love, and the way. Lead on, Lord.*

STEAL AWAY

Jesus repeatedly left the crowds, though, stealing away into the wilderness to pray. . . . Hear me, O God, when I cry; listen to my prayer. You are the One I will call when pushed to the edge, when my heart is faint. Shoulder me to the rock above me.

LUKE 5:16; PSALM 61:1–2 VOICE

There will be times in our lives when we experience trouble, challenges, and seemingly insurmountable obstacles. But we can take heart knowing that while walking this earth, Jesus went through tough times as well. And He has shown us what to do when our hearts are overwhelmed.

When you feel as if you can't go on, when you're too tired to lift your head, when your thoughts are too tangled by worry and fear to make any sense, when you feel no one is on your side, do as Jesus did. Steal away. Remove yourself from the crowds, even those you love, and find a private place to pray.

Ask God to listen to your prayer, to hear your words. Cry to Him for help. Tell Him exactly what you need. Expect God to answer, to provide you with a solution in His time. Ask Him to lead you to the towering rock of safety that is Him.

. . . .

Lord, I come to You alone. Hear my prayer.
Lead me to Your rock of refuge. Hide me in the
shelter of Your presence. In Jesus' name I pray, amen.

CORE STRENGTH

*My salvation and my significance depend ultimately on God;
the core of my strength, my shelter, is in the True God. Have
faith in Him in all circumstances, dear people. Open up your
heart to Him; the True God shelters us in His arms.*

PSALM 62:7–8 VOICE

If we want help from God, we have to open our hearts to Him, to allow ourselves to be vulnerable when in His presence, to give Him control over our lives.

Exercise videos are continually telling us that we need to strengthen our core if we're going to be better balanced and stable physically. The same holds true when we want to increase our spiritual strength.

In our very inner being, deep down in our center, we must concede that all we are and who we are depends entirely on God. We must admit He is our spiritual strength, the one who shelters us, and helps us. No matter what the circumstances—pregnancy, drought, menstruation, flood, war, depression, death, divorce, unemployment, financial hardship, menopause, etc.—we can be true to God, knowing He will and can handle any situation in which we find ourselves.

Today, open yourself up to the God who loves you, who holds nothing but good for you. Allow Him to be the very core of your strength.

* * *

*True and faithful God, core of my strength, light of
my life, to You I open my heart. Shelter me within
Your arms as we share this moment together.*

HOLD OUT YOUR HAND

"Don't be shocked or afraid of them! The LORD your God is
going ahead of you. He will fight for you, just as you saw
him do in Egypt." . . . "Hold out your hand." So the man held
out his hand, and it was restored! . . . O God, you are my
God; I earnestly search for you. My soul thirsts for you; my
whole body longs for you in this parched and weary land.
DEUTERONOMY 1:29–30; LUKE 6:10; PSALM 63:1 NLT

You need not be afraid of anything that comes against you. Because
God has already gone before you, knows what lies ahead of you. And
He has pledged to fight for you, just as He fought to bring His people
out of Egypt.

Yet to make this holy relationship work, you need to trust God
with everything. With each little problem, big and small. And you
need to seek Him, search for Him, thirst for Him with all you are
and desire to be. Only when you hold out your hand seeking His will
will He be able to battle for you. Because as soon as you start seeking,
reaching out to Him, He knows you are ready, willing, and able to let
Him take the lead, fight the battle, finish the conflict.

Are you ready?

Lord, I hold out my entire self—mind, body, soul, and spirit—to You.
Thank You for Your willingness to fight for she who seeks You.

LIKE JESUS

Keep loving your enemies no matter what they do. Keep doing
good to those who hate you. Keep speaking blessings on those who
curse you. Keep praying for those who mistreat you. . . . Think of the
kindness you wish others would show you; do the same for them.
LUKE 6:27–28, 31 VOICE

One surefire way to become a woman of calm, courage, and confidence
is to treat others as you would like to be treated. For when you do,
your spirit begins to blossom, transforming you into the woman God
designed you to be, a woman becoming more and more like Jesus.

Today, this Good Friday, resolve to love your enemies. Do
something nice for those who detest you. Say a blessing over those
who curse you. Pray for those who misuse you. In other words, treat
others the way you would want to be treated: with kindness.

These loving tasks are not, at first, easy to perform. That's because
your earthly self would like to retaliate against your enemies. Acting
like Jesus goes against your nature. Yet the more you do so, the more
you begin building up and strengthening your spirit, training it to
become like that of your God, the one whom we call love.

Give me the strength and resolve, Lord, to treat
others as I want to be treated, no matter what.

MORNING SMILES

Often at night I lie in bed and remember You, meditating
on Your greatness till morning smiles through my window.
You have been my constant helper; therefore, I sing for
joy under the protection of Your wings. My soul clings to
You; Your right hand reaches down and holds me up.
PSALM 63:6–8 VOICE

When you are down-and-out, when you can find no light amid the shadows, when hope seems especially elusive, spend some time before bed thinking about God. Remember all the wonderful things He has done, is currently doing, and promises to do for those who follow, worship, and serve Him. Think back to all the times God has helped you in the past.

Whenever you meditate on the goodness of God, the one who promises to always protect you, your outlook (and in-look) changes for the better. Joy begins to burgeon. And before you know it, you're singing praises to God and greeting the daylight with a morning smile.

Cling to the Lord. Imagine His right hand reaching down in this moment, lifting and holding you up. What joy to be held by Him!

As I lie in bed, Lord, I remember how wonderful and loving You are. Thinking of all the times You've helped me, I find myself singing for joy. Hold me in this moment and in this day to come.

CITY GATES

When the Lord saw her, his heart overflowed with compassion. "Don't cry!" he said. Then he walked over to the coffin and touched it, and the bearers stopped. "Young man," he said, "I tell you, get up." Then the dead boy sat up and began to talk! And Jesus gave him back to his mother.

LUKE 7:13–15 NLT

As Jesus was approaching the city of Nain, He saw a funeral procession coming out of the gate. Knowing that the dead man was the only son of a widow, Jesus couldn't help but be moved. Seeing her sorrow, Jesus encouraged her not to cry. He then approached the coffin, touched it, and spoke over the dead man's body, telling it to rise. And rise he did! Jesus, through His endless compassion, then reconciled the mother to her son.

Later, Jesus would die on the cross so that all believers could be reconciled with their loving Parent. Yet Jesus would rise again as He overcame death, blessing believers with eternal life. All because He loves God's children, sees them through His eyes of compassion.

Up in heaven, Jesus awaits. He sees you at the city gates. And by His powerful words and love raises you up to eternal life! Today, as you celebrate Easter, think on these things. Ponder them in your heart. Take courage and hope from them, from Him!

. . . .

Thank You, Jesus, for loving me so much, for dying so I could live, in Your name. Amen.

DO NOT FORGET

"Do not forget that he led you through the great and terrifying wilderness with its poisonous snakes and scorpions, where it was so hot and dry. He gave you water from the rock! He fed you with manna in the wilderness, a food unknown to your ancestors."

DEUTERONOMY 8:15–16 NLT

The Israelites were hungry—*hangry* even. Complaining and miserable, they whined to their leader, Moses. "Why has the Lord brought us into the wilderness to starve to death? We were better off as slaves in Egypt."

Maybe they had forgotten about the ten plagues. Perhaps their miraculous escape through the parted Red Sea somehow slipped their minds. And when there had been no water to drink? It flowed out from a rock. Yet with every new challenge the Israelites faced, they suffered from selective amnesia about what God had already done.

God continued to show up. He provided manna to eat every day. He made their clothes last for forty years and their feet withstood the long, arduous journey (Deuteronomy 8:4). He gave them what they needed to endure.

If you're waiting on God to act, remember the amazing works He has done in the past. Ask Him for strength to endure today, and trust that He will lead you to a place of wholeness.

. . . .

Father, You have never failed me. I will not forget the blessings of the past. I will lean on Your goodness today, and I look forward to celebrating Your victories to come. Amen.

NO LOST CAUSES

When we were overwhelmed by sins,
you forgave our transgressions.
PSALM 65:3 NIV

Nobody is beyond Christ's redemption.

The woman caught in adultery? Jesus saved her from the justice she deserved (John 8:11). The woman at the well? Jesus offered her truth she desperately needed (John 4). Zacchaeus the swindler? Jesus showed him a better way (Luke 19). The thief next to Jesus on the cross? Christ heard his profession of faith and forgave his sins on the spot (Luke 23:40–43).

Do your sins ever weigh heavy on your conscience, guilt invading your thoughts? Or maybe you worry for a friend or a prodigal child who just can't seem to stop making bad decisions. The truth is that there's not a mistake so huge that the blood of Jesus won't cover it. There are no lost causes in Christ's kingdom.

If you feel overwhelmed today, pray. Confess your sins and your struggles to God, and He will listen, hear, and encourage you while wiping your slate clean. He knows you aren't perfect, and He knows the person you're praying for isn't perfect either—but each are perfectly loved. Ask Him for opportunities to remind others of their worth in God's eyes. Nobody is beyond the forgiveness of Jesus.

* *

I am a sinner, Father. Yet You love me and forgive
me. Thank You for Your unending well of mercy.
Please meet me there today and every day. Amen.

ABUNDANT GENEROSITY

*Barren desert pastures yield fruit; craggy hills are now
dressed for celebration. Meadows are clothed with frolicking
flocks of lambs; valleys are covered with a carpet of autumn-
harvest grain; the land shouts and sings in joyous celebration.*

Psalm 65:12–13 voice

It's amazing to see God's character reflected in His creation. Each year brings a cycle of new life in spring, growth in summer, bounty in autumn, and dormancy in winter—every step along the way offers its own wonder.

Psalm 65—a harvest psalm—describes how God's care of nature is a sign of His love and provision for His people. Jesus confirmed God's gentle care of the birds and splendor of flowers in the field in Luke 12. God blesses us as well—giving us more than we need or deserve.

When you see and experience God's abundant generosity, when you take the time to be thankful for it, you see the perfect example of how to give to others. When you spend your time and resources on God's work, you'll find you're living out Jesus' teaching in Luke 12:34 (niv): "Where your treasure is, there your heart will be also."

. . . .

*Father, You are so good to me. Thank You for taking care of
my needs and blessing me beyond measure. I am not worthy of
Your gifts, but I praise You for the generous God You are. Amen.*

THE STORM WHISPERER

A squall came down on the lake, so that the boat was being swamped, and they were in great danger. The disciples went and woke him, saying, "Master, Master, we're going to drown!" He got up and rebuked the wind and the raging waters; the storm subsided, and all was calm.

LUKE 8:23–24 NIV

Jesus' disciples were frightened. . .and rightfully so. Even today, the Sea of Galilee is the scene of strong storms that sometimes produce twenty-foot waves. The storm that day in Luke 8 was fierce enough to strike terror in the hearts of the expert fishermen among them, and the threat of drowning was real.

When the storms of life blow in, we may assume that God has lost control and that we're at the mercy of fate. But regardless of how it seems, God does not lose control. He was, is, and will always be sovereign in our lives and circumstances. He controls the big picture of history as well as our own personal stories.

Jesus, with just a word, can calm the storm in your life, and what's more is that He wants to calm the storm in your heart and replace it with His peace (John 14:27). Ask Him, in faith, to take care of it all.

Jesus, please calm the storm around me and inside of me. I need Your peace to reign in my life. Amen.

NOT OVERLOOKED

When the woman realized that she could not stay hidden,
she began to tremble and fell to her knees in front of him.
The whole crowd heard her explain why she had touched him
and that she had been immediately healed. "Daughter," he
said to her, "your faith has made you well. Go in peace."
LUKE 8:47–48 NLT

The hemorrhaging woman had suffered physically and emotionally for twelve years, going unnoticed and ignored. According to Old Testament law, a man who touched a menstruating woman became ceremonially unclean (Leviticus 15:19–28). To keep themselves undefiled, Jewish men didn't touch, speak to, or even look at women.

Yet Jesus proclaimed to a crowd of people that this "unclean" woman had touched the hem of His cloak and she was immediately healed. His garment didn't contain mystical healing power; it was her faith in Jesus that healed her.

Jesus did not overlook this woman. As God's beloved child she deserved to be noticed and respected by all. When you feel overlooked or unnoticed, take courage in Jesus' act of love, knowing that He cares for you just the same.

. . . .

Jesus, I am in awe of Your care and kindness for
this woman. Your love for her surpassed the rules and
regulations of the law, and You ushered in a new way of
holy living. Forgive me when I overlook or look down on
others. They are God's beloved children just as I am.

HE'LL MAKE IT HAPPEN

Jesus said, "You feed them." "But we have only five loaves of bread and two fish," they answered. "Or are you expecting us to go and buy enough food for this whole crowd?"

LUKE 9:13 NLT

The disciples planned to send away the crowds to go find something to eat. But Jesus had other plans: "You feed them."

Jesus must've been kidding, right? Because five loaves of bread and two fish is a shockingly small amount of food to feed a multitude of people. But the disciples were focused on what they *didn't* have (food and money) instead of what they *did* have (a miracle-working God standing in front of them).

Have you ever been called to do something that seems impossible? A lack of funds, a lack of help, a lack of space, a lack of fill-in-the-blank—all of these things can blind us from seeing God's power. The truth is that God won't ask you to do something in His name without providing a way to make it happen. It may not come in the form you were expecting, but neither did the disciples expect that five loaves and two fish would result in thousands of full bellies and twelve extra baskets of food.

Jesus, open my eyes to Your power. I believe You are able to do immeasurably more than I can imagine! When I'm tempted to focus on what I lack, remind me of this story.

ON THE MOUNTAINTOP

Jesus took Peter, John, and James up on a mountain to pray.
And as he was praying, the appearance of his face was transformed,
and his clothes became dazzling white. . . . Then a voice from the
cloud said, "This is my Son, my Chosen One. Listen to him."
LUKE 9:28–29, 35 NLT

Peter, John, and James had a life-changing experience on the mountaintop. There they saw who Jesus really is—not just a great prophet and teacher, but God's own Son and the long-awaited Messiah. This moment was so powerful, so awe-inspiring, so affirming to their faith that they didn't want to leave.

Maybe you've had a similar experience. A weekend retreat or a conference or a week of church camp can provide a unique opportunity to spend time studying, praying, and fellowshipping with others. With fewer distractions, it's easier to come face-to-face with God, and we may want to stay there—away from the challenges of daily life. Knowing the struggles that lie in the valley can keep us clinging to the mountaintop, but high above reality we can't minister to others.

Yes, we need times of renewal. We need profound, uninterrupted encounters with God on the mountain so we can return to be a light to the world. Gain hope and courage that you can carry into the valley.

* * *

Jesus, I will meet You on the mountain.
Please lead me through the valley as well. Amen.

THE HARD QUESTIONS

Jesus. . .said to his disciples, "Listen carefully to what I am about to tell you: The Son of Man is going to be delivered into the hands of men." But they did not understand what this meant. It was hidden from them, so that they did not grasp it, and they were afraid to ask him about it.

LUKE 9:43–45 NIV

Even though Jesus' disciples had already seen Him perform amazing miracles—like feeding a crowd of thousands with five loaves of bread and two fish or healing the sick or driving out demons—they didn't fully understand yet who Jesus was. So the disciples couldn't fathom how Jesus could be betrayed and killed. Instead of asking the hard, scary questions about what He meant, they started arguing about which disciple would be the greatest in Christ's kingdom.

Have you ever read something in God's Word that left you scratching your head? Have you ever felt a prompting from the Holy Spirit that left you feeling uncomfortable or uncertain? When that happens, tell God honestly how you feel. He can handle your questions and uncertainty—nothing is too hard or too big—and He will listen with care. Ask Him to reveal His perfect plan, and as you wait for understanding, ask for the faith you need to take each step along the way.

* *

Thank You for being a God who willingly listens to my concerns. I don't always understand, but I trust You to do what is best.

WATER EVERYWHERE

*You sent abundant rain, O God, to refresh the weary
land. There your people finally settled, and with a bountiful
harvest, O God, you provided for your needy people.*
PSALM 68:9–10 NLT

In a season of drought, all it takes is a few days without rain for land to dry up. Cracked, parched, crusty soil and rolling clouds of dust make everything feel a bit more desperate—brittle, fragile, inhospitable.

When we are far away from the life-giving nourishment of Jesus' living water, our hearts can feel dried out like that. But the good news is that a dry spell doesn't have to persist. God is the faithful gardener of our souls, and Jesus is the source of living water who invites us to drink deeply, like in John 4:13–14 (NLT) where He said to the woman at the well, "Anyone who drinks this water will soon become thirsty again. But those who drink the water I give will never be thirsty again. It becomes a fresh, bubbling spring within them, giving them eternal life."

That water is available, free of charge (Revelation 21:6). Accept Jesus' gift of grace anew today and experience the abundant goodness of His life-giving water. You'll soon see new growth in the lush, fertile soil of your heart.

*Jesus, please refresh my weary heart. Help me tap into
the only source of water that will quench my thirst forever.
Thank You for providing an abundant resource for what I need.*

NO QUALIFICATIONS REQUIRED

*Jesus was filled with the joy of the Holy Spirit, and he said,
"O Father, Lord of heaven and earth, thank you for
hiding these things from those who think themselves
wise and clever, and for revealing them to the childlike.
Yes, Father, it pleased you to do it this way."*

LUKE 10:21 NLT

*Must have master's degree and a minimum five years' experience. Qualified
candidates should email a cover letter and résumé to human resources. . . .*
The world loves a list of requirements. Many of life's opportunities
seem available only to the elite, the highly educated, the intelligent,
the rich, the attractive, or the powerful.

But God's kingdom is different. Here in Luke 10:21, Jesus
prayed, thanking the Father that His kingdom is equally available
to *everyone*. Regardless of position or abilities or race or gender or
family tree, we come to Jesus not through our list of qualifications
but through faith like a child: a pure-hearted love for and genuine
trust in the Father.

Thank God that everyone has access to the Creator of the universe,
to the mighty, powerful I AM, and our loving heavenly Father. Trust
in God's grace, rather than your own personal qualifications, for your
role in His family.

*Father God, I trust You. I humbly submit my heart to
Your kingdom. Give me the pure faith of a child who is
meeting You the first time. May my faith be pleasing to You.
Thank You for being available to everyone, everywhere.*

PERSISTENT PRAYER

One of [Jesus'] disciples said to him, "Lord, teach us to pray."
LUKE 11:1 NIV

When the disciples asked for a lesson in prayer, Jesus first launched into a model prayer, what we often call the Lord's Prayer. But He didn't stop with just an example. In Luke 11:5–8 (NLT) He continued to teach them about the importance of persistence in prayer with a story:

"Suppose you went to a friend's house at midnight, wanting to borrow three loaves of bread. . . . And suppose he calls out from his bedroom, 'Don't bother me. The door is locked for the night, and my family and I are all in bed. I can't help you.' But I tell you this. . .if you keep knocking long enough, he will get up and give you whatever you need because of your shameless persistence."

Continually asking for something in prayer is for our benefit, not God's. Practicing boldness does more to change *our* hearts and minds, and it helps us understand and express the intensity of our needs. Persistence in prayer helps us recognize how God works in our lives. In Luke 11:10 (NLT), Jesus said God will hear and respond to our repeated prayers: "Everyone who asks, receives. Everyone who seeks, finds. And to everyone who knocks, the door will be opened."

. . . .

Lord, I come today asking for Your help. And I will come again tomorrow. And the next day. Thank You for hearing me.

YOU ARE A LIGHT

*"No one lights a lamp and puts it in a place where it will
be hidden, or under a bowl. Instead they put it on its
stand, so that those who come in may see the light."*

LUKE 11:33 NIV

Darkness makes everything more challenging. Your house, easy to navigate in the light, transforms into a virtual labyrinth in the dark. Doorjambs are targets for stubbed toes, stairs become a real broken-bone risk, and those Legos strewn on the living room floor. . .more painful than a fire walk. So after you fumble in the dark and click on your phone's flashlight, you wouldn't think of shoving it in your pocket. No, you raise the beam high to let it illuminate everything around you.

God has created you to be a light. Your story, attention, and influence can be an encouragement to others, but only if you share it. Are you taking the time to tell others about what God is doing in your life? Share the light of Christ's impact on your life yesterday, today, and forever. The Holy Spirit living inside you is a beacon that can lead others to both a personal relationship with you and with Jesus.

. . . .

*God, I want to be Your light in the world, but I admit that
I am intimidated. Forgive me when I choose to keep You
to myself. Make me bold and give me opportunities to show
Your love to others in a real, authentic, life-changing way.*

WAITING FOR HELP

*I am exhausted from crying for help; my throat
is parched. My eyes are swollen with weeping,
waiting for my God to help me.*

PSALM 69:3 NLT

David—the writer of Psalm 69—was wrung out like a dishrag. Physically spent and emotionally exhausted, David sounds like he's on the brink of collapse and despair in Psalm 69:3. Yet despite his suffering, he had hope that God would help him.

Throughout scripture, we meet giants of the faith who suffered through seasons of waiting for God's help. Moses led his people through the desert for forty years; Job endured life-altering tragedies; Noah, following God's instructions to build a boat, dealt with his neighbors' ridicule; Hannah agonized while waiting for the blessing of a child; Paul was imprisoned for preaching the gospel. What do these people all have in common? They held on to the hope that God would arrive. And He did!

So when you are waiting for God's help, remember David. Remember Moses and Job and Noah and Hannah and Paul. God sees your tears and swollen eyes, and they are not in vain. Continue to pray, even if you already feel like a wrung-out dishrag. God hears you, and He is coming to help in His perfect time.

*God, I am clinging to the hope that You will help me.
The longer I wait, the harder it is to hope, but I will not
despair. I trust Your timing, even when I don't understand it.*

PRICELESS

*"What is the price of five sparrows—two copper coins?
Yet God does not forget a single one of them. And the very
hairs on your head are all numbered. So don't be afraid;
you are more valuable to God than a whole flock of sparrows."*

LUKE 12:6–7 NLT

How do you measure your worth? The answer might depend on how you're feeling about yourself today.

If we're well-rested and energized, the scale is down a pound or two, and the house is clean and laundry is put away, we might feel like a million bucks. But if the opposite is true, we might struggle to feel like we're worth anything at all. Looking for our personal value in the eyes of others is even more dangerous. The world evaluates us according to what we can do, what we achieve, and how we look. But our true worth doesn't lie in anything that the world thinks about us.

God's estimation of our worth goes much deeper than surface level. Our value to God doesn't rise and fall based on how we act. He knows us and loves us from the inside out. God created us out of nothing, and He cares for all His creatures—because we belong to Him. God values you. So step forward in the confidence of His love and care today and every day.

. . . .

*Lord, when I feel worthless, You call me priceless.
When I feel unworthy, You call me loved and accepted.
May I see my value through Your eyes only.*

EVERYTHING YOU NEED

I keep telling you not to worry about anything in life—
about what you'll eat, about how you'll clothe your body.
Life is more than food, and the body is more than fancy clothes.
Luke 12:22–23 voice

Jesus knows that our list of top-ten worries often includes many physical needs: *Can we stretch the paycheck a bit more? What will we do for dinner tomorrow? The kids' toes are squished in the end of their too-tight shoes. The mortgage comes due soon and the car is making that weird noise again.*

These are valid concerns—after all, we are *physical* beings with *physical* requirements. But sometimes our worries take up so much headspace they crowd out our relationship with God, the thing Jesus tells us is the most important. Jesus puts it this way in Luke 12:29–31 (nlt): "And don't be concerned about what to eat and what to drink. . . . These things dominate the thoughts of unbelievers all over the world, but your Father already knows your needs. Seek the Kingdom of God above all else, and he will give you everything you need."

Trust is the remedy for worry. When you have faith that God knows, cares about, and is actively supplying everything you need, it frees up your mind to focus on what's eternally important.

Father, I give You my worries and ask You
to clean out the clutter so I can focus on You.

YOU HAVE ALREADY WON

Then the LORD said to Joshua, "See, I have delivered Jericho into your hands, along with its king and its fighting men."
JOSHUA 6:2 NIV

Joshua was assessing the towering walls of Jericho when God told him he had already won the battle—even before the Israelite army had started marching around the city. With a guarantee of victory from God Himself, Joshua must've had an extra dose of confidence going into the battle of Jericho.

As Christians, we have the same promise of victory over evil. Christ defeated Satan through His sacrifice on the cross, and scripture reminds us repeatedly of our victory through Him. Romans 8:37 (NLT) says that "overwhelming victory is ours through Christ"; Hebrews 2:14 says that Jesus broke the power of the devil by dying a human death; 1 John 3:8 (NLT) says Christ "came to destroy the works of the devil"—and He certainly did!

Although we still fight battles and have struggles and frustrations and temptations every day, we have the assurance that God wins. Whatever you are struggling through today, Christ conquered it. Whatever is coming tomorrow, God has already handed you the victory. We do not have to fear the power of a defeated enemy. Because of Christ's power we win—now and through all of eternity.

Jesus, I will move forward boldly and with purpose, knowing You have claimed victory in every area of my life.

PLEASE HURRY, GOD!

May all who seek you rejoice and be glad in you; may those who long for your saving help always say, "The LORD is great!" But as for me, I am poor and needy; come quickly to me, O God. You are my help and my deliverer; LORD, do not delay.

PSALM 70:4–5 NIV

Upright, faithful, wise, brave, and kind, David is described in 1 Samuel 13:14 (NIV) as "a man after [God's] own heart." David's urgent pleas for help in many of his psalms show he understood God cared about him on a personal, individual level.

Yet even in David's moment of panic, he still praised God for what He has done and for who He is. Praise is important—especially when we are in the middle of a crisis—because it helps us keep the correct perspective. It allows us to remember who God is, the fact He is all-powerful, and that He is in control of everything.

So when your prayers become urgent pleas, take a moment to breathe and praise. Thank God for how He has worked things out and blessed you in the past. Ask Him to strengthen and comfort you today. Acknowledge His work in your current situation and ask Him to reveal what He is doing—how He is weaving together events for your good and His glory.

Lord, please hurry. Give me the strength to endure. Although I don't understand what's going on, I know You are good, and I praise You for Your kindness to me.

OUR SUPERHERO

For you have been my hope, Sovereign LORD, my confidence since my youth. From birth I have relied on you; you brought me forth from my mother's womb. I will ever praise you.

PSALM 71:5–6 NIV

For many kids, parents are their first heroes. Who's the strongest person ever? Daddy. Who heals every cut and scrape with a bandage and a kiss? Mommy. Then as we get older, we learn stories surrounding superheroes. . .Superman, Wonder Woman, and other fictional characters. These larger-than-life heroes leave us inspired by their greatness and give us hope that we can be like them in some way. But superparents aren't perfect and superheroes aren't real. Too soon we grow up to experience disappointments, failures, and frustrations. The world tells us that we only have ourselves to rely on, so we try to shoulder the burden of self-confidence. But we are fallible, and confidence in ourselves can only go so far.

The truth is that God is the only superhero who is worthy of our praise and awe. God will not disappoint; God will not fail. Reliance on our heavenly Father is the only way to lasting confidence. Put your trust in Him and His mighty power, with childlike faith and hope.

*Sovereign Lord, You are better than a superhero—
You are my Savior. I count on You to rescue me always.*

KEEP ON. . .

*And now, in my old age, don't set me aside. Don't abandon
me when my strength is failing. . . . But I will keep on hoping
for your help; I will praise you more and more. I will tell
everyone about your righteousness. All day long I will proclaim
your saving power, though I am not skilled with words.*

PSALM 71:9, 14–15 NLT

Whether you've celebrated twenty-five birthdays or ninety-five
birthdays, you have a lifetime of blessings to thank God for. When
you remember God's goodness throughout the years, it can help
you see that He is always near, He is a constant source of grace,
and His love never fails.

Remembering how God has come through in the past and
praising Him again and again is one of the best ways to buoy your
hopes in tough times. In the moments you may not see God working,
talk about the instances when God helped you. And when the aches,
pains, fatigue, and ills of aging come (after all, none of us are getting
any younger), when you need God even more, be assured that He is
still your constant help and companion.

Take a lesson from David. No matter what's going on in your
world today, don't give in to despair. Keep on expecting God to come;
keep on praising; keep on serving. Hope in Him will keep you going.

Father, You've never failed me yet, and You never will!

WHOLEHEARTED FAITHFULNESS

"I. . .followed the LORD my God wholeheartedly. . . .
Now then, just as the LORD promised, he has kept me
alive for forty-five years since the time he said this to Moses,
while Israel moved about in the wilderness. So here I am today,
eighty-five years old! I am still as strong today as the day
Moses sent me out.". . . Then the land had rest from war.
JOSHUA 14:8, 10–11, 15 NIV

Caleb was one of the original spies sent into the Promised Land (Numbers 13:30–33). There he saw great cities and intimidating giants, but he believed God would help the Israelites take over the land—even when others doubted. God saw Caleb's faith and promised him an inheritance of land (Numbers 14:24; Deuteronomy 1:34–36), but Caleb didn't receive that blessing until forty-five years later.

Yet Caleb's faith never wavered.

Even when the land he received still had giants, Caleb knew God would help him conquer them. Caleb's wholehearted faith made him a strong leader, a capable warrior, and a servant of God his entire life.

What can we learn from Caleb? Faithfulness matters—both at the start of our walk with God and throughout our lives. A living, thriving relationship with our Savior is one that grows, strengthens, and continues to add to the kingdom of God.

. . . .

Lord, as long as You bless me with air in my lungs,
I will be faithful. There is nothing You can't do.

FLAVOR ENHANCER

Don't be like salt that has lost its taste. How can its saltiness be restored? Flavorless salt is absolutely worthless. You can't even use it as fertilizer, so it's worth less than manure! Don't just listen to My words here. Get the deeper meaning.

LUKE 14:34–35 VOICE

Movie popcorn without butter and salt is like a bowl of hot packing peanuts. And a hot pretzel without a good sprinkling of sea salt is just knot-shaped bread.

The distinctive taste of salt adds zest and flavor depth to the foods we eat. It's also a mineral that our body needs to stay in balance. When it's lacking from our diet, we crave it. Salt is also a natural preservative. So it makes sense that Jesus calls His followers "the salt of the earth" (Matthew 5:13). We are to add an important flavor in the world, preserving the good and helping it from spoiling. Our saltiness should enhance the attractiveness of Christ.

But if salt gets wet and then dries, it loses its flavor. It becomes a colorless, tasteless residue. Deserving no place on the spice rack or on the kitchen table, it is worthless.

Being salty, standing apart from the rest of the bland world, takes commitment and sacrifice. Follow Christ's example in His saltiness: spread love, compassion, truth, and encouragement wherever you go.

Jesus, give me the courage to be more like You every day. I will be the salt in this bland world!

HE'S SEARCHING FOR YOU

"If a man has a hundred sheep and one of them gets lost, what will he do? Won't he leave the ninety-nine others in the wilderness and go to search for the one that is lost until he finds it? And when he has found it, he will joyfully carry it home on his shoulders."

LUKE 15:4–5 NLT

Why would the shepherd in the parable of the lost sheep leave ninety-nine to search for just *one* wayward sheep? He knew the ninety-nine were safe in the sheepfold, but the one lost sheep was in danger. The shepherd placed a high value on each member of his flock, so he knew it would be worthwhile to search for the lost one.

God loves each of us so much that He pursues each person and then rejoices when he or she accepts His love and gift of salvation. Jesus spent time with sinners because He was reaching for people we may consider beyond hope—the lost sheep. But before you believed in Christ, God pursued you too. He didn't just idly wait for you to ask for forgiveness. No, He is a God who searches for sinners and then joyfully forgives them as they enter His family!

If you feel far from God today, don't despair. You are priceless to the Great Shepherd. He is searching for you!

. . . .

God, I am so thankful that You search for me when
I stray and that I am of great value to You.

PROMISES, PROMISES

So the LORD gave Israel all the land he had sworn to give their ancestors, and they took possession of it and settled there. The LORD gave them rest on every side, just as he had sworn to their ancestors. Not one of their enemies withstood them; the LORD gave all their enemies into their hands.

JOSHUA 21:43–44 NIV

God's people had been homeless, wandering in the desert for generations. Many of these Hebrews had been born during the Israelites' forty-year stint as nomads, so all they knew was the desert. The promises God had made to their grandparents may have seemed like a myth. Yet God was faithful, and, as Joshua 21:45 (NIV) says, "not one of all the LORD's good promises to Israel failed; every one was fulfilled."

We can take hope in the fact that God delivered on His promises in the Bible. The more we learn about the promises God fulfilled in the past, the easier it is to hope He will fulfill those same promises today.

When you feel the tug of impatience, wanting God to act in a certain way *now*, choose instead to trust in the faithfulness of God and His perfect will for yesterday, today, and forever.

. . . .

God of the promise, I praise You for Your faithfulness. You are reliable. You are trustworthy. I have nothing to fear when it comes to putting my life, my heart, and my soul in Your hands.

THE IMPORTANCE OF INTEGRITY

*"If you are faithful in little things, you will be faithful
in large ones. But if you are dishonest in little things,
you won't be honest with greater responsibilities."*

LUKE 16:10 NLT

Matters of money are often where our integrity is put to the ultimate test. Dishonest financial gain, even a small one, can be especially tempting when we think nobody will ever miss the money.

But God calls us to a higher standard, even in the minor infractions we could easily rationalize away. The choices we make and the actions we take when no one is looking make a difference now and in our future decisions. When we are honest and responsible in small earthly riches, God will increasingly trust us with the things that have eternal value—the riches of His kingdom.

The good news is that every day brings new opportunities to be a woman of integrity. If you've made an error in the past, do what you can to right the wrong and seek forgiveness if necessary. No matter what bad choices you've made, your next choice can be the right one . . .the one that honors God above money.

Father, I choose You as my master. Help me to remember that my life is much more than my money and possessions. Riches in Your kingdom are what truly matter. Guide me in integrity in all things, and help me make the right decision no matter how hard it is.

FAITH TO DO THE IMPOSSIBLE

The apostles said to the Lord, "Increase our faith!"
He replied, "If you have faith as small as a mustard seed,
you can say to this mulberry tree, 'Be uprooted and
planted in the sea,' and it will obey you."

LUKE 17:5–6 NIV

Just before the apostles asked Jesus to increase their faith in Luke 17:5, Jesus taught them the importance of forgiveness by saying, "If another believer sins, rebuke that person; then if there is repentance, forgive. Even if that person wrongs you seven times a day and each time turns again and asks forgiveness, you must forgive" (Luke 17:3–4 NLT).

Repeated forgiveness like that probably felt impossible, even for Jesus' closest friends and companions. The disciples realized the only way they could forgive like that was with Christ's help, so their request for more faith in Luke 17:5 was sincere; they wanted the faith they needed for such radical forgiveness. The faith they asked for is the ability to do God's will even when it feels impossible. This kind of faith is a complete obedience and readiness to do whatever He calls for.

Jesus explains the power of faith with the mustard seed illustration, showing that the amount of faith isn't as important as the right kind of faith—faith in God that is alive and growing.

Lord, instead of asking for more faith, I am asking for
real, genuine, living and growing faith. With Your
help, I know I can do anything in Your will.

GRATITUDE LEADS TO GREATER FAITH

One of them, when he saw he was healed, came back,
praising God in a loud voice. He threw himself at Jesus'
feet and thanked him. . . . Jesus asked, "Were not all ten
cleansed? Where are the other nine? . . ." Then he said to
him, "Rise and go; your faith has made you well."
LUKE 17:15–17, 19 NIV

When Jesus told the ten lepers to show themselves to the priests in Luke 17:14, He sent them to the temple *before* they were healed. This was strange, because a leper would normally only go to a priest if his leprosy was in remission so the priest could declare him clean (Leviticus 14). Although Jesus' instruction didn't make much sense, the lepers responded in faith and were miraculously healed on their way.

But only one of the ten returned to thank Jesus.

This story shows us it's possible to receive God's great gifts with an ungrateful spirit—nine out of ten lepers did. But the one who returned and thanked Jesus learned that his faith had played a role in his own healing.

God doesn't demand our thanks, but we please Him when we have a grateful heart and express that gratefulness to Him. Through that gratitude, we learn more about Him and recognize His healing, provision, and care in our lives.

Father, my heart overflows with
thanks for everything You do for me.

TWO PRAYERS

*"The Pharisee. . .prayed. . . 'I thank you, God, that I am not
like other people—cheaters, sinners, adulterers. I'm certainly
not like that tax collector! I fast twice a week, and I give you
a tenth of my income.'. . . [The tax collector] beat his chest in
sorrow, saying, 'O God, be merciful to me, for I am a sinner.'
I tell you, this sinner, not the Pharisee, returned home justified
before God. For those who exalt themselves will be humbled,
and those who humble themselves will be exalted."*

LUKE 18:11–14 NLT

In Luke 18, Jesus gives examples of two vastly different prayers. First
the Pharisee, a highly regarded Jewish leader, prays in a way that
shows his prideful attitude. As he lists his holy habits—loudly in the
middle of the temple—we hear disdain for those he considers lower
than himself.

Next is the pitiful cry of the tax collector, an outcast from the
religious community, as he weeps and beats his chest in sorrow for his
own shortcomings. He's done wrong, and although he isn't worthy of
it, he humbly begs for God's forgiveness.

God heard both prayers, but the Pharisee's self-righteous attitude
cut him off from learning anything from God. The tax collector
humbled himself and acknowledged his need for mercy, a request
God faithfully filled (2 Chronicles 7:14).

. . . .

*Father, please be merciful to me. I am a sinner,
and I need Your healing power to make me whole.*

EVERY OPPORTUNITY

As Jesus approached Jericho, a blind beggar was sitting beside the road. When he heard the noise of a crowd going past, he asked what was happening. They told him that Jesus the Nazarene was going by. So he began shouting, "Jesus, Son of David, have mercy on me!"

LUKE 18:35–38 NLT

When the blind beggar in Luke 18 heard that Jesus was walking by, a glimmer of hope must've flickered in his desperate heart. That hope compelled him to shout toward Jesus for mercy. The crowd tried to hush the blind beggar, but he would not waste the opportunity to get Jesus' attention.

"What do you want me to do for you?" Jesus asked. "Lord," he said, "I want to see!" (Luke 18:41 NLT).

It was such a straightforward request. But combined with the beggar's faith that Jesus *could* heal him, he *immediately* could see and he *immediately* followed Jesus, praising God. Jesus' healing of the blind beggar changed this man's life and the lives of the people who witnessed it, who also praised God for what they saw (Luke 18:43).

What has Jesus done in your life that you need to share with others? Your stories of God's help can be a huge source of encouragement in your faith as well as the people around you.

. . . .

Jesus, give me the faith of the blind beggar. I need Your help every day, and I will take every opportunity to cry out to You.

THE POWER OF LOVE

*Zacchaeus stood up and said to the Lord, "Look, Lord! Here
and now I give half of my possessions to the poor, and if I have
cheated anybody out of anything, I will pay back four times
the amount." Jesus said to him, "Today salvation has come
to this house, because this man, too, is a son of Abraham. For
the Son of Man came to seek and to save the lost."*

LUKE 19:8–10 NIV

Tax collectors were some of the most despised people in Israel.
Although Jewish by birth, Zacchaeus was considered a traitor because
he chose to work for the Roman government and was a known crook.

Yet where others saw a greasy little cheat, Jesus saw a man worthy
of His time and attention. Jesus loved Zacchaeus and showed him
kindness and honor in His words and deeds. Zacchaeus' response was
immediate and shocking: he promised to give to the poor and make
restitution with generous interest to those he had swindled. The tax
collector demonstrated his inward heart change by outward action.

Jesus' love changed the course of Zacchaeus' life, but it also
changed the lives of all the people Zacchaeus had cheated. Don't
underestimate the power of a loving word or deed. God can use the
simplest kindness for amazing transformation!

*Jesus, thank You for examples in the Bible like Zacchaeus
that remind me that no one is out of Your loving sphere.
Help me to love the unlovable in Your name.*

THE SYMPHONY OF PRAISE

"Blessed is the king who comes in the name of the Lord!"
"Peace in heaven and glory in the highest!" Some of the Pharisees
in the crowd said to Jesus, "Teacher, rebuke your disciples!" "I tell
you," he replied, "if they keep quiet, the stones will cry out."
LUKE 19:38–40 NIV

The Pharisees thought the crowd's praise was blasphemous and asked Jesus to hush His followers. But even though the palm branch–waving people misunderstood what kind of king Jesus was, their worship was directed toward the right person.

Scripture tells us that all of God's creation worships the Creator. Psalm 148 includes a lengthy list from nature, each of which cries out in worship: from the sun, moon, and stars to the fire, hail, snow, and wind. Mountains and trees and oceans and animals and kings and rulers and young men and young women. . .the passage urges every corner of creation to praise the name of the Lord.

What is your favorite way to worship? Whether it's through song, prayer, spending quiet time in His presence, or some other way, don't let your own inhibitions or the criticism of others keep you from worshipping. Join in with the stones and play your part in the symphony of praise.

. . . .

Father, I praise You for who You are—the master.

THE RIPPLE EFFECTS OF GRATITUDE

*We thank You, O True God. Our souls are overflowing
with thanks! Your name is near; Your people remember
and tell of Your marvelous works and wonders.*

PSALM 75:1 VOICE

One of the best ways we can show God our love is to have a heart full
of gratitude. From it, we can share stories about how His goodness
has manifested in our lives. We can encourage the weary by reminding
them God is still full of works and wonders. We can boost others
and ourselves with a dose of gratitude for yesterday and one of hope
for tomorrow.

Even more importantly, we can be women who are quick to
give God credit. Consider how much it means to you when someone acknowledges you or tells you about something you did that
made a difference in that person's life. When you adopt an attitude of
gratitude and it spills out to others in conversation, the ripple effects
are far-reaching.

Has the Lord restored a broken marriage or opened the door to
a dream job? Have you found a community of friends after months
of asking God for help? Did the treatment work? Have you seen a
change of heart in your child? Right now, thank God for making a way
when you thought there was none. Share the news of His blessings
with others. And be ready for more!

*Lord, You're amazing and I am so thankful for
the ways You love me! Help me spread the news!*

LONGING FOR A MIRACLE

*A certain man of Zorah, named Manoah, from the clan
of the Danites, had a wife who was childless, unable to
give birth. The angel of the LORD appeared to her and
said, "You are barren and childless, but you are going
to become pregnant and give birth to a son."*

JUDGES 13:2–3 NIV

What miracle are you hoping for right now? Where do you need
God to intervene on your behalf? The God who made motherhood
available to Manoah's infertile wife is the same God who hears your
cry for help today. And He is able to do the miraculous in your life too!

If you're longing for a husband, tell God of your heart's desire.
If you've been unable to get pregnant, ask for divine intervention. If
you are lonely, trust Him for like-minded and faith-filled friends. If
you want to be free from fear, ask God to remove it. If you're battling
a life-threatening disease, tell Him about your longing to be healed.

Just like He did in the days of old, God still does miracles. You
have every reason to hold on to hope because your God is magnificent.
So, cry out to Him for what you're wanting. And trust His will and
ways in each circumstance. Remember, there is always hope!

. . . .

*Lord, it feels risky to hope for big miracles
because I don't want to be disappointed.
Help me accept Your will, whatever it may be.*

A HEART TO GIVE

*While Jesus was in the Temple, he watched the rich people
dropping their gifts in the collection box. Then a poor widow
came by and dropped in two small coins. "I tell you the truth,"
Jesus said, "this poor widow has given more than all the rest
of them. For they have given a tiny part of their surplus,
but she, poor as she is, has given everything she has."*

LUKE 21:1–4 NLT

The poor widow's small act of faith shook the heavens. And Jesus
recognized it immediately. He knew the sacrifice she made by dropping
those two small coins in the coffer. He saw the selfless motives and
her desire to make a difference, even if it meant she would go without.
And Jesus knew the faith it took to give more than most would have
thought wise. What a beautiful example of loving God through giving.

There are many ways to bless His kingdom, so don't let any
condemnation pollute your heart. Do you love to volunteer your time?
There are countless ministries and other nonprofits that need your
time to help further their mission. Do you have treasures to share?
Maybe you have tangible items that need a new home or you feel
led to give financially. Let God stir your heart to bless as He sees fit.
And do so with a glad heart.

* * * * *

*Lord, make my heart tender to Your leading.
Show me where and how to bless Your kingdom.*

NEVER LEFT BEHIND

*"People will be terrified at what they see coming upon
the earth, for the powers in the heavens will be shaken.
Then everyone will see the Son of Man coming on a cloud
with power and great glory. So when all these things begin
to happen, stand and look up, for your salvation is near!"*

LUKE 21:26–28 NLT

If you're a believer, you can be certain you won't be left behind. Just as He vowed, and at the appointed time, Jesus will come back to take you into eternity with Him. There may be a lot of promises unkept in this life, but the gift of salvation is not one of them. So, take heart! The hardships you must face here will come to an end and a beautiful life in heaven will be yours forever.

How do you know you'll be in eternity with the Lord? Romans 10:9 says that if you truly believe God raised Jesus from the grave and if you confess Jesus is Lord with your voice, then you will be saved. The words themselves hold no power—it's the deep belief in the truth and acceptance of God's gift of grace that secures your salvation.

Today, make certain your eternity has been settled. Talk to God and admit your need for a Savior. Repent of your sins. Doing so will ensure you'll spend forever and a day in the unmatched presence of God.

* *

Lord, thank You for the gift of salvation.

OUR OPEN WOUNDS

I yell out to my God, I yell with all my might, I yell at the top of my lungs. He listens. I found myself in trouble and went looking for my Lord; my life was an open wound that wouldn't heal.

PSALM 77:1–2 MSG

What a powerful image painted by today's verses. Can you relate? For the psalmist, he likened his life to an open wound that won't heal. While we don't know what events caused him to feel this way, we can certainly understand the cruelty of life.

Our time on earth isn't easy. Guaranteed. Scripture even tells us straight-out that we should expect hardships. From moments of trauma to epic failures to deep insecurity, no one escapes this life unscathed. Maybe you have a child who's been difficult from the get-go. Maybe your marriage has been abusive emotionally or physically. Or maybe you've prayed for a husband and kids, and the lack of either has made you overwhelmingly discouraged.

Be encouraged to know God sees you! He loves you! And He understands every feeling as He collects every tear. Run to the Lord in your pain and let Him comfort you. He is the one who can restore your hope.

. . . .

Lord, I'm hurting. I feel battered and beaten by life. Today, I lay it all at Your feet and wait for You to heal the wounds I can't.

IN HOT PURSUIT

Simon, Simon, how Satan has pursued you, that he might make you part of his harvest. But I have prayed for you. I have prayed that your faith will hold firm and that you will recover from your failure and become a source of strength for your brothers here.

LUKE 22:31–32 VOICE

It's the plan of Satan and his minions to pursue every one of us. What he really wants is to destroy God. But because he can't do that, God's children are the next best thing. We are his target.

Don't let that unsettle you! Jesus is praying for our faith to rise up in strength so we can stand strong through every trial and temptation. We may be shaken, but the enemy cannot destroy us. We may face unsettling situations, but we won't be broken. God is ready to give us everything necessary to navigate these times with confidence and courage.

And here's the coolest part. Scripture says that once we emerge victorious, we'll be a source of strength to those around us. Our faith will encourage others to have faith too! That we got through a difficult season intact will help others find hope they will as well. That's the beauty of community. That's the power of faith.

· ·

Lord, thanks for the heads-up! Give me the strength in hard times so I can be a beacon of hope to others.

HEART CONNECTIONS

But Ruth replied, "Don't urge me to leave you or to turn back from you. Where you go I will go, and where you stay I will stay. Your people will be my people and your God my God."
RUTH 1:16 NIV

Ruth had a great heart connection to her mother-in-law. Even though she'd lost her husband to death and had every right to go back to her people, Ruth's love for Naomi was unbreakable. And she vowed to stay with her to the end. Her loyalty was evident and beautiful.

We can replicate that same kind of devotion today. It's important we understand how to love others well. Investing time and energy in those we care for strengthens our bond to one another. It helps us feel safe and secure, giving us courage in the hard moments. It makes us feel worthy of good things. And it offers an earthly support system to weather the storms.

It's because of God's mighty love for us that He brings people into our lives. Their presence blesses us in magnificent ways. And truth be told, there is nothing so sweet as earthly community to do life with.

. . . .

Lord, would You bless me with good friends and family? I long to have the kind of heart connection Ruth and Naomi had. I want to experience its goodness. Open my eyes to see the right people at the right time.

SAVED THROUGH FAITH

*"We deserve to die for our crimes, but this man hasn't done
anything wrong." Then he said, "Jesus, remember me
when you come into your Kingdom." And Jesus replied,
"I assure you, today you will be with me in paradise."*

LUKE 23:41–43 NLT

For any of us who get caught up in the idea we must be *works focused*
to earn our salvation, let today's verses settle the matter once and for
all. Because the truth is we can't do anything to make it happen. The
Word tells us in Ephesians 2:8 that it's by grace through faith we are
saved. It's nothing we do. Salvation is a gift of God.

What's so comforting about the scripture reading above is that
it proves this to be true. One of the two criminals being crucified
with Jesus chose to believe He was who He said He was. He didn't
have the ability to work for it. He couldn't do anything to make His
salvation a reality, except ask for it. And right then and there, the
criminal became a believer. He was saved by his faith.

So, take heart and take a deep breath. It's not your job to earn
your way into heaven. It's your job to believe first and then pursue
righteous living.

. . . .

*Lord, what a relief to know I'm unable to earn my way
into heaven. Thank You for knowing I'm imperfect and
for making a way for me to be with You forever regardless.*

GOD ANSWERS PRAYERS

"I prayed for this child, and the LORD has granted me what I asked of him. So now I give him to the LORD. For his whole life he will be given over to the LORD." And he worshiped the LORD there.

1 SAMUEL 1:27–28 NIV

Hannah's story is a powerful example of God answering prayer. It's reminding us that what may be impossible in the natural way is always possible when the Lord chooses to move. And while He isn't a genie in a bottle—always ready and willing to give us our heart's desire—God hears our cries and promises to do what is best.

What are you asking for right now that feels unattainable? Do you need a better job that pays more money? Do you need to finish your education? Are you asking God to remove the disease threatening your life? Do you need justice in a court case to prevail? Or are you praying for salvation for someone special? Like Hannah, don't give up asking God for your heart's desire.

Be encouraged today, knowing He hears your prayers. And even more, that nothing is impossible with the Lord.

. . . .

Lord, it's a privilege to pray and know You're listening. Thank You for that! Because You know what my heart longs for, I trust You to move on my behalf.

HE DREW NEAR

*He entered our world, a world He made; yet the world
did not recognize Him. Even though He came to His
own people, they refused to listen and receive Him.*
John 1:10–11 voice

God went to unfathomable lengths to bridge the gap sin left between us and Himself. He didn't want to let anything keep us separated. God loved us—His creation made in His image—so deeply that He sent His Son to make things right. He drew near by stepping out of heaven and into the world. And even though He was unappreciated, abused, deserted, and disregarded, rest assured He would do it all over again to be with you.

Be encouraged knowing how deeply God loves you. There is nothing you can do that would make Him love you any *more* or any *less* than He does right now. He delights in your life as heaven cheers you on from above.

So today, meditate on the sacrifices the Lord made for you. Imagine what it must have felt like to be treated so badly by so many. Or what it must have felt like being a supernatural, eternal life force confined by a human body. Or how difficult it must have been His knowing the fate that awaited Him. Jesus' willingness to sacrifice in such ways lets us know how valuable and worthy we are to Him.

. . . .

*Lord, You gave up so much for me.
Thank You for Your deep and sacrificial love.*

FOREIGN GODS

*Then all the people of Israel turned back to the L*ORD*. So Samuel
said to all the Israelites, "If you are returning to the L*ORD *with
all your hearts, then rid yourselves of the foreign gods and the
Ashtoreths and commit yourselves to the L*ORD *and serve him
only, and he will deliver you out of the hand of the Philistines."*

1 SAMUEL 7:2–3 NIV

Our God is a jealous God. He doesn't want anything in our life to
be above Him. The Lord wants Himself to be our priority, without
compromise. And when we stray, God is ready for our return with
open arms.

Let Samuel's edict to the Israelites resonate with you. The idea
of God's people ridding themselves of foreign gods applies to all
believers—including you. Let's face it: We all entertain foreign gods.
It may just look different today than it did back then.

Ask yourself what you place above the Lord. What gets top
billing each day? Social media? That new series on Netflix? Time out
with friends? Shopping? Exercise? Family? Be intentional to reset
your priorities so God gets your best. Find the courage to rearrange
your time or focus. And return to the Lord with all your heart,
recommitting your life to serving Him with passion.

* *

*Lord, I confess my priorities have been off and I've given my time
and focus to other things above You. Help me change that.*

PURSUING RIGHTEOUSNESS

Oh, how often they disobeyed Him in the wilderness and frustrated Him during their time in the desert! Over and over again, they tested God's patience and caused great pain for Israel's Holy One.
PSALM 78:40–41 VOICE

Even though the Israelites disobeyed continually, God never gave up on them. He punished them, yes. He brought His wrath at appropriate times. And ofttimes they paid the consequences for their disobedience. But the Lord never disowned them for their bad choices. Let this be an encouragement and a comfort, knowing there's nothing you can do to make God walk away either.

That being said, let's still choose to be women who pursue righteous living. We may not get it perfect. We won't always make the right decisions and lead with the best motives. And we'll most certainly act in ways that frustrate God and others. But we can seek to love the Lord with our lives.

The truth is that our salvation is settled, and no bad behavior can take it from us. We can't lose it. God's unwavering love ensures it. But when we follow His will and ways, a beautiful blessing will follow. And our obedience will delight Him!

....

Lord, forgive me for the times I've behaved like an Israelite. And help me choose to follow and obey You instead.

FOR GOD SO LOVED

"For this is how God loved the world: He gave his one and only Son, so that everyone who believes in him will not perish but have eternal life. God sent his Son into the world not to judge the world, but to save the world through him."

JOHN 3:16–17 NLT

You may deeply love those closest to you, but you'd never sacrifice a child to prove it. You probably wouldn't cash out your retirement funds, give up your home, or commit a crime to prove it either. Our love, as humans, has understandable limits. But God's love has no boundaries.

As a matter of fact, Ephesians 3:18–19 (VOICE) says His love is "infinitely long, wide, high, and deep, surpassing everything anyone previously experienced." Knowing that amazing truth helps us to believe that God *would* send His Son to make a way for restoration. He just loves us that much.

Stand strong in faith in this crazy world, knowing you are deeply loved. Understand that the Lord is unwilling to let anyone fall away. And believe God would—because God did—go to extraordinary lengths to prove it. He sent Jesus to reconcile the world and save it. And you're blessed because of it.

. . . .

Lord, I'm humbled by the depth and width and height of Your love for me. Let my confidence be anchored in it.

DECLARING GOD'S RIGHTEOUSNESS

The Eternal One is our witness, the One who first raised Moses
and Aaron to be leaders of the people, the One who brought
your ancestors here out of the oppression of Egypt. Now
stand ready as I will present to you, before the Eternal
One, a declaration of all the righteous acts the Eternal
has done on behalf of you and your ancestors.

1 SAMUEL 12:6–7 VOICE

The sweetest memories any of us can muster are the times God intersected in our situations or the situations of those we love. When we think back on how He saved a marriage or healed an addiction or restored a fractured family, it's humbling. We've seen God remove a disease. We've watched money appear in the nick of time. And our eyes have seen a hardened heart soften in the most tender way. God is amazing.

So when you need it most, take the time to declare all the righteous acts of God you have witnessed. Do it to strengthen yourself. Do it to strengthen your friends and family. Do it to praise Him, being purposeful to recognize God's goodness. There is something powerful that happens when you choose to remember.

. . . .

Lord, when I look back at all Your blessings in my life,
there are too many to count. I'm overwhelmed by the ways
You've healed, restored, saved, and loved me. Thank You!

AUTHENTICALLY YOU

"It's who you are and the way you live that count before God.
Your worship must engage your spirit in the pursuit of truth.
That's the kind of people the Father is out looking for: those who
are simply and honestly themselves before him in their worship."

JOHN 4:23 MSG

God appreciates authenticity. We don't need to put on airs or try to be something we're not. He isn't expecting us to be anything more than who we are—who He created us to be. And while we may feel pressure from the world to be magnificent, God already knows we *are* magnificent, simply because we are His.

It's when we embrace this truth that we're able to worship honestly and simply before Him. Since we're not trying to pretend to be holier or better or different than others, our praise is organic. And the aroma is sweet.

Be emboldened to be yourself, not only to God, but also to others. Your authentic self—with all its coolness and quirkiness—is His purposeful design. He thought you up. God chose who you would be. He intentionally pieced you together, to make you expressly unique, to be the woman you were meant to be.

Lord, thank You for reminding me that who I
am is good and planned by You! Give me the
courage to be authentic in every area of life.

TAKING GOD AT HIS WORD

The king's officer pleaded with Him, Sir, do come down at once
before my little child is dead! Jesus answered him, Go in peace;
your son will live! And the man put his trust in what Jesus said
and started home. But even as he was on the road going down,
his servants met him and reported, saying, Your son lives!

JOHN 4:49–51 AMPC

The king's officer took Jesus at His word. Rather than trying to manage the miracle by insisting He come home with him, this father
simply chose to believe. He honored the Messiah by believing that
He was who He said He was and that He'd do what He said He'd
do. That's faith!

The stress this father must have been under, knowing his child
was deathly ill. The desperation to find solutions. The pressure to
uncover healing. And even with all that weighing on him, the man
was able to set it aside and. . .*trust*. That's an extraordinary feat no
matter how you slice it.

Let that build confidence in us today. We don't need to beg
God to come with us. We don't need to see anything in writing.
Our faith doesn't require a sworn statement. If God says He will do
something—if He makes a promise—*it will come to pass*. We can
take heart because our Father is faithful!

* *

Lord, I choose to take You at Your word.

WHEN YOU NEED QUICK COMPASSION

*Do not hold the sins of our ancestors against us, but send
Your compassion to meet us quickly, God. We are in deep despair.
Help us, O God who saves us, to the honor and glory of Your name.*

PSALM 79:8–9 VOICE

Sometimes we need God's compassion to meet us *quickly*. Like when we betray a friend, and our apology isn't received. Or when we give in to sin again, especially knowing it's a destructive decision. Or when we are exhausted from trying to make right what we made wrong, and we're left feeling hopeless. Or when life throws one curveball after the next and we can't seem to find our footing.

The good news for every believer is that our despair matters to the divine. We are deeply loved and cherished by the Creator. And God sees our predicament and all the ways it destabilizes our heart. He understands how it ushers in fear, sadness, and insecurity. He misses nothing. So, when we need quick compassion from our heavenly Father, we will find it. God will be the one to save us. He will rescue His beloved.

Today, cry out and ask for God's peace and comfort. Ask for His compassion. Make no mistake. . .you are worthy of it.

*Lord, thank You for knowing there are times I need quick
compassion from You. And thank You for blessing me with it.*

THE GIFT OF FRIENDSHIP

*And Jonathan made a covenant with David because
he loved him as himself. Jonathan took off the robe he
was wearing and gave it to David, along with his
tunic, and even his sword, his bow and his belt.*

1 SAMUEL 18:3–4 NIV

David and Jonathan had a beautiful and powerful friendship. God knit their hearts together, and they stood in solidarity. Even though his father, Saul, had a love/hate relationship with David, Jonathan's care for his friend never wavered. His loyalty was never in question. And it created a special bond between them that was unbreakable.

Many of us envy this kind of friendship because we don't have it in our life. We long for it, but it's never materialized. Nonetheless, take heart, friend! God made us for community. He understands its importance to our heart, happiness, and mental health. We need friends to hold us up in hard times, grieve with us in sad times, and celebrate with us in good times. Yes, His desire is for us to be surrounded by loving family and friends as we navigate life!

Make it a daily plea until it comes to be. Our pursuit for a Jonathan is a worthy one!

*Lord, true friendship is such a gift and something
I deeply desire. Please hear my cry for a Jonathan
and bring one my way. Thank You!*

TURNING LAMENT INTO PRAYERS

Then we will not turn away from You. Bring us back to life!
And we will call out for You! O Eternal God, Commander of
heaven's armies, bring us back to You. Turn the light of Your face
upon us so that we will be rescued from this sea of darkness.

PSALM 80:18–19 VOICE

Today's scripture is a communal lament after the fall of Israel. In their sin, God's people felt the rift in their heart and were desperate to reconnect with Him in meaningful ways. They knew His displeasure in their choices. And they wanted to make it better.

In these two short verses, notice they twice asked the Lord to bring them back to Him. They asked God to turn His face toward them again, acknowledging He is their rescuer. The realization of their bad choices was evident. And in His great love and compassion, their relationship was eventually restored.

Take a deep breath. You may be freaking out over your sin, afraid it will cause you to be ostracized and rejected by God. But that simply isn't the truth. God doesn't work that way. He loves you and wants a relationship. So, turn your lament into prayer and let Him know how you're feeling. Repent. Ask Him to settle your heart with His compassion and love. And then feel God's embrace of goodness on your life as you commit to righteous living.

Lord, I'm sorry. I love You.

THE LORD FULLY SATISFIES

Jesus replied, "I am the bread of life. Whoever comes to me will never be hungry again. Whoever believes in me will never be thirsty."

JOHN 6:35 NLT

The bottom line from today's passage of scripture is that the Lord fully satisfies. When you decide He's the solution to every problem, the answer to every need, and the fulfillment of every longing, the result will be a contentment unmatched by anything the world may try to offer. You won't feel a lacking. You won't feel deprived. And there won't be a longing for something more. He is everything. God is everything.

Today, be encouraged to know this powerful truth. No matter where you are in life right now, regardless of where you feel deficient and wanting, pressing into God will remedy it. And this choice will bring perspective and hope to your weary heart. It may not make all your trouble go away, but it will remind you God is in full control and His plans are for good.

Embrace your faith in new and fresh ways and choose to see the Lord of all as your source and provider. You're not alone or left to your own devices. Invite God into every part of your life and experience the blessing.

Lord, help me always see You as my everything. No matter what I'm facing, You're the solution. What a gift!

HE'S EXPERIENCED IT ALL

At this point many of his disciples turned away and deserted him. Then Jesus turned to the Twelve and asked, "Are you also going to leave?" Simon Peter replied, "Lord, to whom would we go? You have the words that give eternal life. We believe, and we know you are the Holy One of God."

JOHN 6:66–69 NLT

While we aren't glad Jesus felt abandoned by His followers, it does help us realize we're completely understood by Him. Because Jesus was both fully human and fully God at the same time, He would have experienced the full range of human emotions. So that means when we go to the Lord with our challenges and frustrations, He can authentically sympathize.

In those moments when you don't feel comfortable sharing your innermost feelings and struggles with others for fear of judgment, let the Lord be your refuge. You can tell Him anything. Truth be told, He already knows it anyway. God is omniscient. And He will protect your heart, your secret, your fears and insecurities and bring comfort too.

Trust the Lord to be a confidant, even when you can't trust anyone else. Know that He won't judge you. He won't condemn or make you feel silly. Nor will He hold it against you. Better than all others, God understands, and His love never changes.

. . . .

Lord, You endured so much pain in the world and understand all I go through. That brings so much relief and hope to my heart.

CARING FOR THE MARGINALIZED

"Stand up for the poor and the orphan; advocate for the rights of the afflicted and those in need. Deliver the poor and the needy; rescue them from their evil oppressors."
PSALM 82:3–4 VOICE

While this passage of scripture is the image of a moment in heaven where God is accusing His messengers of a lackluster performance, it's a call we should heed too. He is faulting them for not caring for the poor. He's indicting them for not pursuing justice. And because the marginalized obviously matter greatly to God, today's reading provides an opportunity to see if we are caring for the orphan, the afflicted, the needy, and the poor.

We're called to love with abandon. The Lord's desire is for us to be His hands and feet in the world. That's why we financially support organizations who serve these groups. It's why we volunteer our time to help meet the needs of the less fortunate. The call to love is why we take mission trips and start local ministries. In God's eye, everyone matters.

Heed God's call. Be strong in your commitment to love the marginalized so no one can accuse you of not caring. When you step out in obedience, they will be encouraged, knowing God not only sees them but also cares.

. . . .

Lord, tender my heart to care for humanity.
Let me be a woman who loves well.

TIMING

*Then the leaders tried to arrest him; but no one laid a
hand on him, because his time had not yet come.*

JOHN 7:30 NLT

Here's the gold nugget to take from today's scripture reading: nothing can go against God's plan and timing. If it's His will, it will happen. When the time is right, His plan will come to pass. And we can trust the Lord's schedule to be binding. In this crazy world, the one and only thing we can be sure of is that God's in control.

Consider that while you were still in the womb, the Lord made plans for your life. He planned the timing of your entrance onto the world stage. He planned the timing of your successes and failures. He planned the day you'd see Him face-to-face. And when the hour strikes, it will all come to pass.

Be comforted by this truth today! Experience the relief of knowing God's blueprints are valid and withstanding. Be reassured in knowing nothing can knock His plan off course. Take heart in knowing He's leading with certainty, following the design He determined long ago. If what you've been waiting for hasn't happened yet, rest knowing the time has not yet come.

. . . .

*Lord, I love knowing there is a time for everything.
Let that powerful truth bring me comfort and courage.*

STRENGTH THROUGH GOD

*David was greatly distressed because the men were talking of
stoning him; each one was bitter in spirit because of his sons and
daughters. But David found strength in the LORD his God.*
1 SAMUEL 30:6 NIV

When it all hit the fan, David strengthened himself in the Lord. His
men were turning on him in anger, blaming David. While they were
out on a mission, hostiles had taken their wives and children, and
he was about to be the scapegoat. Without one friendly face around
him, David went to God for hope and wisdom. In that moment, he
was strengthened.

So often we think our strength comes from our bestie. We look
to our significant other for help. We lean on a parent or coworker or
neighbor. And while they are all awesome and important, they aren't
our savior. The very best they have to offer pales in comparison to
what we receive through faith.

Let David's example rejuvenate you today! With no one around to
bring encouragement, he had no option but to take his needs directly
to God. No matter what situation we're in or challenge we face, this
will always be our best option anyway. There is no substitute for what
the Lord can (and will) do for those who love Him.

. . . .

Lord, thank You for the reminder that You are all I need.

HOW FORTUNATE YOU ARE

*For the Eternal God is a sun and a shield. The Eternal grants
favor and glory; He doesn't deny any good thing to those
who live with integrity. O Eternal One, Commander of
heaven's armies, how fortunate are those who trust You.*

PSALM 84:11–12 VOICE

Let the words in today's passage wash over you like a tidal wave
of truth. The psalmist saw God correctly and documented Him as
a blessing and left a reminder for those who would come next. Be
expectant for the Lord to be these for you too.

Let God both shine His glory into your day while shielding you
from the harmful rays of life. Feel the warmth of His favor as God
blesses your good choices and intentional obedience. Can you see
this playing out in your circumstances? Have you been awake and
aware of all the ways He has captured your heart? As a believer, how
fortunate that you have a loving Father who dotes on His daughters.

So be full of confidence, knowing God won't deny His beloved as
you walk out—albeit imperfectly—righteous living. Be assured that
when you live with intention and integrity, good things will follow.

*Lord, thank You for seeing my pursuit of upright
living and blessing it. I know I'm fortunate to receive
Your favor as I trust You each step of the way.*

CAN'T FIGURE HIM OUT

Some of the Pharisees said, "This man Jesus is not from God,
for he is working on the Sabbath." Others said, "But how
could an ordinary sinner do such miraculous signs?"
So there was a deep division of opinion among them.
JOHN 9:16 NLT

There is comfort in knowing we cannot figure out God. No matter how much we try to make sense of Him, we simply can't. The Lord doesn't fit into the box. His actions aren't easily determined or defined. We can't often explain His decisions or timing. And, in all actuality, that's a good thing. What a relief to know His ways are not our ways. Would you want to serve a God you could figure out?

So let your heart be at rest today. Your inability to comprehend the complexity of the Lord is good! It's normal. And rather than beat your head against a wall trying to decode the divine, choose instead to trust His plans. Embrace the mystery that surrounds His magnificence and fall into the safety of His mighty arms.

We don't have to be in charge, because He is. And we don't have to dissect His every move, because faith reminds us God works for our good and His glory.

Lord, it's oddly comforting to just let You work in my
life. I trust You to make all the loose ends come together,
providing clarity. Until then, I'll cling to peace.

THE WAY

*"Yes, I am the gate. Those who come in through me will
be saved. They will come and go freely and will find good
pastures. The thief's purpose is to steal and kill and destroy.
My purpose is to give them a rich and satisfying life."*

JOHN 10:9–10 NLT

The most amazing part of this scripture is understanding the intentional decision of God to make a way for believers to have eternal life. Jesus became a gate for us to walk through to find redemption. He gave us an option to be restored. He created a path to salvation. He loved us—loves us—that much.

God didn't throw His holy hands in the air and give up when sin entered the world. He didn't let out a huge exhale in disgust. God didn't entertain the idea of walking away. And He never considered letting the thief's plans of stealing, killing, and destroying prevail. Instead, a way for liberation was created.

No terrible decisions you may currently be making, nor any past seasons of sinning, will keep you from heaven. If you're a believer and follower of Jesus, once you have walked through the gate, it's a done deal. You have everlasting life.

. . . .

*Lord, thank You for Jesus making a way
for my salvation. My life is Yours. I love You!*

YOUR PRAYERS AND PLEAS

O Eternal One, lend an ear and hear my prayer; listen to my pleading voice. When times of trouble come, I will call to You because I know You will respond to me.

PSALM 86:6–7 VOICE

Let your faith be steadfast, wholeheartedly believing God is working all things for your good and His glory. Choose to believe He hears the depths of your prayers and pleas. Be a woman full of faith, trusting and waiting for God to act on your behalf. It's His honor and privilege to shepherd His sheep, taking care of every need, every time.

Are you scared by a diagnosis? Did your finances fall through? Is your marriage stuck in a rough patch? Is parenting toddlers or teenagers wearing you out? Do you feel unqualified for the new job? Are you afraid for the future? Has the state of the world unsteadied your heart?

Go right to God and let Him comfort you. Let Him bring a fresh perspective for you to grab on to. Let every time of trouble drive you to the Lord, knowing He will always respond in the perfect way needed, in that moment.

. . . .

Lord, thank You for hearing my prayers and pleas.
Thank You for being a reliable God who is trustworthy and
faithful to meet me in my need, ready to fulfill my heart's desires.

ACKNOWLEDGING GOD'S POSITION

*But Lord, You are a God full of compassion, generous in grace,
slow to anger, and boundless in loyal love and truth. Look
at me, and grant me Your favor. Invest Your strength in me,
Your servant, and rescue me, Your handmaiden's child.*

PSALM 86:15–16 VOICE

Did you notice the approach to prayer the psalmist took? Before asking for help, the writer acknowledged the splendor and majesty of God. He unpacked His awesomeness. And then he proceeded to ask for what was needed.

No, this is not manipulative. It's reverent. It's respectful and humble. It's worshipful. The psalmist wasn't trying to butter God up for the ask. Instead, he was solidifying the Lord's position in relation to his own. He was letting God know His leadership was understood. And then once his perspective was established, the requests followed.

Let this be a powerful example for you to follow. Why not consider this format in your own prayer life? It will set your heart right first and foremost while simultaneously boosting your confidence in God's greatness. So as you ask for His favor or strength or help, you will have already reminded yourself that God is all-powerful, fully capable, and always willing.

. . . .

*Lord, let me always approach You with humility,
wholly aware of Your unwavering magnificence.*

FULL RANGE OF EMOTIONS

*When Jesus saw her sobbing, and the Jews who came with her [also]
sobbing, He was deeply moved in spirit and troubled. [He chafed
in spirit and sighed and was disturbed.] And He said, Where have
you laid him? They said to Him, Lord, come and see. Jesus wept.*

JOHN 11:33–35 AMPC

The Bible tells us Jesus was able to experience the entire range of
emotions as a man during His time on earth. From righteous anger
to joy to grief and everything in between, becoming human allowed
Jesus a firsthand experience of what we regularly feel. So when His
friend Lazarus died, scripture says He was deeply moved and troubled,
and it made Him weep.

Do you see the gift in that? Today's verses remind us that no
matter what we are feeling—be it frustration, rejection, fear, worry,
or insecurity—Jesus is able to truly understand. And with that
understanding comes compassion. And with that compassion comes
action.

So be encouraged to unpack the depths of your heart with God. Be
confident, holding back nothing. And take heart in Him because He
gets it. There is no better sounding board and no one better qualified
to handle your struggles and frustrations than the Lord.

*Lord, I'm humbled by the lengths You've gone to in Your love
for me. Thank You for knowing me fully and completely.*

A CONFIDENT SACRIFICE

*A dinner was prepared in Jesus' honor. Martha served, and
Lazarus was among those who ate with him. Then Mary took
a twelve-ounce jar of expensive perfume made from essence
of nard, and she anointed Jesus' feet with it, wiping his feet
with her hair. The house was filled with the fragrance.*

JOHN 12:2–3 NLT

What a beautiful picture of selfless love. Mary poured out a treasured possession as a sacrifice, washing Jesus' feet with a jar of expensive perfume. To make it even more meaningful, she used her own hair to wipe His feet.

Yet one disciple was vocal about his disapproval of Mary's actions. Judas thought it would have made more sense to sell the perfume and feed the poor. He looked right past her compassion and criticized instead. But Jesus defended her sacrifice because He saw her heart behind it.

Don't worry about what others think. There will always be someone ready to complain or condemn. The world is full of nitpickers. When you feel led to show your love and care in meaningful ways, be courageous about it. Remember who you're ultimately serving. And let your selflessness shine a spotlight on God's goodness.

*Lord, give me confidence to love with abandon even when
naysayers pass judgment or find fault with my actions.
My desire is to always serve You and those You send my way.*

NO FLOWERY WORDS

*I'm standing my ground, GOD, shouting for help, at my prayers
every morning, on my knees each daybreak. Why, GOD, do you
turn a deaf ear? Why do you make yourself scarce? For as long as
I remember I've been hurting; I've taken the worst you can hand
out, and I've had it. Your wildfire anger has blazed through my
life; I'm bleeding, black-and-blue. You've attacked me fiercely
from every side, raining down blows till I'm nearly dead.*
PSALM 88:13–17 MSG

The writer of this psalm is in deep despair. He holds nothing back in
his communication to God. He doesn't use flowery words. He doesn't
make light of his situation. In fact, he's talking tough—he's standing
his ground with God. And he means business!

So often we take the soft approach with God. Christians are
supposed to be sweet, gentle and soft-spoken...right? And sometimes,
that flows into our relationship with God. We forget that we can
be 100 percent real with Him, 100 percent of the time. So, we hold
back our feelings in our prayers. But God is big enough to handle
whatever we lay on Him. Our anger. Our fears. Our worries. Our
disappointments. Our hurts. He can take it! He only cares that we
bring it *all* to Him. Because that's where our troubled hearts should
go—directly to our heavenly Father.

*God, I have no flowery words to share with You today.
I am hurting. I need You now! Please help me!*

MORE JESUS

"I did not come to judge the world but to save the world."
JOHN 12:47 ESV

We Christians are often hypercritical of others, aren't we? . . .

"I wouldn't associate with her. She's been divorced—twice!"

"Did you see the way her daughter dresses? What terrible parenting!"

"They call themselves Christians? They haven't been to church in weeks!"

Now imagine that Jesus looks at us the very same judgmental way:

"No way would I save her. Did you hear what she said about her husband yesterday?"

"Um. . .I know what she was thinking in her meeting at work this afternoon. What a terrible human being!"

"Now why would she go and let her kid do something like that? She's the worst!"

We need a little perspective from time to time, don't we? What a relief that Jesus came to save and not to judge—or we'd all be in some serious trouble! The truth of the matter is we *all* need Jesus. The more Jesus in our lives, the better! So rather than spend our time judging each other, let's take more time getting to know each other. Serving each other. Loving each other. Supporting each other. Celebrating— *together*—the Savior who came to save *all*.

. . . .

Beautiful Savior, thank You for the reminder that I am far from perfect, and so I have no right to judge anyone else. If You don't judge, Lord, I certainly shouldn't. Thank You for coming to save everyone!

KNOWN BY LOVE

*[Dear] little children. . . You are not able to come where
I am going. I give you a new commandment: . . . Just as
I have loved you, so you too should love one another.
By this shall all [men] know that you are My disciples.*

JOHN 13:33–35 AMPC

After Jesus explains to His disciples that they can't go with Him to the cross, He gives them a new commandment: "Just as I have loved you, so you too should love one another." He had already told the Jews they should love each other, but this "new" commandment came with a higher standard: to love *as He loves*. Jesus assures the disciples this is how all people will know they are His true followers. Their love will be what sets them apart from the rest of the world.

You might be thinking, *How is it possible to love like Jesus? Christ's love is a divine, unconditional love. . .and human love has limits.* There is truth to this. . . . While humans, left to their own devices, *can't* love like Jesus, humans *with Jesus can love like Jesus*. He makes all things possible, including our ability to love like Him! (See Matthew 19:26; Luke 1:37; Philippians 4:13; Mark 10:27.) Today, set a new, higher standard for yourself as you show others the love of Christ. Ask God for His help!

. . . .

God, I want to be known by my love—a love that looks like Yours!

PASSWORDS OF PRAISE

Blessed are the people who know the passwords of praise.
. . . Delighted, they dance all day long; they know who
you are. . .they can't keep it quiet! Your vibrant beauty
has gotten inside us. . . . We're walking on air!
PSALM 89:15–17 MSG

Read these verses from the Psalms. Surely you want to be one of *those* people. A delighted soul? . . . Joyful dancing? . . . Walking on air? . . . More of it *all* please! It's not just wishful thinking. If you know the "passwords of praise," you can be—in fact, you *are*!—one of *those* people!

What are these "passwords of praise," exactly? . . . The pure joys of Jesus! Worship. Obedience. Experiencing the power of the gospel.

If life has been dark and dreary for far too long, perhaps you should take stock of your spiritual status. While life isn't all sunshine and rainbows—the storm clouds and rains *will* come—it is possible to experience perpetually sunny days when you walk with Jesus. Each storm presents an opportunity to experience the warmth and light of the Son. So, when the skies darken, the lightning flashes, and the thunder booms, pull closer to the heavenly Father. Don't allow the storms to distract you from the divine. Grab hold of God's hand and don't let go. His goodness and love will light up your whole world!

Today, Lord, I ask You to light up my world!

A JIGSAW PUZZLE LIFE

*GOD made my life complete when I placed all the pieces before him.
. . . He gave me a fresh start. . . . I haven't taken God for granted.
Every day I review the ways he works. . . . I feel put back together.*

2 SAMUEL 22:21–24 MSG

Sometimes life feels like a giant jigsaw puzzle with lots of teeny-tiny pieces—and many of them have gone missing.

David knew what a "missing puzzle pieces" life was like. He experienced it firsthand. But instead of lamenting and keeping his focus on how bad things were, he chose to turn everything over to God. He gave God his whole life—every single puzzle piece—and submitted to Him. David, though imperfect, lived for God. He kept God's rules and fully depended on God. And though he sometimes failed, David never turned away from Him. And so, God rewarded David for his righteousness. He took the pieces of David's life and put it all back together.

Like David, we too can make the wise choice to give our puzzle pieces to God. When we ask for help, God hears. He will put the puzzle of our lives back together, creating a complete and beautiful picture of beauty, hope, and faith.

*Father God, my life sometimes feels like a jumbled mess,
and I need Your help! Today, I give all the pieces of
my life to You. I trust You to put it all together.*

JOY-GIVER

"A woman giving birth to a child has pain because her time has come; but when her baby is born she forgets the anguish because of her joy that a child is born into the world. So. . .now is your time of grief, but I will see you again and you will rejoice, and no one will take away your joy."

JOHN 16:21–22 NIV

Jesus was getting ready to go to the cross. But before He did, He explained this astounding truth from the book of John to His disciples: their grief would turn to joy. The *very* thing that would cause them pain would be the same thing that ultimately brought them lasting joy. Because this probably wasn't clear to the disciples how this could be, Jesus used the example of childbirth.

The laboring of a mother, as she brings a child into the world, is unbelievably hard and painful—this is the "grief" part of what Jesus was talking about. But the ultimate feeling of joy takes over once the mother holds her child in her arms. Childbirth brings pain. . .and joy! Just like the cross brings grief. . .and joy!

Our grief here on earth is temporary, dear one. But joy with Jesus is eternal!

. . . .

Joy-giver, thank You for the promise of eternal rejoicing. It encourages my heart to know that any grief I experience serves a greater purpose and will one day be turned to joy that lasts forever.

IN HIS HANDS

Jesus answered them, "Do you finally believe? In fact, you're about to make a run for it—saving your own skins and abandoning me. But. . .The Father is with me. I've told you all this so that. . .you will be unshakable and assured, deeply at peace. In this godless world you will continue to experience difficulties. But take heart! I've conquered the world."
JOHN 16:31–33 MSG

As Christ-followers, it's easy to become discouraged in a world that seems to move farther and farther away from Jesus. The gap becomes more pronounced by the day. Wars. Disease. Natural disasters. Political unrest. It seems there's one crisis after another. And even those who follow Christ could be pulled into the fray if our focus is too much on the world and not enough on Jesus. Our anxiety and depression may threaten to spiral out of control. We may even lose hope.

But. . .just as God didn't abandon His Son on the cross, Jesus assured His disciples that He was still in control and always would be—because He conquered the world! So, take heart. As bad as things might seem, our heavenly Father has us in His hands—today, tomorrow, and for eternity! With the unfailing promise of Jesus, we have lasting joy, peace, comfort, and hope!

Lord, because of Your unfailing promises, I always have hope. As the world grows apart from You, draw me closer to Your heart. Thank You for Your love and salvation!

OUR FOREVER HOME

Lord, through all the generations you have been our home!
Before the mountains were born, before you gave birth to the
earth and the world, from beginning to end, you are God.
PSALM 90:1–2 NLT

Here, the psalmist is praising God. He is celebrating the consistent character of the heavenly Father, who does not change (Hebrews 13:8)—who has been the "home" of humanity since the beginning of time, and who will continue to be our home for all eternity (Deuteronomy 33:27).

When you think of *home*, what comes to mind? What emotions do you feel? . . . Comfort, love, calm, family, warmth, acceptance, forgiveness, joy, fun. . . For some, there really is no place like home. But for others, home isn't warm and fuzzy—instead, it's been filled with hardship and strain, sadness and chaos.

No matter what your home is like right now—or has been like in the past—there is good news: we've all received an invitation to a *forever home* with Jesus. And home with Him offers everything our souls crave—peace, beauty, tranquility, grace, love without limits . . . It's the home we've always longed for, and the door is wide open, complete with a WELCOME mat outside. Take a step inside your forever home today.

. . . .

Father God, I accept Your invitation to my forever home with
You. Thank You for being such a good Father, for giving me love
and grace, peace and comfort—all the things my soul craves!

A SELFLESS REQUEST

God said to [Solomon], "Because you. . .have asked for the ability to lead and govern well, I'll give you what you've asked for—I'm giving you a wise and mature heart. . . . As a bonus, I'm giving you both the wealth and glory you didn't ask for. . . . And if you stay on course, keeping your eye on the life-map and the God-signs as your father David did, I'll also give you a long life."

1 KINGS 3:11–14 MSG

Why would God give Solomon whatever he asked for? Was Solomon a perfect servant of God? Did Solomon know something we don't? . . . Maybe Solomon had a secret. . . .

Solomon didn't have insider information, but he *did* do something very right. When he made a request of God, it wasn't selfish. Instead, Solomon asked for wisdom. In fact, his request was solely focused on others—the people in his kingdom, to be exact. He wanted to lead his people well. And Solomon knew he'd need God to help him do just that.

Like Solomon, when we walk in God's way, when we obey His Word and make requests according to His will, He will grant us what we ask for. And He might just add in some extra blessings along the way! Praise Him!

Wisdom-giver, thank You for answered prayer.
Remind me that when I follow Your will and
Your ways, You will bless me beyond measure.

TAKE COVER

Those who live in the shelter of the Most High will find rest in the shadow of the Almighty. . . . He alone is my refuge, my place of safety. . . . He will rescue you. . .and protect you. . . . He will cover you with his feathers. He will shelter you with his wings.

PSALM 91:1–4 NLT

Imagine a helpless baby bird snuggled up safe and cozy in the warm, fluffy feathers of his mama. There, under her wings, he is protected, cared for, sheltered from the dangers of the outside world. In the nest, mama bird will shield her baby from the storms and deliver daily meals to keep him healthy and growing stronger every day.

This is a beautiful picture of how the heavenly Father cares for us. There will always be danger in the world. There will be troubles and worries that plague our minds and pain our hearts. Yet, when we know Jesus, we live in "the shelter of the Most High." And there, we are safe and secure. He will cover us and rescue us from the hard things. . .and in the safety of His presence, we can truly rest and find comfort for our weary souls.

When you find yourself in need of rescue, run to the Most High! Take cover under His wings of protection and love!

. . . .

*My refuge, my God, thank You for being my safe place.
In You, I take comfort. In You, I find sweet rest.*

YOUR FAVORITE GO-TO

The LORD says, "I will rescue those who love me. I will protect
those who trust in my name. When they call on me, I will answer;
I will be with them in trouble. I will rescue and honor them.
I will reward them with a long life and give them my salvation."
PSALM 91:14–16 NLT

Who do you call when you need advice? Who listens when you need to talk? Who has your back, lending unwavering support or a helping hand when you need it most? Surely there's one person who is your go-to, most trusted human being of all time.

But has your go-to person ever broken a promise? Left your urgent text unopened or unanswered, your important call unreturned? . . . Humans, even the very best of them, let us down sometimes.

But there is one who can be trusted every second, every minute, every hour of every day of every year. His name is Jesus. And when we trust Him wholly, when we love Him completely, He makes good on all His promises and—even better!—He offers us many wonderful things in return. He assures us of His presence. His rescue. His honor. His reward. His salvation.

Have you chosen to follow Jesus? If you have, praise Him! If you haven't, it's not too late! . . .

My Lord and Savior, I trust You. I love You. Come into my heart.
I want to follow You, praise and honor You, all my days.

CELEBRATE!

*It is a good and delightful thing to give thanks to the Lord,
to sing praises. . .to Your name, O Most High, to show forth
Your loving-kindness in the morning and Your faithfulness
by night. . . . For You, O Lord, have made me glad by
Your works; at the deeds of Your hands I joyfully sing.*

PSALM 92:1–2, 4 AMPC

Some people record their blessings. They keep a journal where they write down the good things that happen every day. This helps them maintain a positive outlook on life and serves as a great reminder that the bad days really aren't *all* bad. There is some good in every bad day too!

Here, in Psalm 92, something good has happened, and the psalmist is celebrating and showing his delight in song: "You, O Lord, have made me glad by Your works; at the deeds of Your hands I joyfully sing." Journaling your blessings or singing about them—both are wonderful expressions of the heavenly Father's goodness in everyday living.

This world, while often difficult, doesn't have to leave us down and depressed. When we belong to Jesus, we have the promise of His blessing. We have the benefit of His kindness and goodness. And if we keep our focus on those things, our emotional wellness will benefit mightily. Praise Him!

. . . .

*God, You are so, so good. Help me to keep my
focus on Your loving-kindness. Thank You for
these wonderful things that happened today. . .*

WAY-MAKER

*"Blessed be GOD, who has given peace to his people Israel.
. . . Not one of all those good and wonderful words that he
spoke through Moses has misfired. May GOD. . .continue to
be with us just as he was with our ancestors—may he never
give up and walk out on us. May he keep us centered and
devoted to him, following the life path he has cleared."*

1 KINGS 8:56–58 MSG

When we're staring trouble in the face or having a conflict with a difficult person, it's human nature to want to run. . .to give up or give in. . .to do whatever it takes to escape a less-than-desirable situation. Better yet, it would be nice if we could avoid conflict altogether, wouldn't it? But life this side of heaven will never be trouble-free.

So, when trouble comes, instead of running away. . .run *into* the arms of the heavenly Father. He is the strong and steady rock, who was with you yesterday, who is with you today, and who will be with you tomorrow. He will *never* run out on you. He will *never* give up on you. And He will *always* make a way for you.

Like He promised (verse 56), God will give you peace despite the pandemonium. Cling tight to His promise and keep your face turned toward Him today and all your days to come.

. . . .

*Way-maker, thank You for Your constant
presence in my life. I cling to Your promises.*

WHEN DOUBT CREEPS IN

*[Thomas said,] "Unless I see in his hands the mark of
the nails, and place my finger into the mark of the nails,
and place my hand into his side, I will never believe."*
JOHN 20:25 ESV

If you've ever experienced feelings of doubt when it comes to God,
you're in good company. The Bible shares numerous true stories of
doubters who needed an extra boost of faith:

- Thomas, who doubted Jesus had risen from the dead
  (verse 25)

- A desperate father, whose son was possessed by an evil
  spirit (Mark 9:24)

- Sarah, who laughed when God promised to give her a son
  in her old age (Genesis 18:11–12)

While we know (in our minds) that we can trust God, we often
feel (in our hearts) that He might not come through for us. When
doubt creeps in and begins to take root, tell God you're struggling.
Be honest. This makes room for Him to step in and meet your need.
Then, spend time in His Word. Immersing your heart and mind in
God's beautiful, unchanging truth is one of the best ways to free
your spirit from doubt. Never forget that *all things are possible* with
God (Matthew 19:26)!

. . . .

Lord, I believe!

INTO THE SEA!

Jesus stood on the shore; yet the disciples did not know that it was Jesus. Jesus said to them, "Children, do you have any fish?" They answered him, "No." He said to them, "Cast the net on the right side of the boat, and you will find some." So they cast it, and now they were not able to haul it in, because of the quantity of fish. That disciple whom Jesus loved therefore said to Peter, "It is the Lord!" When Simon Peter heard that it was the Lord, he. . .threw himself into the sea.

JOHN 21:4–7 ESV

The disciples didn't know the man on shore was Jesus. Yet, they listened when He told them to cast their net on the other side of their boat. And the payoff was big: more fish than their net could possibly hold! While the description of this catch is quite impressive, perhaps more notable is the reaction of Peter. When he recognized Jesus, he didn't waste any time; he wanted to get to his Lord right away! And so, Peter jumped into the sea!

Anytime you find yourself struggling, remember this story of Jesus calling to the disciples from the seashore. Just as He called out to them, He calls out to you today. Will you be like Peter and, without pause, jump into the sea with both feet?

. . . .

Lord, I am so thankful for Your Word that reminds me of Your greatness and power and love.

SOUL-SOOTHER

Who will protect me from the wicked? Who will stand up for me against evildoers? Unless the LORD had helped me, I would soon have settled in the silence of the grave. I cried out, "I am slipping!" but your unfailing love, O LORD, supported me. When doubts filled my mind, your comfort gave me renewed hope and cheer.

PSALM 94:16–19 NLT

What stresses you out? What doubts seep into your heart and fester? This world is full of hard things that add layers of anxiety to our already stressful lives. If you were to make a list, you'd probably need an extra-large sheet of paper with line...*after line*...*after line* of writing space.

When you experience stress and doubt, what calms your anxiety-filled heart? Quiet time with tea and a good book, perhaps? Lunch and conversation with a lifetime bestie? An after-dinner power nap? A warm bubble bath? . . . Certainly, these feel-good things can offer a temporary reprieve from life's chaos. And yet...there is something—*someone*—better. This someone offers a lasting, permanent hope for your doubting heart and calm for your anxiety-ridden soul. This someone is the one and only true soul-soother, Jesus.

The writer of Psalm 94 knew his help, hope, and protection would always be found in the unfailing love and comfort of the Lord. You can trust in that same life-changing truth today! Isn't Jesus wonderful?

. . . .

Comfort-giver, Soul-soother, You alone are all I need today and all my days to come!

RAISE THE ROOF

Come, let's shout praises to GOD, raise the roof for the Rock who saved us! . . . GOD is the best, High King over all the gods. In one hand he holds deep caves and caverns, in the other hand grasps the high mountains. He made Ocean. . . ! His hands sculpted Earth! So come, let us worship: bow before him, on your knees before GOD, who made us! . . . He's our God, and we're the people he pastures, the flock he feeds.

PSALM 95:1, 3–7 MSG

Nations surrounding Israel would have been bewildered by a God who is ruler over all things and creator and sustainer of everything. After all, they worshipped gods of the sun, moon, stars. . .gods of the mountains and forests. . . You name it, they had a god for it. And so, they would have had a difficult time grasping the concept of one supreme God above their imaginary gods.

This psalm sets God apart as the Creator—naming Him as "the best" and "King over all the gods." Its words are overflowing with appreciation and thanksgiving for God's creation, His care, His provision, and His saving grace.

Join your heart in the worship. "Raise the roof" with your praises to the one who made you. . .the one who leads you. . .the one who feeds you!

. . . .

My Shepherd, I sing Your praises today. My heart is thankful for all You are and for all You do!

GOD OF SIGNS AND WONDERS

*"And I will show wonders in the heavens above and signs on
the earth below, blood, and fire, and vapor of smoke; the sun
shall be turned to darkness and the moon to blood, before the day
of the Lord comes. . . . And it shall come to pass that everyone
who calls upon the name of the Lord shall be saved."*

ACTS 2:19–21 ESV

A blood-red moon hanging in the sky. . . How curious! The crowds
of people who had gathered to listen to Peter had already witnessed
several strange events—including Jesus' crucifixion and resurrection
three days later, as well as a daytime sun turned dark. . .and so, it
wouldn't have been altogether unimaginable to believe the cosmos
would announce the coming arrival of the day of the Lord.

If you believe the Bible is God-breathed—His holy, truth-filled
Word—then you're not unfamiliar with the astonishing ways of God.
Nothing about Him is typical, from His love to His power to His
grace. He works and communicates in mysterious ways—that's part
of His beautiful character.

How well are you acquainted with the wonder-working God?
Have you fully embraced and accepted His gift of eternal life? He
came for you. He came for all. Call on His name today!

*Wonder-working God, I am in awe of Your mysterious
ways. Even the cosmos follows Your lead and obeys
You! I call on Your name, Father. Save me!*

ALTAR SHOWDOWN

"O LORD. . .let it be known this day that you are God. . .and that I am your servant. . . . Answer me. . .that this people may know that you. . .are God. . . ." Then the fire of the LORD fell and consumed the burnt offering and the wood and the stones and the dust, and licked up the water that was in the trench. And when all the people saw it, they fell on their faces and said, "The LORD, he is God."

1 KINGS 18:36–39 ESV

Elijah's words show a no-holds-barred trust in his faithful God—even when God told Elijah to do something crazy, like soak an altar with water right before he was going to ask God to set fire to the sacrifice. . . . Most of us would have thought, *Are You serious, God? This is nuts!* But not Elijah.

And so, Elijah trusted. God answered. Fire fell. The water-soaked sacrifice was consumed. Wood, stones, soil—gone! The water in the trench—dried up! In one miraculous moment, the people in the crowd fell to their faces. They believed!

What seemingly impossible task is God asking you to undertake for His kingdom? Do you trust He will equip you to succeed? Be like Elijah. Say yes to whatever He asks of you. You won't regret it!

. . . .

Father, show me what You would have me do to further Your kingdom, and I will trust and obey!

WHAT CAN *YOU* DO?

*Many wonders and signs were being done through the apostles.
And all who believed were together and had all things in
common. And they were selling their possessions and belongings
and distributing the proceeds. . . . And day by day, attending
the temple together and breaking bread in their homes, they
received their food with glad and generous hearts, praising
God and having favor with all the people. And the Lord added
to their number day by day those who were being saved.*

ACTS 2:43–47 ESV

It's difficult to share the message of Jesus in a world distracted by culture and conflicting voices. Getting the attention of the unsaved isn't easy, is it? Especially when many of our family, friends, and neighbors have already bought stock in the world's lies.

Yet, perhaps, there's something to be learned from the early church. Here in Acts, church growth was exploding. What were these believers getting right? . . . They were devoted in their faith. They practiced what they preached. They lived according to their needs, not their wants. They stood apart in their generosity, their positive attitude, and dedication to their relationships.

Put simply: they lived their faith every day, and people couldn't help but notice! What about you? . . . How can you stand out for Jesus today? Ask Him. . .He'll show you the way!

*God, help me to stand out so my friends,
family, and neighbors want what I have. . .You!*

PERFECT JUDGMENT

All who serve handcrafted gods will be sorry—and they were so proud of their ragamuffin gods! On your knees, all you gods— worship him! And Zion, you listen and take heart! . . . Sing your hearts out: GOD has done it all, has set everything right.

PSALM 97:7–8 MSG

Here in Psalm 97, we get a look at two groups of people: those who love and worship the one true God, and those who worship false idols. These groups experience very different consequences for their actions. For those who know and serve God, the promised outcome—joy and righteousness—comes as no surprise. The true shock is reserved for those who don't know God and are put to shame. And sadly, our world is filled with people who have little to no desire to connect with the heavenly Father.

And yet. . . Imagine a coming day when the Lord reigns and His powerful presence demands that righteousness and holiness become the standard. It's hard to fathom while living in a world focused on self and deluged by mounting cultural pressures, isn't it? However, that's exactly what scripture promises. Our Lord is perfect, and therefore, His judgment is also perfect. We will no longer be the unfortunate victims of faulty, human-heart judgment—judgment that accepts bribes and twists truth. And so, we can rejoice in the faithful assurance of God's promise! Take heart! He has set everything right!

Perfect Lord, I rejoice in Your fair, faithful judgment!

BEAUTIFUL MUSIC

Shout your praises to GOD, everybody! Let loose and sing!
Strike up the band! Round up an orchestra to play for GOD,
add on a hundred-voice choir. Feature trumpets and big trombones,
fill the air with praises to King GOD. Let the sea and its fish give
a round of applause, with everything living on earth joining in.
Let ocean breakers call out, "Encore!" And mountains harmonize
the finale—a tribute to GOD when he comes. . . . He'll straighten
out the whole world, he'll put the world right, and everyone in it.
PSALM 98:4–9 MSG

If you've been paying attention to world events over the last several years, you'll likely agree that the world's "orchestra" is *way* off-key. Instead of an ear-pleasing, harmonious symphony, the atmosphere has been overcome by nothing but noise—a loud, dissonant, disagreeable racket. And it's no wonder. . .with all the fear, anxiety, anger, and sadness that drowns out every bit of hope and joy. You can't even hop on social media for a minute without multiple, anxiety-inducing posts flooding your feed.

With all the negativity, what can you do? . . . For starters, find hope and encouragement in these verses from Psalm 98. The promise that God will straighten out the world—He'll set it right—should calm your troubled heart. And when He sets things straight, there will be nothing but beautiful music floating on the breeze!

God, thank You for the promise that You'll make things right.

GREAT EXPECTATION

*The apostles performed many signs and wonders among
the people. . . . More and more men and women believed. . . .
People brought the sick into the streets and laid them. . .so that
at least Peter's shadow might fall on some of them as he passed by.*

ACTS 5:12, 14–15 NIV

The signs and wonders of the apostles were many. And though the
Bible doesn't explain in detail what those "signs and wonders" were,
we can assume they were the usual healings, casting out of demons,
and other miracles. The fact that the apostles did these miracles in
clear view of the people most definitely moved the minds and hearts
of those watching. As unbelief turned to belief, more and more people
joined the early church.

People had such faith in the healing miracles of Jesus that they
took their sick friends and relatives and placed them so that even a
part of Peter's *shadow* would fall on them when he passed by. While
we know the power to heal didn't come from Peter's shadow—or even
from Peter himself—this demonstrates a deep level of faith. They just
knew healing would take place!

How about you? Do you have the kind of faith that comes
free of doubt and full of great expectation? If you're struggling to
wholeheartedly believe, talk to Jesus. He's listening.

*Lord, erase all doubt from my mind. Help me to
trust You fully—always expecting great things!*

GOD IS GOD!

Know this: GOD is God. . . . He made us; we didn't make him. We're his people, his well-tended sheep. Enter with the password: "Thank you!" Make yourselves at home, talking praise. Thank him. Worship him. For GOD is sheer beauty, all-generous in love, loyal always and ever.
PSALM 100:3–5 MSG

"God is God." Is there any message more powerful, more beautiful, more hopeful than that?

We all struggle at times with our thoughts and emotions. Sometimes our minds swirl with negative thoughts. Our souls drown in doubt. Our courage is squashed by fearful feelings. Hope is elusive. We feel discouraged and lost, depressed and beaten down.

But. . . If we follow Jesus, if we truly *know* Him, we can reach out to Him in faith and ask Him to soothe our troubled hearts. And He will come through. Why? Because God is God. He made us. He cares for us. He is beautiful, loving, and loyal—forever!

If you don't already know Him, start right now. Begin by reading these scriptures: Romans 3:10, 23; 6:23; 5:8; 10:9–10; 10:13.

If you do know Him, tell Him, "Thank You"! Praise Him for His generous love and loyalty.

. . . .

God, thank You for all You are to me—my Creator, Savior, and friend. No matter what's going on in the world or inside my heart, I can rejoice because You are who You are. . .and You will never let me down.

WAY MAKER

*"These patriarchs were jealous of their brother Joseph, and they
sold him to be a slave in Egypt. But God was with him. . . .
And God gave him favor before Pharaoh, king of Egypt."*

Acts 7:9–10 nlt

The only thing Joseph had done "wrong" was to be on the receiving
end of his father's favor. No one else in the family had been gifted a
beautiful, colorful coat to wear. And his jealous brothers didn't like it
one bit. To further strain their relationship, Joseph shared a dream—of
his brothers bowing down to him—and his brothers' hatred grew.
This led them to commit a heinous act: selling their brother into
slavery and convincing their father that Joseph had been devoured
by a wild animal. How tragic!

And yet. . .when trouble and hardship hit Joseph from all sides
and his future looked uncertain and grim, God was there, working
His *good* plan behind the scenes. Then, in time, Joseph rose from lowly
slave to respected governor over all of Egypt! His status even put him
into a position to provide food for his brothers and father during a
time of famine in their land. The family was reunited, forgiveness
granted, and broken relationships mended.

No matter how bad things get, know that God is still working. Still
caring. Still providing. Still making a way. His plans for you are good!

. . . .

Father God, thank You for the reminder that Your plans are good!

DESPERATE PRAYERS

*LORD, hear my prayer! Listen to my plea! Don't turn
away from me in my time of distress. Bend down to
listen, and answer me quickly when I call to you.*

PSALM 102:1–2 NLT

When was the last time you prayed a desperate prayer? You poured out
your heart and soul. You ranted. You cried. You put it *all out there*—not
so much the good, but definitely the bad and the ugly. You begged
God to respond, not in His timing but *right now*! . . .

Such is this prayer of the psalmist. His words are coming from
a place of desperation. He is pleading with God to hear. . .to listen.
And he isn't asking nicely: "Lord, would You mind listening to me
today? If You have time, there are some things I'd like to share with
You. Oh, You're busy? That's okay. Just get back to me later." Nope!
This guy means business, and he doesn't hold back.

Sometimes life's situations make us desperate—for comfort. . .
for healing. . .for a quick answer from our heavenly Father. . . And
while it might be our practice to approach God quietly and calmly,
the truth is He can handle the ranting, "I can't take it anymore!"
prayers. He is a *big* God. Whatever you say to Him in prayer, He can
handle it! He is faithful, and He is so, so good.

*Faithful Father, I need You! Please comfort me,
protect me, and give me Your peace.*

FROM DESPAIR TO HOPE

*Nations will fear the name of the L*ORD*,*
and all the kings of the earth will fear your glory.
*For the L*ORD *builds up Zion; he appears in his glory.*
PSALM 102:15–16 ESV

This psalmist is under a lot of stress. He's in agony. (Read verses 1–12.) Yet, through the pouring out of his distressed heart and soul, something wonderful stirs in his spirit—a light begins to shine in the darkness. And, as he begins to think on the power and promises of the living God, his desperate words take a turn—from despair to hope.

There is comfort in knowing that God will make good on all He has promised. God is committed to building His church, and the psalmist has a heart for the same. This helps the psalmist hold on to hope and confidence, even in the middle of his personal trials.

Can you relate? . . . Perhaps you're having a personal struggle of your own. Maybe you're in utter agony. . .or maybe you're just a little stressed with the state of things. Either way, you could use some positivity in your life! What joy to know the same hope and comfort the psalmist experienced can also shine a light into your darkness. Take heart! Claim the power and promises of God as your very own!

Heavenly Father, I am in distress! Please soothe my troubled soul.
I claim Your promises of hope, peace, comfort, and love today.

UNSETTLING OPPORTUNITY

Forced to leave home base, the followers of Jesus all became missionaries. Wherever they were scattered, they preached the Message about Jesus. Going down to a Samaritan city, Philip proclaimed the Message of the Messiah. When the people heard what he had to say and saw the miracles. . .they hung on his every word.
ACTS 8:4–6 MSG

Due to persecution of the church, Jesus' followers were forced to leave the comforts of their "home base"—the place where they did life together. No one had need for anything in the community of the early church. So, this abrupt shift surely caused some unexpected financial hardship and fear of the unknown.

Yet this scattering of church members served a monumental purpose in God's plan. What seemed like the breaking up of the church was really an opportunity for the *growing* of the church. As new communities were formed, and as Jesus' followers shared the good news in faraway places, more people joined the church.

If you've ever experienced change—like a new job or a cross-country move—then you know how unsettled it can make you feel. But there is beauty to be found in the unexpected—especially when Jesus is at the center of your life. People most often come to know Jesus through people just like you. . .just like the members of the early church.

Jesus, remind me that everywhere I go, I have a fresh opportunity to share You with someone new.

NEVER FORGET

*O my soul. . .don't forget a single blessing! He forgives your sins—
every one. He heals your diseases—every one. He redeems you
from hell—saves your life! He crowns you with love and mercy—
a paradise crown. He wraps you in goodness—beauty eternal.
He renews your youth—you're always young in his presence.*

PSALM 103:2–5 MSG

Where are you right now? . . . More specifically, where are you in life? Your career? Your relationships? Your financial goals? Your hopes and dreams?

Odds are, no matter how far we've come, we probably aren't quite where we'd like to be. And often, we get stuck there. We become unsettled. We grow discontented. We want to be anywhere but where we are.

And, in our discontent, we lose sight of our blessings. We forget how far God has brought us. We forget that, with Him by our side, we have *everything*. We forget that He has saved us, washed us whiter than snow, and is preparing a forever home for us in heaven.

Friend, no matter where you are, always remember:

You're forgiven.

You're healed.

You're saved.

You're crowned with love and mercy.

You're wrapped in goodness.

You're forever young!

. . . .

*Father God, I'm sorry for getting stuck in my own discontented
thoughts. Help me shift my focus. Help me never forget how far
You've brought me and how far You promise to take me.*

ALWAYS IN REACH

Saul was still breathing out murderous threats against the Lord's disciples. He went to the high priest and asked him for letters to the synagogues in Damascus, so that if he found any there who belonged to the Way. . .he might take them as prisoners to Jerusalem. As he neared Damascus. . .a light from heaven flashed around him. He fell to the ground. . . . "Who are you, Lord?" Saul asked. "I am Jesus, whom you are persecuting," he replied. "Now get up and go into the city, and you will be told what you must do."
ACTS 9:1–6 NIV

Have you ever felt so far away from Jesus that you thought you were beyond saving? In our humanness, we've all fallen short—we're all sinners in need of redemption. We've cheated. We've lied. We've stolen. We've broken one—or more—of the Ten Commandments.

But. . .how do your shortcomings stack up against Saul's? Saul had breathed "murderous threats against the Lord's disciples." Saul *hated* God's followers. He imprisoned and punished them. If anyone on earth was beyond saving, Saul would have been the guy.

And yet. . .God had a purpose for even someone like Saul. And on that road to Damascus, he had an encounter with Jesus that forever changed him.

Rest assured, your beautiful soul is never beyond saving. The Lord is waiting for you to take His hand. You are *always* within His reach.

Lord, I'm never beyond Your saving grace. Thank You.

GOD ALONE

"But worship only the LORD, who brought you out of Egypt with great strength and a powerful arm. Bow down to him alone, and offer sacrifices only to him. . . . You must worship only the LORD your God. He is the one who will rescue you from all your enemies."

2 KINGS 17:36, 39 NLT

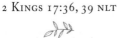

Some people adore their possessions. They spend their lives getting more and more of what they desire, what they think will make them happy. Then, when theft, fire, and flood come along, taking all they'd accumulated, they feel destitute and desolate.

Other people worship money, for the power and prestige it gives them. They work day in and day out, making their jobs and their status their priority, shoving others out of the way in their lonely pursuit of the almighty dollar. Yet when the banks or stock markets fail, when inflation rises and their money is lost, they realize their souls were lost a long time ago.

The Lord warns repeatedly that He alone should be your center, your idol, your one and only God. That it's He alone who redeems, rescues, and provides for you. It's He alone who can hold and protect you—heart, head, spirit, and soul.

. . . .

Lord, I want to worship You alone. For You're the only one who can truly rescue me, strengthen me, empower me, and love me—on earth and in heaven. Amen.

HARD OF FEARING

*The servants of King Hezekiah came to Isaiah. Isaiah
said to them, Say to your master, Thus says the Lord:
Do not be afraid because of the words you have heard.*

2 KINGS 19:5–6 AMPC

Words can cut you to the quick. They can cause seen and unseen pain that can leave an ache that lasts forever. For words once spoken can never be taken back.

Especially harmful are words that are said against your God. Even more painful is when those words are spoken by people you love.

So, what's a woman to do? Trust in, lean on, and keep your confidence in the Lord (2 Kings 18:5). Take heart and listen to God. Remember that He doesn't want you to be afraid of any words you hear, either against you or Him. Nor should you be in any way hurt by them. Just let them fall from your ears as you remember who your God is, that He has a plan, a good plan, for you. And He will work spoken words of evil into something good.

*Lord, help me not to get so caught up in the words of
others. In the myriad of voices I hear throughout the day,
there's only one I will attend to: Yours. For You and Your
Word are the light, love, truth, and the way I follow.*

HEARD AND SEEN

[God to Isaiah:] Go back and tell Hezekiah, the leader of My people, "This is the message of the Eternal One, the God of your ancestor David: 'I have listened to your prayer and have witnessed the tears falling down your face; therefore I am going to heal you.'"

2 Kings 20:5 voice

Feeling alone? Confused about your purpose? Feeling less than? Suffering from loss, grief, or any other kind of pain? Wondering where to go from here? Everything that you feel and fear, God knows about. He sees the tears running down your face. He knows the thoughts going through your mind, the feelings that fuel your body or cause you to trip up.

No matter where you are or what you're doing, no matter how far or near home you may be, no matter what the hour or the day, God hears your prayer. He knows the feelings you cannot put into words.

So go ahead and cry. Allow the words to God to fall off your lips. Take heart knowing that He sees and hears. He knows what you're going through. And it's His desire and aim to help, to heal you.

. . . .

Thank You, Lord, for listening to my prayers, for wanting to assuage the tears falling down my face, the fears preying on my mind. Remind me that I need not feel so alone, that You are with me, to help and heal me.

ALL WELCOME

*It is clear to me now that God plays no favorites, that God accepts
every person whatever his or her culture or ethnic background,
that God welcomes all who revere Him and do right.*

ACTS 10:34–35 VOICE

There may be times when you feel like you don't really belong to anyone or anything. That because you are who you are, somehow you don't fit into God's plan.

God is here to tell you that you do belong—to Him! He cares not what your social status is. He cares not what race you are or what country you come from. He cares not what political party you belong to or what laws or positions you support. It matters not to Him how much money you have or don't have. All God cares about is you. What Peter proclaims here in Acts and what the apostle Paul makes clear in Romans 2:11 is that God accepts all who come to Him, no matter what their country, culture, or color.

Rest in the knowledge that God accepts you. He calls you into His family of love and light. He welcomes all who worship Him and do right.

. . . .

*Thank You, Lord, for accepting me into Your family,
for including me in Your plan. Help me to serve and
worship You by doing right by You. In Jesus' name, amen.*

THE UNEXPECTED

Suddenly an angel of the Lord appeared [standing beside him], and a light shone in the place where he was. And the angel gently smote Peter on the side and awakened him, saying, Get up quickly! And the chains fell off his hands. . . . Then Peter came to himself and said, Now I really know and am sure that the Lord has sent His angel and delivered me from the hand of Herod and from all that the Jewish people were expecting [to do to me].

ACTS 12:7, 11 AMPC

Time and time again, God comes through for His people. When there seems to be no good road ahead, no successful way out of a situation, God sends His angel to stand beside you, to shed light on your situation, to get you moving, to free you from whatever's holding you back from doing what God would have you do.

So come to your senses! Take courage in knowing that God will deliver you from whatever and whoever has entrapped you. He will do what no one would ever expect or predict. All you need to do is open your ears and eyes to His miraculous power and love.

. . . .

Thank You, Lord, for always being there when I need You, for setting me free, for reminding me that You are the God of not only the impossible but the unexpected! Amen.

SEEK, LOOK, AND REMEMBER

Seek the Eternal and His power; look to His face constantly.
Remember the wonderful things He has done,
His miracles and the wise decisions He has made.

PSALM 105:4–5 VOICE

It's relatively easy to get caught up in the machinations of this world. But God would have you take another tack.

To keep attuned with God, to keep your confidence up in what He does and who He is, seek Him. Crave His presence. Make it a point to commune with Him, one-on-one, each day.

Look to God's face not just once in a while but constantly, continually. Think about all the wonderful things He has done, the wonders He has performed, the rivers and seas He has parted so that His people could walk through on dry land. Think about the misfits He has embraced. Think about the way He sees people not so much as who they are but as who they will one day be.

Consider the promises and wise decisions God has made, the way He works things so that good will come to those who follow Him, seek Him, look to Him, and remember Him, who live their lives with an awareness of His presence everywhere they go and in everything they do.

. . . .

Lord, may I be a woman who continually seeks Your presence, looks to Your face, and remembers Your wonders. Thank You for giving me purpose, seeing me as the woman I will one day be. Amen.

A DIFFERENT PATH

*When they were but a few men in number, in fact, very
few, and were temporary residents and strangers in it,
when they went from one nation to another, from one
kingdom to another people, He allowed no man to do them
wrong; in fact, He reproved kings for their sakes.*

PSALM 105:12–14 AMPC

Ever felt that you were a stranger here, walking amid even stranger
people? That's only natural. Because this world is not the world you
belong to. This kingdom of man is not the realm your spirit aches for.

You are a woman of God. You have chosen a different path than
many others. Because you are a follower of God, chosen by Him to
be a part of His plan, you march to a different drummer, you whistle
a different tune.

So take heart. It's okay if you feel different from those among
whom you live. God has got His eye on you. He'll make sure no one
does you any real harm. His angels have got you covered. Your God
is ready, willing, and able to bring out the best in you for His kingdom. Your job is to walk His way. He'll do the rest.

*Thank You, Lord, for choosing me to walk a different path,
to be a part of Your kingdom. You alone are
my true hearth and home. Amen.*

THE POWER OF PRAYER

There was a man named Jabez who was more honorable than any of his brothers. His mother named him Jabez because his birth had been so painful. He was the one who prayed to the God of Israel, "Oh, that you would bless me and expand my territory! Please be with me in all that I do, and keep me from all trouble and pain!" And God granted him his request.

1 Chronicles 4:9–10 NLT

The first few chapters of the book of 1 Chronicles are filled with names of those who begat and those who were begat. Yet one name stands out from all the others: Jabez.

Jabez was a man whose birth caused his mother much pain. To commemorate the event, she named him Jabez, which means "sorrow maker" or "pain." Not a wonderful appellation to begin life with. But Jabez was, apparently, a praying man. He cried out to God, asking that He would bless his life, enlarge his territory, be with him in all endeavors he undertook, and keep him from harm. And God granted Jabez all he'd requested.

Don't let the life you were born into or the name you were given define you. Instead, reach beyond what seems expected of you. Dedicate your life and your future to God. Pray constantly. Ask God for spiritual blessings to come upon you, for Him to stay by you in all you do, for Him to keep you out of trouble.

Lord, hear my prayer.

AMID THE BATTLE

They were given help against them, and the Hagrites or Ishmaelites were delivered into their hands, and all who were allied with them, for they cried to God in the battle; and He granted their entreaty, because they relied on, clung to, and trusted in Him.

1 CHRONICLES 5:20 AMPC

When the battle is going against you, what do you do? Do you give up? Do you run? Do you fight even harder?

As today's verse reminds us, when we're in the thick of trouble, we need to take stock of what we're relying on. Are we depending on our own abilities, luck, talents, and timing? Or are we counting on God's power, plan, prowess, and promptness?

If we're putting all our trust and hope in God, if we're clinging to Him with all our strength, if we're trusting in Him to see us through whatever comes our way, if we go to Him in prayer knowing that we will not see victory unless we have His help, He will answer our entreaties.

Today, consider the battles that are currently being waged in your life. Think about areas where you may be relying on yourself more than God. Then cling to Him, pray to Him, trust Him to see you through. And He will!

. . . .

You know the battles before me, Lord. Putting all my trust in You, I cry out for Your help, counting on You alone to deliver a victory! Amen.

NEVER LEFT BEHIND

*Then He brought His people out of slavery, weighed down
with silver and gold; and of all His tribes, not one of them
stumbled, not one was left behind. . . . He spread out a cloud
to cover His people and sent a fire to light their way at night.*

PSALM 105:37, 39 VOICE

You belong to a God who cares for you and will never abandon you.
He will cover you with His cloud of protection and give you light
so you can find your way. If you are hungry and thirsty, He will send
you manna from heaven and split a rock from which water will gush
out. And He will do all this with joy in His heart. Why? Because
you believe. Because you're His daughter. Because you trust Him to
make good on His promises.

Always remember that you have a link to a supernatural being,
one who is all-powerful, one who created all things, one who put the
breath in your lungs and will be there to lead you further on when
that breath is gone.

Today, take heart from the fact that you belong to a God who
looks upon you with not just love but joy. A God that will answer
as you ask.

*Thank You, Lord, for always providing for me,
looking out for me, loving me. You are my all in all.*

THE NEVERTHELESS GOD

The inhabitants of Jebus said to David, "You shall not come here." Nevertheless David took the stronghold of Zion, which is the city of David. . . . And he built the city all around, even from Millo all around. . . . So David grew greater and greater, for the LORD of hosts was with him.

1 CHRONICLES 11:5, 8–9 SKJV

God has a plan for your life. A good plan. The only thing is that to realize that plan, to be a part of God's scheme, you need to trust Him entirely, no matter how bleak your situation looks nor how much bravado and mocking is acted out and spoken against you.

When David went to establish a place from which to rule both Judah and Israel, the people inhabiting the city of Jebus mocked him. Trusting in themselves and the strength of their fortress, they made it clear to David that he and his army would be easily repulsed. What they didn't know is that David belonged to a "nevertheless" God.

When you trust in God's presence and power more than you trust in anything or anyone else (including yourself), God enables you to grow. To become stronger. To have success. . .nevertheless.

What are you trusting in?

. . . .

You, Lord, are the "nevertheless" God. Nothing. . .no one can match Your love and power. May I trust in You more than anyone or anything else in heaven or on earth. Amen.

SPIRITUAL SENSES

They sensed the Holy Spirit telling them not to preach their message in Asia at this time. . . . They came near Mysia and planned to go into Bithynia, but again they felt restrained from doing so by the Spirit of Jesus. So they. . .went down to Troas. That night Paul had a vision in which a Macedonian man was pleading with him. Macedonian Man: Come over to Macedonia! Come help us!
ACTS 16:6–9 VOICE

Knowing we cannot walk through this life on our own, God continually sends us messages, telling us where to go, what to do. And when we open ourselves to His leading, to His truths, we're never steered wrong.

The only time we may find ourselves in dire straits is when we forget about God. When we ignore His urgings, when we treat Him as someone other than our ally.

Although the Israelites witnessed all God's mighty deeds, they soon forgot about Him and all He'd done for them (Psalm 106:13, 21). Deaf to His promptings, His people wandered around the desert for forty years, becoming not only discourag*ed* but discourag*ers*. Not so with Jesus' apostles, who sensed the Spirit among them and followed His leadings. Their doing so led to visions as God's firm hand directed their every move and effort.

Take heart by opening yourself up to God's Spirit. Go where He bids you go, rerouting when He deems appropriate.

Lord, I open myself to the leading of Your Spirit. Where would You have me go?

GOD OF BREAKTHROUGHS

*Around midnight Paul and Silas were praying and singing
hymns to God, and the other prisoners were listening.
Suddenly, there was a massive earthquake, and the prison
was shaken to its foundations. All the doors immediately
flew open, and the chains of every prisoner fell off!*
ACTS 16:25–26 NLT

When things get hard, you have two choices. You can moan, groan, and complain to God, surrendering to whatever has come against you. Or you can praise anyway!

The latter is what Paul and Silas did after they'd been attacked by a crowd, stripped of their clothing, beaten with rods, and thrown into jail. Despite what was happening, the men praised God. They prayed and sang hymns. The other prisoners were listening to their songs and prayers. And suddenly, the earth quaked, the prison shook, the cell doors opened, and every prisoner's chains fell off!

Your God is a God of breakthroughs (1 Chronicles 14:11), so no matter what comes against you, never give up, never give in to the dark side. For Jesus is with you—all the way!

*Thank You, Lord, for allowing me to be a part of Your family and
kingdom. With You behind me, going before me, and walking
with me, I need never fear any situation but simply praise You,
knowing no barrier or person can keep Your strength, love,
and power at bay. Praise to the God of breakthroughs!*

TWISTED TRUTHS

*And the people of Berea were more open-minded than those
in Thessalonica, and they listened eagerly to Paul's message.
They searched the Scriptures day after day to see if Paul and
Silas were teaching the truth. As a result, many Jews believed,
as did many of the prominent Greek women and men.*

ACTS 17:11–12 NLT

There are some proclaimers of the Word who twist its message to
fit their own ideologies. Fortunately, we have the scriptures we can
search to see if the proclaimers' message match the veracity found
in God's Word.

God has provided His Word as a light in this world, one that will
keep the darkness of evil at bay. His Word is to direct us and guide
us, be as a beacon for our journey, a lamp to our feet and a light to
our path (Psalm 119:105). But that beacon, that light, is of no use to
us if we don't seek it and allow it to illuminate our minds and hearts.

Today, consider some of the conflicting messages you've been
hearing. Then dive into the scriptures to determine if the message is
from the mind of God or that of man.

*Protect me, Lord, from the twisted truths of others.
Give me insight into Your scriptures. Shed Your light into
my life, heart, and mind. Help me determine Your truths.*

GOD KNOWS BEST

Joab (to Abshai): If the Arameans are too strong for me, then you will help me; and if the Ammonites are too strong for you, then I will help you. Be strong. Let us show courage for the sake of our people and for the cities of our God. May the Eternal do what He knows is best.

1 Chronicles 19:12–13 voice

Joab, the commander of King David's army, knew his forces were at a disadvantage from the enemy armies that had come against them. So "he asked the most skilled Israelite soldiers to prepare for battle against the Arameans. His brother Abshai commanded the remainder of the forces, who prepared to fight the Ammonites" (1 Chronicles 19:10–11 voice). Joab then determined that if either he or his brother needed help, the one would come to the other's aid.

Before they parted company, Joab reminded his brother to be strong. To take heart. To leave the results of the battles in God's hand, assured He would do what was best.

As a child of God, you have the same assurance. You can live your life making best-laid plans, remaining strong, taking courage, and leaving the results to God. For He alone knows best.

Thank You, Lord, for filling me with the assurance that You will work all things out for the best. Because of You, I can and will be strong and courageous, leaving the results of my efforts to You!

A CONTINUAL REMINDER

*"Be strong and courageous; do not be afraid or lose
heart! . . . The LORD your God is with you." . . .
"Don't be afraid! Speak out! Don't be silent! For I am
with you, and no one will attack and harm you."*
1 CHRONICLES 22:13, 18; ACTS 18:9–10 NLT

Time and time again, God finds a way to remind His children to be
strong and courageous. He repeatedly tells them to neither be afraid
nor lose heart.

God wants you to understand that because you are a believer,
because you are a woman of the Way, He is with you. And because
He's with you, you have all the strength and courage you need to do
what He has called you to do!

Write down these words in your journal: *I am a strong and
courageous woman. Because God is with me, I need not be afraid nor lose
heart!* Post them on a piece of paper and stick it on the fridge or the
dashboard of your car. Do whatever you need to do to get these truths
to stick in your mind, heart, spirit, and soul. Then walk forward with
confidence and strength!

. . . .

*Lord, help me to engrave in my mind and heart the fact that I am a
strong and courageous woman. That I need not be afraid. That I can
take heart because You, the Lord of my love and life, are with me!*

OUR RESCUER

*In their distress, they called out to the Eternal; He saved
them from their misery. He rescued them from the darkness,
delivered them from the deepest gloom of death; He shattered
their iron chains. May they erupt with praise and give
thanks to the Eternal in honor of His loyal love and all
the wonders He has performed for humankind!*

PSALM 107:13–15 VOICE

God is amazing! No matter how rebellious we may become, no matter how many wrong roads we might take, He will still answer our cries when we call out to Him in distress!

At times we may be too embarrassed to ask God for help. For all too often, the trouble we find ourselves in has come from our own words and actions, or our silence and inactions. Regardless of the circumstances and situations that cause us distress, we must never hesitate to call out to God in prayer, to ask Him for help. When we do, He, in His infinite love and compassion, will rescue us from the blackness of the pit. He will lead us to the light, free us from whatever has bound us, deliver us from the end we deserve.

Today, call out for God's help. Understand that He will save you. Allow Him to free you from your fetters. And praise His name!

. . . .

*I thank You, Lord, for continually being there
for me, for answering my call, for loving me beyond
measure. All praise, thanks, and honor to You!*

STORM SETTLER

*In their distress, they called out to the Eternal, and He saved them
from their misery. He commanded the storm to calm down, and
it became still. A hush came over the waves of the sea, the sailors
were delighted at the quiet, and He guided them to their port.*

Psalm 107:28–30 voice

When you feel as if you are lost at sea, trying to ride through an
incredibly strong storm, no longer able to navigate the winds, currents,
and tides, call out to the Lord.

When you're caught up in a force that is so much larger than you
are, when you're so far adrift, so far beyond the shore that you have
no idea what to do or what to steer toward, pray that your faith will
rise up within you and bring Jesus' name to your lips.

Jesus can settle any storm. He can calm any chaos. With one word,
He can still the sea. And when He does so, when all the tumult in
our lives is hushed, we feel closer to Him than ever. In His calming
company, we find our joy and are reminded once more that He is our
true north. Jesus is our sure guide to the port of our delights, for His
name is power (Acts 19:17).

. . . .

*Your name, Lord, is power. So I pray You would
calm the rising tide within me. Guide me to
the port of Your calling and my delight.*

DO THE WORK

"Be strong and courageous, and do the work. Don't be afraid or discouraged, for the LORD God, my God, is with you. He won't leave you or forsake you until all the work for the service of the LORD's house is finished."

1 CHRONICLES 28:20 HCSB

David had once thought he'd be the one to build a temple to house the Lord's presence. But God had another plan in mind.

Although David's intentions were good and his heart in the right place, although he was the apple of God's eye, the Lord wanted His temple built not by a man of war but by a man of peace. So although God promised David's "descendants will rule continually" (2 Samuel 7:16 VOICE), it would be Solomon who would be charged with building the Lord's house.

David accepted that news with great humility. He then spent the rest of his days acquiring the materials his son would need to complete the holiest of building projects.

So take heart; God has a plan for you. All you need to do is be strong and brave and do what He's calling you to do. Know that He is with you and will not leave your side until your work of service to Him on earth is completed.

. . . .

Give me courage and strength, Lord, to do all You have called me to do. Thank You for Your faith in me and Your presence by my side. Amen.

TAKING ADVANTAGE OF EVERY MOMENT

Our True God is more powerful than all the other gods.
Though no one can build a house for Him because He inhabits
the heavens and beyond, I am humbly building a place where
we can encounter Him and burn incense before Him. . . . Paul
is carrying on an extended dialogue with the believers, taking
advantage of every moment since we plan to leave at first light.

2 Chronicles 2:5–6; Acts 20:8 voice

David's son Solomon began the construction of the temple of God four years into his rule, a building project that would take seven years to complete. (His own palace took thirteen years.) By the time Solomon died, he had ruled for a total of forty years.

Although Solomon was wise, in the end he did fall away from God. Some say it was because of the many foreign wives he had married. Whatever the reason, Solomon didn't stay true to the Lord throughout his life. Yet he did accomplish much.

We only have a certain amount of time allotted to us. God alone knows when we too will part from this mortal coil (Job 14:5). Yet He would have us be like Paul, staying true to God to the end and taking advantage of every opportunity we can to serve Him and spread the good news of His love for all.

. . . .

Lord, help me not while away the hours but
take advantage of every moment to serve You!

THE POWER OF PRAISES

At the sound of the music, the Eternal's temple was filled with a cloud, the glory of God. . . . My heart is committed, O God: I will sing; I will sing praises with great affection and pledge my whole soul to the singing. . . . Only through God can we be successful. It is God alone who will. . .bring us victory!

2 CHRONICLES 5:13; PSALM 108:1, 13 VOICE

After completion of the temple, the priests carried the ark of the covenant into its new home. As the musicians played, the singers began singing, "He is good! His loyal love will continue forever!" (2 Chronicles 5:13 VOICE). In response, God's cloud of glory filled the temple!

God loves to hear praises. Whether one's day is going well or not, committed hearts of courage and love cannot help but sing to Him, thanking Him for all He has done and promises to do.

Only through God will you be successful. He alone can and will bring you victory. So today, take heart and sincerely raise your voice in praise to God. Allow His presence to fill you to overflowing as He works to not only love you and provide for you but to bring you victory over whatever comes against you!

. . . .

Lord, hear me sing my praises to You. Fill me with Your presence as I revel in Your love!

THIS AMAZING GOD

"There is no God like You in heaven or on earth, who keeps
Your covenant and shows mercy to Your servants who
walk before You with all their hearts. You who have
kept with Your servant, my father, David, what You have
promised him, and You have spoken with Your mouth and
have fulfilled it with Your hand, as it is this day."

2 CHRONICLES 6:14–15 SKJV

Those who follow God, who walk wholeheartedly in His ways, are sure to receive His mercies, forgiveness, and love. For they belong to a God who is all-powerful, a keeper and fulfiller of promises.

Know that your God is one whose word is a ready source of encouragement on those days when you are downhearted. This God's ears are perked, waiting to hear the strains of your songs of praises. This God will shed His own tears when you're sorrowful, render aid when you apply to Him, pray to Him, yearn for Him in faithfulness and truth (2 Chronicles 6:29).

This God is one who knows your heart, perhaps better than you yourself (2 Chronicles 6:30). He knows what brings you sorrow and pain, what gives you joy and ease.

If you need help, if you need aid, strength, courage, or just someone to talk to, you need go no further than your prayer closet. There you can have a heart-to-heart conversation with this amazing God.

. . . .

Lord, hear my prayer, examine my heart, render Your aid.

YOUR POTENTIAL

Blessed be the Eternal One your God, who favored your
potential as a great ruler and placed you on His throne. . . .
Paul greeted them and then reported account after account of
what God had done through him among the outsiders.
2 CHRONICLES 9:8; ACTS 21:19 VOICE

God has a purpose for you. God sees who you are, knows what you're capable of, has a plan for your particular talents and situation.

The queen of Sheba recognized that God had put Solomon on the throne for a reason. God saw his potential, knew he was the right man for this particular job in this particular place and time.

Thousands of years later, the Lord knew Saul, a former persecutor of people of the Way, was just the man for bringing people into the fold. He knew Saul would not only have a name change (to Paul) but a heart change, and he would also change the world for God's good.

So if you feel as if you're wasting your time and talents, that there's something better for you out there, apply to God for help. Ask Him to make your potential clear. Then, with courage, hope, and faith, go where He calls you to go. And change the world.

. . . .

Lord, use me, Your humble and loving servant, to my full
potential. Then give me the courage, hope, and faith to do
what You would have me do, to go where You would have me go.

KNOW, SEE, AND HEAR

"The God of our ancestors has chosen you to know his will and to see the Righteous One and to hear words from his mouth."

ACTS 22:14 NIV

Saul (the persecutor of people of the Way before he transformed into the apostle Paul) had a life-changing encounter with Jesus. Blinded by the light of Christ as he traveled on the road to Damascus, Saul was led away by his companions. When Ananias came to see Saul, as God had instructed, he stood by his side and said, "Brother Saul, look up and receive back your sight" (Acts 22:13 AMPC), and in that moment, Saul regained his vision.

That's when Saul learned that God chose him—as He has you—for three things: to know His will, to see Jesus, and to hear His voice.

It's God's will that you learn about Jesus and from His Word discover His will for your life. God has chosen you to see Jesus, to look for His light in every situation. It's God's will that you hear His voice speaking to you, leading you, directing where He would have you go.

So take heart. You're not lost or left on your own. God has provided you with His Word, your companion as you make your way through this world.

. . . .

Lord, open my mind so I may know You, my eyes so I may see You, my ears so I may hear You.

HOLY ENCOURAGEMENT

*You, who are devoted to being with God and searching
for God, be strong and do not lose courage because your
actions will reap rewards. . . . That night the Lord came
near and spoke to him. The Lord: Keep up your courage,
Paul! You have successfully told your story about Me in
Jerusalem, and soon you will do the same in Rome.*

2 CHRONICLES 15:7; ACTS 23:11 VOICE

Time and time again, the Lord reminds His followers to keep up their
courage, to be strong, to do what God would have them do.

In 2 Chronicles 15, the Spirit of God spoke through the prophet
Azariah to let His people know that when they are with Him, He is
with them; that when they actively seek God, He will be found by
them; that those devoted to Him should continue to be strong and
brave, and live as He called them to live. In so doing, they would
reap their reward!

Jesus encouraged Paul in the same way. Paul was doing what God
had called him to do and the Lord wanted to make sure he would
continue walking in the Way.

Now it's your turn. Spend some time with the Lord. Give Him
the opportunity to draw near to encourage you, to strengthen you for
the work He has prepared for you.

. . . .

*I need Your encouragement and strength, Lord.
Draw near and lift my heart and spirit.*

FULLY COMMITTED HEARTS

*"The eyes of the LORD search the whole earth in
order to strengthen those whose hearts are fully
committed to him. What a fool you have been!"*

2 CHRONICLES 16:9 NLT

Sometimes it takes a prophet to point out the obvious. That's what
Hanani the seer did for King Asa of Judah.

When King Baasha of Israel invaded Judah, Asa didn't trust
God to save him. Instead, he took silver and gold from the temple of
God and his own house and sent them to the king of Aram, asking
for him to help him.

Three years later, "Asa contracted a severe foot disease. Once again,
he had the opportunity to look to the Eternal, but instead he relied
on physicians" (2 Chronicles 16:12 VOICE). A few years later, Asa died.

Through these and many other accounts, the scriptures make
clear that God gives us ample opportunities to trust in Him, to seek
guidance, relief, and comfort through Him, to turn to Him when our
hearts need strength.

God continues to search the entire earth to give strength to those
who have hearts fully committed to Him. Will yours be one of them?

*Help me, Lord, to turn to You at the first sign of a problem.
For I know You hold all solutions and remedies. I recognize and
acknowledge that all power and strength is in Your hands. Amen.*

SECURE HEARTS

Surely the righteous will never be shaken; they will be remembered forever. They will have no fear of bad news; their hearts are steadfast, trusting in the LORD. Their hearts are secure, they will have no fear; in the end they will look in triumph on their foes.

PSALM 112:6–8 NIV

These words of wisdom and encouragement were written after the Jews were exiled from their land. Here God's people are reminded of the benefits that come for those who follow Him, who are just in their dealings with others.

The Lord assures us that the woman who is and does right in God's eyes will never be rattled. Even if she's afflicted for a season, she will not be utterly and forever distraught nor destroyed. In fact, she who remains calm and secure through all her trials and tribulations will always be remembered by others. No matter what bad news arises, the woman of God will trust Him, knowing that because she's in His hands, God will give her victory.

Allow God to write today's verses upon your heart and soul. Then, trusting in God alone, stand firm no matter what this life brings your way.

I come to You today, Lord, asking You to help me trust in You alone, to never be shaken, nor fearful. May I rest—calm, cool, and collected—in You forever.

LIFE LESSONS

Listen to me, Judah and inhabitants of Jerusalem. Trust in the Eternal One, your True God, not in your own abilities, and you will be supported. Put your trust in His words that you heard through the prophets, and we will succeed.

2 Chronicles 20:20 voice

Second Chronicles 20 relates an amazing, faith-building story, one that has so many life lessons it cannot help but linger in your mind.

After receiving the message that three massive armies were heading to Judah, King Jehoshaphat immediately sought help from and consulted with God, humbly admitting to Him: "We can do nothing to stop this huge army from attacking us; we don't know what to do, so we are asking for Your help" (2 Chronicles 20:12 voice).

God answers Jehoshaphat's prayer by speaking through Jahaziel: " 'Do not fear or worry about this army. The battle is not yours to fight; it is the True God's. . . .' Do not fear or worry. Tomorrow, face the army and trust that the Eternal is with you" (2 Chronicles 20:15, 17 voice).

Early the next morning, Jehoshaphat tells his people to trust in God, not in their own abilities, and He would come through for them. And God did so in a miraculous way. He'll do the same for you.

. . . .

Lord, when I don't know what to do, remind me to come to You for help, to trust in You for miraculous success, and to praise Your miracle-working power.

MAKING A PATH FOR GOD TO MOVE

Ahaziah's sister Jehosheba, the daughter of King Jehoram, took Ahaziah's infant son, Joash, and stole him away from among the rest of the king's children, who were about to be killed. She put Joash and his nurse in a bedroom. In this way, Jehosheba, wife of Jehoiada the priest and sister of Ahaziah, hid the child so that Athaliah could not murder him.

2 Chronicles 22:11 nlt

Imagine for a moment that your dead half brother's mother is literally slaughtering all her grandchildren so that she can rule the roost, which, in this instance, is the kingdom of Judah. Imagine that somehow, you garner the courage to step in and save the infant son of your brother. You gather him up and steal him and his nurse away, taking them to a bedroom where the maniacal Athaliah could not reach him. And, in so doing, make a path for God to move.

Where would you garner the hutzpah to perform such an act of courage? From God. Where would you get the vision to do such a thing? From the Lord, who clearly shows what is good and what is evil.

When just and righteous women take a stand against evil, when instead of cowering they take heart, only God knows how much good they can do, how much they may change the world!

. . . .

Lord, give me the courage and vision to take a stand against evil and work for good. In Jesus' name, I pray, amen.

GOD'S POWER

*A man of God came to him, saying, O king, do not let all this
army of Ephraimites of Israel go with you [of Judah], for the
Lord is not with you, for if you go [in spite of warning], no
matter how strong you are for battle, God will cast you down
before the enemy, for God has power to help and to cast down.*

2 CHRONICLES 25:7–8 AMPC

You have a solution to a problem. And you think it's a really good
one. After all, wouldn't God want to see you succeed? So, you start
making plans. You begin building up your forces, making sure you
have what you need to triumph. There's only one problem: you haven't
asked God for advice.

The prophet advising King Amaziah provides a lesson for us. We
need to seek, listen to, and then heed God's advice. We need to consult
with Him every step of the way, to leave a door open for Him to come
through if we've taken a wrong turn. For He has the power to both
help us if He's for our plans and ruin those plans if He's against them.

When you have a plan, take it to God, seek His approval. And
if it's a go—and *only* if it's a go—ask Him for the courage to see
things through.

....

*I have a plan, Lord. Can we talk? Because I
don't want to take one step without You.*

SAIL THROUGH THE STORM

"Last night an angel of the God to whom I belong and whom
I serve stood beside me, and he said, 'Don't be afraid, Paul, for
you will surely stand trial before Caesar! What's more, God in
his goodness has granted safety to everyone sailing with you.'
So take courage! For I believe God. It will be just as he said."

ACTS 27:23–25 NLT

The apostle Paul and his companions (Luke and Aristarchus) were on a ship carrying 276 men. A storm arose. Eventually, to save themselves, they threw the cargo overboard, then some of the ship's equipment. "Days passed without relief from the furious winds. . . . Despair set in, as if all hope of rescue had been cast overboard as well. On top of all this, the crew had been unable to eat anything because of the turmoil" (Acts 27:20–21 VOICE).

That's when Paul gave comfort and encouragement to the men, telling them they would not lose one life. For God had come alongside him and told him not to be afraid. That He would make sure they all made it to safety.

When you need courage, when you need strength and to find some sense of hope in what appears to be a hopeless situation, seek God's voice, His Word, His face. Believe things will be just as He said. And you'll sail through your storm.

. . . .

I need courage, strength, and hope, Lord. Help me
find a way to make it through this storm.

THE BEST LISTENER

*I love the LORD, for he heard my voice; he heard
my cry for mercy. Because he turned his ear to
me, I will call on him as long as I live.*
PSALM 116:1–2 NIV

Listening attentively is a skill that doesn't come naturally to most people. Being an exceptional listener who hears and understands is a trait that can strengthen relationships and cultivate peace and harmony. If you have a good listener in your life, they are probably someone you enjoy talking to.

God always hears the prayers of His children (John 9:31), but more than just listening, He is attentive to the words you say. Because He created you, He understands the essence, context, and story behind what you're feeling and expressing. Even if you're repeating a familiar refrain in your prayers, God doesn't tune it out. God doesn't have selective hearing, and you can be sure He hears your cries of frustration as clearly as your songs of praise with the same attentive ear.

If you feel discouraged and unheard by the people around you today, remember that God is near, listening attentively to your every prayer and answering each prayer to give you His best for your good.

. . . .

*Thank You for always listening to my prayers, Father,
even when my words are fumbling and ineloquent. Guide me
in Your wisdom today, as You lead me in Your will for my life.*

SIMPLE FAITH

*The Lord protects those of childlike faith; I was facing
death, and he saved me. Let my soul be at rest again, for
the Lord has been good to me. He has saved me from
death, my eyes from tears, my feet from stumbling. And so
I walk in the Lord's presence as I live here on earth!*

Psalm 116:6–9 nlt

We all go through seasons when life feels overly complicated. Whether
it's rooted in relationship problems, health issues, job stress, or family
drama, these are the times when we are our most anxious, agitated,
and adrift.

Sometimes life *is* complicated and we may not have the ability
to simplify it, but even in the midst of life's wildest twists and turns,
we can rely on the power of a simple, childlike faith in our Father
God. Today, dig into the promises of scripture and return to this
powerful faith:

Are you feeling anxious? Tell God about it (Philippians 4:6–7).

Is the weight of the world on your shoulders? Give your burdens
to God (Psalm 55:22).

Are you tired? Find rest in Jesus (Matthew 11:28).

Are you paralyzed by guilt? You are not condemned (Romans 8:1).

Are you feeling overlooked and unappreciated? The Lord delights
in you (Zephaniah 3:17).

*Father God, when life gets complicated, keep my
faith rock solid and simple, like the faith of a child.*

GENEROUS GIVING

"Since the people began to bring their contributions to the temple of the LORD, we have had enough to eat and plenty to spare, because the LORD has blessed his people, and this great amount is left over."

2 CHRONICLES 31:10 NIV

King Hezekiah generously gave to the priests and asked the Hebrew people to give a tenth of their income as well—so that the Levites could be free to serve God and minister to the people. The Bible says that for nearly five months they generously gave grain, wine, oil, honey, field crops, and animals from their herds and flocks. Great heaps of all these offerings piled up—plenty to sustain the ministry and more to share with those who had need.

Generous giving is an important part of a vibrant faith, and the Bible tells us it's less about *how much* we give and more about *our attitude* as we give. Second Corinthians 9:7 (NLT) says that "God loves a person who gives cheerfully." Cheerful giving starts by realizing how much God has given to us. From daily little blessings to the ultimate gift of our salvation, He is worthy of our praise and generous giving. Also, giving generously often goes along with sound financial habits. A budget that prioritizes giving offers peace of mind and follows the example of the Old Testament tithing of firstfruits. How can you become a more cheerful giver?

You are a generous Father, Lord. I gladly give You my first, my best offering to further Your kingdom.

TALK ABOUT HIM

Shouts of joy and victory resound in the tents of the righteous:
"The LORD's right hand has done mighty things! The LORD's right
hand is lifted high; the LORD's right hand has done mighty things!"
PSALM 118:15–16 NIV

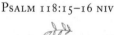

Home is a place where a family finds shelter from the storms of life. Although no family is perfect, it's a place where we can be ourselves and celebrate each other, work through challenges, frustrations, and heartbreak, and ultimately be a place of healing and refuge for all who enter.

You can make your home a place where God is praised. That doesn't necessarily mean that you break out the guitars and drums and keyboard to sing together (although if that's your style, go for it!). Your home can be a place where you talk about the things God is doing in your life. Share the ways that God has provided for you in the past—ways that He has done amazing things! With your children, talk about the things that scare them and how God gives them strength (Philippians 4:13; Matthew 19:26). Your insight into God's presence in your life will encourage your family members to see God at work in their lives too.

Practice this at home, at work, at school, and out in the world; it'll be easier—even natural—to proclaim His goodness to everyone you meet.

. . . .

Lord, I will make my home a place where You hear shouts of victory!

A REASON TO REJOICE

This is the day that the LORD has made;
we will rejoice and be glad in it.

PSALM 118:24 SKJV

Some days the sun is shining, the birds are singing, and all is right with the world. Rejoicing comes naturally on days like that. But other days—maybe *most* days if we're honest—it's just plain hard to rejoice.

The psalm writers understood that struggle. David, especially, poured out his frustration when he felt like God was far away (Psalm 10, 13). But no matter how low David felt, he was always honest with God. And his prayers always concluded in praise—praise that made all the difference in his outlook and outcome.

Psalm 118:24 is a simple truth to change your current outlook and outcome, even when you don't feel like rejoicing. Tell God how you truly feel and then find at least one small thing to praise Him for: God has given you breath in your lungs today to live for Him.

When I am sad and frustrated, I don't want to bring an offering
of whining to Your feet, Lord. I know I can be honest with You.
I am frustrated and at the end of my rope! I need You to come
and take care of the problems that are all around me. Today
is a new day, God, and I will step forward in the confident
hope that You are working, even when I can't feel it.

RIGHTEOUS AND WORTHY

People are counted as righteous, not because of their work,
but because of their faith in God who forgives sinners.
ROMANS 4:5 NLT

When God's Word tells us that we are saved through faith, it's not a matter of how much faith we have or how strong our faith is. It's not about saying the right prayer or acting the right way or completing some spiritual checklist. We can know our salvation is alive and real because Jesus paid the debt of our sins by dying on the cross. When we believe, the forgiveness of Jesus is more than strong enough to save us no matter how weak or strong our faith is.

Ephesians 2:8 (NLT) puts it this way: "God saved you by his grace when you believed. And you can't take credit for this; it is a gift from God." Jesus offers us the gift of salvation because He loves us, not because we have earned it through our powerful faith. Instead, He invites us to believe in Him and accept that gift of grace.

If the world has you feeling less than worthy today, remember this truth: Jesus calls you His beloved sister, made righteous and worthy because He's holy and perfect.

. . . .

Jesus, Your grace elevates me to a place that I know I don't
deserve—right by Your side. But I'm so thankful You made a
way for me to be Your sister. I praise You for Your goodness,
Your holiness, and Your unending love for me.

OVERCOME TO BECOME

We can rejoice, too, when we run into problems and trials, for we know that they help us develop endurance. And endurance develops strength of character, and character strengthens our confident hope of salvation. And this hope will not lead to disappointment.

ROMANS 5:3–5 NLT

Paul didn't sugarcoat reality when he wrote Romans 5; we will have hard times in life. But, thankfully, that's not the end of the story. The trials we face can help us grow in our faith. And when we overcome obstacles we can become more like Jesus.

So when you're living through a difficult season, you can *choose* to rejoice as James encourages believers to do: "For you know that when your faith is tested, your endurance has a chance to grow. So let it grow, for when your endurance is fully developed, you will be perfect and complete, needing nothing" (James 1:3–4 NLT).

You can find joy in hard times not because the pain is pleasurable or that tragedy brings happiness but because God is using life's challenges and Satan's attacks to build your character. Today's problems will result in tomorrow's endurance and perseverance, which in turn will strengthen you, deepen your faith in God, and give you more confident hope about the future.

. . . .

Jesus, give me the wisdom to see past my immediate circumstances. I trust in Your timing to make things right. In the meantime, please give me the strength to endure.

DEBT-FREE

*The payoff for a life of sin is death, but God is offering
us a free gift—eternal life through our Lord Jesus,
the Anointed One, the Liberating King.*

ROMANS 6:23 VOICE

The average American has tens of thousands of dollars of debt. From car notes and student loans to credit cards and mortgages, debt ranges from a minor annoyance to a crippling burden. The Bible warns of the dangers of debt, and Proverbs 22:7 (NIV) tells us that "the borrower is the slave to the lender."

The world runs on borrowing and repayment, but God's kingdom is radically different. Our loving Father offers salvation as a gift. And a gift, by its very nature, is free. It is not something we can earn, and it's not something that we can borrow and pay back. Salvation comes to us without monetary cost.

What is the appropriate response to a thoughtful gift? Humble acceptance and gratitude. His offer of grace is unlimited, and when we tell others about God's mercy, they too will find a mysterious, seemingly too-good-to-be-true gift. Praise God today for the overwhelming gift of His grace!

. . . .

*Father, I am so thankful for Your gift of salvation, that all
I can do is sincerely thank You. The truth is that Your grace
is priceless, and if I had to take out a loan to secure it,
I would—but You bless me without asking for any payment
in return. I am Your servant. Do Your good work in me.*

WILLPOWER'S WEAKNESS

I don't really understand myself, for I want to do what is right, but I don't do it. Instead, I do what I hate.

Romans 7:15 nlt

Most children learn the fundamentals of right and wrong at a very young age. But put them in a tempting situation—like within reach of a forbidden candy stash, unsupervised—and you'll see an inward struggle between a desire to follow rules and a desire for delicious candy. Adam and Eve struggled when faced with Satan's temptation of the forbidden fruit, and Paul describes that same experience in Romans 7:15.

Every Christian struggles between the desire to sin and the desire to please God by keeping His rules and laws. But our own willpower is limited, and we should never underestimate the power of sin. If we attempt to fight it with our own strength, we're sure to fail.

Instead of trying to defeat sin with our flawed willpower, we must ask God to take hold of the situation. God alone has victory over sin, and He sent the Holy Spirit to live in us and give us access to that power. And when we fall short, He lovingly reaches down to help us back up.

. . . .

It's difficult for me to admit my own weakness, Father, but I too often feel helpless to do what is right. Instead of feeling guilty for my shortcomings, I will rely on Your strength to overcome sin. With the Holy Spirit alive in me, I will stand in Your victory!

SILENCE THE JUDGE

*There is now no condemnation for those who are in Christ
Jesus, because through Christ Jesus the law of the Spirit who
gives life has set you free from the law of sin and death.*
ROMANS 8:1–2 NIV

Our harshest critic and judge is often the voice in our own head. *Lost
your temper again, eh? I see you shoveling that junk food into the temple of
the Holy Spirit. If you'd just try harder, you could get it together. You didn't
pray at all yesterday! What kind of a Christian are you?*

Each of us should be judged and found guilty for our sin. . .
for breaking God's holy law. But thank God for Jesus! Because of
His sacrifice on the cross, we're not condemned. We're free from
the consequences of sin and given the power to do His will and live
for Him.

So when the judge in your head pipes up, remember that you're
covered in God's grace and free from all condemnation! Ask the
Holy Spirit to speak boldly on your behalf. He's your helper (John
14:26), will guide you in truth (John 16:13), and will lead you in
power, love, and self-discipline (2 Timothy 1:7).

. . . .

*I'm not waiting in fear while the jury deliberates. You've already
declared me not guilty, God! Help me live confidently in this truth.
Spirit, silence the liar in my mind. I'll hold tight to reality and
look to Your Word for the loving promises You supply there.*

TRUE FREEDOM

I will keep on obeying your instructions forever and ever.
I will walk in freedom, for I have devoted myself
to your commandments. . . . How I delight in
your commands! How I love them!
PSALM 119:44–45, 47 NLT

It's the mantra of every rebel: rules are meant to be broken.

But the writer of Psalm 119 talks about keeping God's rules yet still being free.

How is that freedom possible?

The world tells us that obeying God's laws is restraining and stifling. Following His instruction, we're told, inhibits our own choices and liberty. God's rules, people say, will force us into a mold that keeps us from being who we really are.

But the psalm writer understood the truth of the matter. By obeying God's laws, we find the freedom to be who God designed us to be. We find safety in the guardrails of His instruction that keep us headed in the right direction. By seeking the Father's salvation and grace, we're free from sin and the guilt that results from sin. Instead of wandering aimlessly through the world, we can live confidently on the path God lays before us.

It's a paradox the world can't understand: obeying the life-giving instructions of God is the way to true and everlasting freedom.

Father, too often I believe Satan's lies that You are a dictatorial, unfeeling God. The truth is You love me so deeply that You guide me in Your ways gently, as a shepherd with His sheep.

NOT ABANDONED

*I am convinced that nothing can ever separate us from God's
love. Neither death nor life, neither angels nor demons,
neither our fears for today nor our worries about tomorrow—
not even the powers of hell can separate us from God's love.
No power in the sky above or in the earth below—indeed,
nothing in all creation will ever be able to separate us from
the love of God that is revealed in Christ Jesus our Lord.*

Romans 8:38–39 nlt

When Paul writes in Romans 8 about his firm belief that nothing can separate us from God's love, he's speaking from experience.

God loved Paul when he was still called Saul, the cruelest of Christian killers (Acts 7:54–60). Jesus cared so much for Saul that the Messiah confronted him on the road to Damascus, leaving Saul temporarily blind but his name and heart changed forever (Acts 9). And though Paul's ministry included death threats and imprisonment and poverty and illness and shipwrecks and personal challenges, Paul exclaims that it is *impossible* to be separated from Christ's love. Why? His sacrifice on the cross for us is proof of His never-ending love.

What are you facing today, sister? No matter how big, how terrifying, how ugly your situation is, God is with you, He is for you, and He loves you.

*Thank You for the comforting words penned by Paul,
Father. He was convinced and so I am convinced:
nothing can come between Your love and me.*

WHEN BAD NEWS COMES

They said to me, "Things are not going well for those who returned
to the province of Judah. They are in great trouble and disgrace.
The wall of Jerusalem has been torn down, and the gates have been
destroyed by fire." When I heard this, I sat down and wept. In fact,
for days I mourned, fasted, and prayed to the God of heaven.
NEHEMIAH 1:3–4 NLT

Nehemiah broke down and wept when he heard the news that Jerusalem's walls were still in shambles decades after the Jews had returned from Babylonian exile. While the significance of the city's walls may not mean much to us today, in Nehemiah's day they were essential—by offering safety from enemy raids and in a symbolic way by signaling strength, peace, and beauty.

Yes, Nehemiah's heart was broken for his people, but he didn't dwell on his grief. Instead, he prayed, pouring out his heart to God (Nehemiah 1:5–11). And then he was proactive in making plans to rebuild the walls, giving all his passion, ability, and knowledge to that end.

When you're blindsided by bad news, pray first. Then, with God's guidance, work toward moving beyond grief to specific steps that help those who need it. His comfort and power will help you through anything!

Lord, when bad things happen, I don't want to be
paralyzed in my grief. With Your help, I will use
every resource I have to make the situation better.

LOOKING AHEAD

*I am worn out waiting for your rescue, but I have put
my hope in your word. My eyes are straining to see your
promises come true. When will you comfort me?*

PSALM 119:81–82 NLT

The writer of Psalm 119 doesn't mince words. He's tired of waiting for
God to act. Maybe you're right there too. Whether you're waiting for
a job offer or a proposal or a positive pregnancy test or reconciliation
or healing or a prodigal child, it's exhausting when we can't see God
working.

Our loving Father welcomes our honesty about being worn out
and frustrated in the waiting. Even Jesus, just hours before His trial
and crucifixion, anguished over His impending agony and separation
from the Father. He begged God to take away His cup of suffering.

Yet for both the writer of Psalm 119 and Jesus in the garden
of Gethsemane, their suffering wasn't the end of the story. Instead
they reaffirmed their hope and reliance on God's plans. "Not my will,
but yours be done," Jesus prayed in Luke 22:42 (NIV).

How can you overcome a season of worn-out waiting? First, be
honest with God about how you feel. Then look to the promises of
scripture with confident hope that even when you can't see it, He is
working in your situation.

· ·

*Lord, You are so good and so faithful to me.
Be with me and comfort me as I wait for You to act.*

A LIFELONG PURSUIT

It is the same today, for a few of the people of Israel have remained faithful because of God's grace—his undeserved kindness in choosing them. And since it is through God's kindness, then it is not by their good works. For in that case, God's grace would not be what it really is—free and undeserved.

Romans 11:5–6 nlt

A child born into an esteemed family may experience major advantages as she grows. Whether it's wealth or education or career advancement, a child of a similar age born to another family may not have as many opportunities.

Thankfully, God's kingdom doesn't operate like the world. We are saved through our faith in Jesus alone—not because of what we look like, how we act, or the total in our bank accounts.

In his letter to the Romans, Paul gently reminds us to beware of pride—pride that makes us think that God chose us because we deserve His grace. For grace, by its very definition, is undeserved—a free gift. No matter what we do, it cannot be earned, in whole or in part. Understanding the mystery of God's overwhelming kindness is a lifelong pursuit. Let's accept it with thankfulness and praise.

Father, forgive me when I wrongfully think I am better than another sinner. Because the truth is none of us is deserving of Your grace. Yet You continue to shower us with kindness and the confident hope of salvation.

THE BIGNESS OF GOD

For who can know the LORD's thoughts? Who knows enough to give
him advice? And who has given him so much that he needs to pay
it back? For everything comes from him and exists by his power
and is intended for his glory. All glory to him forever! Amen.
ROMANS 11:34–36 NLT

God is big. Huge. All-encompassing, ever-present, and all-knowing. So immense our human brains cannot fathom Him.

But God doesn't ask us to understand Him fully, and when we acknowledge that fact, we can find peace in knowing He's more than capable of being in control of it all. "My thoughts are nothing like your thoughts," God says in Isaiah 55:8–9 (NLT). "And my ways are far beyond anything you could imagine. For just as the heavens are higher than the earth, so my ways are higher than your ways and my thoughts higher than your thoughts."

Yes, we serve a big God, but even though we cannot fully understand Him, we *can* know Him and be known by Him. God is faithful (2 Timothy 2:13) and loving (1 John 4:16) and keeps His promises (2 Corinthians 1:20). He cares deeply for the entire world (John 3:16) and each individual (Luke 21:18). He created us as individuals (Psalm 139:13–16) and has plans for our lives (Jeremiah 29:11).

Take comfort in the bigness of God today.

* *

Thank You for being both the God of
the universe and my loving Father.

DON'T FORGET

Do not forget to rejoice, for hope is always just around the corner. Hold up through the hard times that are coming, and devote yourselves to prayer.
ROMANS 12:12 VOICE

Whether we make to-do lists or use a day planner or set alarms on a phone, we all need reminders so we don't forget important details. Appointments, deadlines, grocery lists, projects, lunch dates, special events, and birthdays—all these things (and more!) are easy to forget if we don't make them a priority.

Romans 12:12 includes a simple but important reminder: "Do not forget to rejoice." "Rejoice in the Lord always," Paul wrote in Philippians 4:4 (NIV). Paul understood how hard it is to rejoice when life is difficult, but he also wrote in Romans 5:3–4 (NLT) that finding joy in difficulties helps us grow endurance that "develops strength of character, and character strengthens our confident hope of salvation." Developing an attitude of rejoicing helps us remain grateful and more hopeful as we rely on the goodness of God—which can help buoy us during difficult times to come.

Don't forget to rejoice today. Start early in the day, start small, and soon you'll discover more reasons to sing God's praises!

God, I will rejoice in Your goodness, even when I don't feel like things are going well. I will find joy in the details of my days, for I know Your Spirit is with me, strengthening me in every step.

LOVING EVERYONE

The commandments say, "You must not commit adultery. You must not murder. You must not steal. You must not covet." These— and other such commandments—are summed up in this one commandment: "Love your neighbor as yourself." Love does no wrong to others, so love fulfills the requirements of God's law.

ROMANS 13:9–10 NLT

Do you ever feel guilty for practicing self-care? Loving on yourself may be a difficult thing to manage between the busyness of life and the feeling you don't deserve it, but taking the time to relax, unwind, and rejuvenate your mind, spirit, and body is important, and it's essential in living out Christ's calling to love others.

Even the most basic forms of caring for ourselves translate over to loving those around us. We don't let ourselves starve, we clothe ourselves reasonably well, and we make sure we have a roof over our heads. We try not to be cheated or physically hurt by others. These things and more are the basic points of fulfilling the second greatest commandment.

You are a cherished daughter of God. Ask Him to show you how to love yourself, your family, and the world in the ways He wants you to. When you are actively showing care to others, you'll find your self-care an extension of God's care.

I love You, Lord. Thank You for the reminder that You love me and that I should love me as well.

THE STORIES OF OTHERS

Such things were written in the Scriptures long ago to teach us. And the Scriptures give us hope and encouragement as we wait patiently for God's promises to be fulfilled.
ROMANS 15:4 NLT

When we're waiting for God to move, we can feel very isolated. After all, nobody else can know exactly what we're going through, how difficult the wait is, and how it's affecting other aspects of life, right?

Firsthand experiences of others who've gone through similar situations can help us feel less alone and give us hope for the future. Scripture also includes stories of heroes of the faith who endured seasons of waiting to eventually experience God's fulfilled promises.

Consider Sarah (Genesis 17), Hannah (1 Samuel 1–2), and Elizabeth (Luke 1), who each struggled to bear children. Although each woman's struggles were different, each received the blessing of children who grew up to do great things for God's kingdom. Add to that the stories of Esther and Ruth, and you'll see the Bible is full of women who waited and found victory through the promises of God!

Are you waiting? Read the stories of scripture. Listen to the experiences of people around you. Do you see someone struggling in their waiting? Share *your* story. Tell her what God has done in your life and share your confident hope that He is working in every situation.

Father, thank You for Your Word. I cherish the eternal wisdom You've given me. Help me spread hope to others.

PERFECT TRUTH

All your words are true; all your righteous laws are eternal.
PSALM 119:160 NIV

"I read it on the Internet, so it must be true." Maybe you've uttered this tongue-in-cheek statement when you've come across some piece of unbelievable information on a screen. Fact-checking websites and watchdog groups spend time, money, and resources to help us distinguish truth from lies, fact from fiction. Yet still it's sometimes impossible to know what is real.

One of God's characteristics is truthfulness. Scripture tells us He cannot and does not lie (Numbers 23:19; Hebrews 6:18). He does not change His mind (1 Samuel 15:29). He is who He says He is—in the past, in the present, and forever (Revelation 22:13). Because of all these things, we can trust that He will do what He says He will do and keep His promises.

Because God embodies perfect truth, we can trust the Bible to be perfect truth as well. That truth is living and active and powerful in our lives today (Hebrews 4:12). How can we use it? Second Timothy 3:16 (NLT) says, "All Scripture is inspired by God and is useful to teach us what is true and to make us realize what is wrong in our lives. It corrects us when we are wrong and teaches us to do what is right."

God, thank You for the gift of Your Word.
When the world feels confusing and I don't know
what to believe, I will stand on the truth of the Bible.

THE STRUGGLE

I urge you, brothers and sisters, by our Lord Jesus Christ and by the love of the Spirit, to join me in my struggle by praying to God for me.
ROMANS 15:30 NIV

Prayer is a beautiful, precious privilege we have in talking with God. There we can find comfort and guidance and refreshment—a reset of our hearts and minds as we focus on Him.

But prayer is not always easy. Here in Romans 15, Paul asks the Roman Christians to join in his struggle through prayer. Although he is physically separated from them, he asks the church to pray for him as he works to spread the good news of Christ across the world. Throughout his ministry, Paul experienced ridicule and persecution and arrests and criminal trials and shipwrecks and imprisonment. Even though the churches Paul wrote to didn't know exactly what hardships he was facing, they knew his work carried great risk.

Who can you join in their struggle through prayer? Maybe you know missionaries who serve in a place where it's risky to be a Christian. Ask God to protect them and move mightily in their work. Maybe you know of a hard situation with a friend or family member. Urgently and earnestly join in their struggle by asking God to help them.

* * *

Father, the struggle of others is my struggle as well.
Help me to be a faithful prayer warrior for others.
We need Your strength in the struggle.

SECURITY

I look up to the mountains—does my help come from there?
My help comes from the Lord, who made heaven and earth!
He will not let you stumble; the one who watches over you will not
slumber. Indeed, he who watches over Israel never slumbers or sleeps.
PSALM 121:1–4 NLT

Personal security is something we often take for granted until something happens that robs us of peace. Yet every day we face situations that can do just that—accidents, fraud, theft, financial loss, floods, fires, betrayal. . .Satan has an arsenal of ways to devastate our peace of mind and heart.

But as Christians, our security doesn't lie in financial stability. It doesn't lie in our family or friends or our car's safety features or the dead bolt on the door. True safety and security come from God. He is our rescuer (Galatians 1:4), refuge and protector (Psalm 91:4), and He is always there in difficult times (Psalm 46:1). Ever on watch, God's vigilance on our behalf doesn't take a break—not even to sleep.

Is your heart exhausted from constant worry of what might happen? The Lord is on the watch. Give Him your anxious thoughts and find your security, your safety, and your rest in Him.

. . . .

Father, You are the security guard of my heart, mind,
and body. I have nothing to fear because You are
faithful to keep me safe. Though the troubles of this
life may trip me up, You will not let me fall.

PARADOXES

You can count on this: God's foolishness will always be wiser than mere human wisdom, and God's weakness will always be stronger than mere human strength.

1 CORINTHIANS 1:25 VOICE

Jesus died in our place. He rose again. He offers forgiveness for our sins and eternal life when we accept His gift of grace.

Those twenty-four words may sound like foolishness to the world, yet for Christians, they hold the priceless wisdom of God's plan. Society worships power, influence, and money, but Jesus came as a humble, penniless servant who offers His kingdom to those who believe. That's the beauty of God's upside-down kingdom.

Here are just a few of the paradoxes in God's plan—His wisdom that leaves the world-wise scratching their heads:

- God's strength works best when you are the weakest (2 Corinthians 12:9).

- To be exalted you must display humility (Luke 14:11).

- If you lose your life for Jesus' sake, you will save it (Luke 9:24).

- The last will be first, and the first will be last (Matthew 20:16).

- Love those who hate you (Matthew 5:43–44).

If you struggle with any of these paradoxes, you aren't alone. But that's where faith steps in. Ask God for His understanding, trusting that His wisdom is eternal and His Word is true.

. . . .

Lord, I don't fully understand Your mysteries, but I trust in Your goodness. I trust in Your might. And I trust in Your love for me.

STRONG LIKE A MOUNTAIN

Those who trust in the LORD are like Mount Zion,
which cannot be shaken but endures forever.

PSALM 125:1 NIV

Every day you have a choice of what you will put your trust in. Will you set your hope in the newest recovery package going through Congress? What about the bestselling self-help book that everyone's talking about? The stock market? A friend or family member? Yourself and your own ability?

While some of these things are more reliable than others, none is perfect and each will ultimately let you down. True wisdom means building a foundation of trust in Jesus because He never changes (Hebrews 13:8). It means to seek guidance in God's Word that endures forever (Isaiah 40:8). We can trust God because even when we are faithless, He is faithful because that's who He is (2 Timothy 2:13). He never sleeps (Psalm 121:3–4) and He doesn't get tired (Isaiah 40:28).

How can you rely more fully on God today? Give Him your worries, big and small, and willingly give Him control over those things. When you choose to trust Him, you're standing on a powerfully unmovable, rock-solid foundation that will weather any storm!

. . . .

God, I trust You. Thank You for being the constant in my life.
No matter if the winds of life blow and the earth shakes,
I know that when I am rooted in Your Word and in
tune with Your Spirit, I will not be moved.

A HARVEST OF JOY

Restore our fortunes, Lord, as streams renew the desert.
Those who plant in tears will harvest with shouts
of joy. They weep as they go to plant their seed,
but they sing as they return with the harvest.
PSALM 126:4–6 NLT

We can see God's amazing ability to restore life all around us. Wildfires burn down forests, leaving a desolate landscape. Yet over time, the trees and underbrush grow back lusher and more robust than before. Broken bones fuse back together and heal. Trees that lose their leaves in the fall lie dormant in winter bud and grow new life in spring.

We all experience pain, grief, and heartbreak, but none of these have to be our permanent state. God can use our tears as seeds that will grow into a harvest of joy because He can bring good out of any tragedy. . .if we let Him.

Are you burdened with a heavy heart today? If life is weighing you down, lift your head and look to God. He wants you to know that this season of difficulty is not for forever. Trust in His perfect timing, ask Him to strengthen you as you wait, and praise Him for the harvest of joy that is coming.

Lord, I give You this season of struggle and I ask You
to redeem it. Turn this hard time into something good,
something miraculous. I claim Your promise in Romans 8:28
that You are working all things together for my good.

THE HARD TRUTH OF SUFFERING

*Job: I hate my life, so I will unload the full weight
of my grievance against God. Let me speak and
reveal the bitterness I am harboring.*

JOB 10:1 VOICE

Job had lost his possessions, his children, and his health. . .and he didn't have a clue why. His three friends told him he must be suffering because of some sin that he committed, even though Job knew that wasn't the case. Here Job is wallowing in self-pity as he rails against a God who would allow him to suffer so greatly.

When we face suffering, our pain can make us fall into the trap of self-righteousness, where we label ourselves a victim and see only the injustice of what's happening.

But the hard truth is that no one, not even Christians, is exempt from trouble. Although there's an explanation for our suffering, we may not know it while we're here on earth. For Job, this was the hardest part of his story. But when Job had nothing left, he had God, and that was enough.

Difficult times are painful, but the result can be a deeper relationship with God. And people who endure the testing of their faith will experience God's great rewards in the end.

. . . .

*Father, when hard times come, please help me to keep the
proper perspective. You are God and I am not. No matter
what happens in my life, I will remain faithful and hopeful
that You have a better tomorrow in store for me.*

CLEAN SLATE

LORD, if you kept a record of our sins, who, O Lord, could ever survive? But you offer forgiveness, that we might learn to fear you.
PSALM 130:3–4 NLT

Imagine a running tally of every sin you've committed. Whether arranged chronologically, topically, or alphabetically, it would be a long list. Any one of these wrongs could separate us from God (Romans 3:23; 6:23), yet scripture tells us that our forgiving Father holds no grudge against our sins.

"I am He who wipes the slate clean and erases your wrongdoing," God says in Isaiah 43:25 (VOICE). "I will not call to mind your sins anymore." We never have to fear that God will bring up past sins that He has already forgiven, because to Him, they are gone completely. God explained it this way in Hebrews 8:12 (VOICE): "I will be merciful when they fail, and I will erase their sins and wicked acts out of My memory as though they had never existed."

When we realize God has completely removed our past sins and forgiven us forever, we know we can talk to Him about anything in prayer. The lines of communication are wide open.

. . . .

Father, I cherish Your forgiveness, and I am so thankful that You remove my sins completely. When I am tempted to hold a grudge against someone who has wronged me, help me to follow Your example of complete forgiveness so I can find true freedom in my relationships.

THE CORRECT PERSPECTIVE

O Eternal One, my heart is not occupied with proud thoughts;
my eyes do not look down on others; I don't even begin to get involved
in matters too big, matters of faith, state, business, or the many
things that defy my ability to understand them. Of one thing I am
certain: my soul has become calm, quiet, and contented in You.

PSALM 131:1–2 VOICE

If anyone had the right to think well of himself, it was King David. Among his list of accomplishments, David was anointed by God to lead His people (1 Samuel 16), wrote no fewer than seventy psalms, and is described as "a man after [God's] own heart" (1 Samuel 13:14 NIV). Quite a spiritual résumé.

Yet throughout his life, David struggled with pride. Pride caused David to sleep with a married woman and then have her husband killed (2 Samuel 11). Pride shows up when we think we're better than others, and it breeds anxiety and turmoil and discontent. Proverbs 8:13 says that God *hates* pride. The only remedy for pride? Humility.

David found joy in humility and sought it out, as we see in Psalm 131:1–2. His humble spirit helped him admit he didn't know everything. That humility led to contentment in God.

Pride leads to chaos; humility leads to peace. Seek the calm, quiet contentment God provides when you let humility reign.

. . . .

Father, You are God and I am not. Give me the correct
perspective. Help me to see myself through Your eyes.

MARITAL STATUS

*I wish everyone were single, just as I am. Yet each person
has a special gift from God, of one kind or another.*
1 CORINTHIANS 7:7 NLT

Whether you are married or unmarried, your relationship status is a gift from God.

That might be a tough pill to swallow if you aren't happy with your current state, but the truth is that both wives and single women are equally valuable in God's kingdom.

When Paul wrote in 1 Corinthians 7 that he wished all people were single like him, his desire was that more people would devote themselves completely to the ministry. Without the added responsibilities of a spouse and family, Paul had time to focus on the unique calling God had for him. He wasn't criticizing marriage—after all, God created marriage. A single woman or a wife and husband who are like-minded in their faith can be equally as effective in God's family.

Loving God and loving others are the two greatest commandments—and regardless of a person's marital status, God provides opportunities every day to do just that. Pray and ask God to show you those opportunities so you can fully live out your life on mission with Him.

*Father, thank You for giving me a purpose in life. I want
to live out Your mission every day. I love You, Lord,
and I want to share that same love with others.*

HERE AND NOW

*Each person should remain in the situation they were in when
God called them. Were you a slave when you were called? Don't
let it trouble you—although if you can gain your freedom, do so.*
1 CORINTHIANS 7:20–21 NIV

God can use anyone, anywhere for His glory. It doesn't matter your
age, education, income level, race, or gender. Whatever skills you bring
to the table, whatever resources you have at your disposal, God can
use you here and now. All you need is a willing and humble heart.

Not all of us are called to minister in foreign mission fields. God
can and will create perfect opportunities to do His work wherever
we are! In Paul's letter to the Corinthian church, he's reinforcing
this idea even more. He writes in 1 Corinthians 7:17–21 that when
someone becomes a Christian, they should usually continue doing the
work they are already doing (as long as it isn't sinful or unethical, of
course). Every career can become work in God's kingdom when we
make the purpose of our job to love, serve, and share Jesus with others.

God has placed you where you are for a reason. Live confidently
for Him where you are, here and now.

*God, when I feel inadequate to do good in Your kingdom,
remind me that You've placed me where I am to be Your
light. Help me see opportunities to serve You and others.
Let my family, friends, and coworkers see Jesus in me.*

LOVE OVER KNOWLEDGE

All of us have knowledge, but knowledge can be risky.
Knowledge promotes overconfidence and worse arrogance,
but charity of the heart (love, that is) looks to build up others.
1 Corinthians 8:1 voice

The Old Testament has a lot to say about knowledge. "Intelligent people are always ready to learn. Their ears are open for knowledge," Proverbs 18:15 (NLT) says. Proverbs 1:7 tells us that the beginning of knowledge is reverence and respect for God. And God's wisdom, Proverbs 8:10 says, is even more valuable than silver or gold.

Yet amassing knowledge just to be smart isn't the goal. Knowledge can lead to pride, making us feel superior to other people. That pride can develop into an arrogant, know-it-all attitude. And if we're unwilling to listen and learn from God and others, then knowing things is meaningless.

Love is more important than knowledge. And God's love always leads to a wisdom that puts Him and others ahead of our own desires (James 3:17–18). The greatest example of this kind of love is Jesus Himself, who sacrificed His life for others (John 15:13).

To strengthen your faith, love more deeply. And by growing love, you will grow to know God better and more fully (1 John 4:7–8).

....

Loving Father, thank You for being the example of pure love.
Help me prioritize love over knowledge in every interaction.
I can possess all the knowledge in the world, but I know that
only Your unconditional love can change the world.

WITHOUT EXPECTATIONS

*If I were doing this on my own initiative, I would deserve
payment. But I have no choice, for God has given me this
sacred trust. What then is my pay? It is the opportunity to
preach the Good News without charging anyone. That's why
I never demand my rights when I preach the Good News.*

1 CORINTHIANS 9:17–18 NLT

Did you know that Paul made and sold tents in addition to starting
churches? It's how he supported himself and his travels. Imagine how
hard he worked every day. And while he could have charged to share
the good news, Paul never did. He knew God called him into service,
and he considered it a privilege.

Let's be careful to love on others without expecting something in
return. Our kind and encouraging words should be free of expectation. Acts of service, like bringing meals or volunteering our time in
ministry, don't require a payback. And if we adopt a servant's heart,
we'll find that our *payment* will be knowing we helped another. Being
God's hands and feet is payment enough.

So be courageous in your faith. Be confident as you share God's
goodness with others. And know that every act of obedience yields
a blessing, according to multiple scriptures in the Bible. When He
gives you a sacred trust like He did Paul, let it be your privilege to
walk it out.

. . . .

*Lord, it's my joy to love on others
and further Your kingdom on earth.*

REMEMBERING

To Him who split the Red Sea in two and made a path between
the divided waters, for His faithful love lasts forever. Then allowed
Israel to pass safely through on dry ground, for His faithful love
lasts forever. To Him who crushed Pharaoh and his army in
the waters of the Red Sea, for His faithful love lasts forever.

PSALM 136:13–15 VOICE

This powerful recount is from what the Israelites experienced. From time to time, they would revisit all the ways God intervened in their lives. They needed to remember time of deliverance. They needed to remember their God was a miracle-worker. Why? Because they wanted a reminder that He is faithful and loving.

Maybe you need to do this exercise today. Maybe you're in a tough spot and in need of a refresher of God's goodness. Are you hopeless? Scared? Worried? Nothing will help refuel your faith like recalling the ways and times the Lord has shown up in your life.

Remember how He removed your bitterness. How He restored that relationship. Consider the opened and closed doors that came at the right times. Reminisce about the financial help, the health breakthrough, the desire to forgive, and the favor at work. Let all these memories encourage you to take heart for what's happening right now.

. . . .

Lord, You have a perfect track record in
my life. Thank You for loving me so boldly!

QUESTIONING GOD

"Where were you when I laid the earth's foundation? Tell me, if you understand. Who marked off its dimensions? Surely you know! Who stretched a measuring line across it? On what were its footings set, or who laid its cornerstone—while the morning stars sang together and all the angels shouted for joy?"

JOB 38:4–7 NIV

Job probably didn't expect this firm response from God. We understand his life had just fallen apart, but questioning the Lord didn't go over well. The truth is that we're unable to comprehend the will and ways of God. We cannot figure Him out or appreciate His magnificence with the human mind. Instead, we're to remember who God is and trust Him.

Maybe the right question for us to ask when it seems things are falling apart is simply. . .*what now?* Unless God chooses to reveal it, we may never know the *whys*. We may never learn the *hows*. But we can always know God works with our best in mind. His plans are for our good and His glory.

So be steadfast in your faith and let God be God. Believe He is actively in control of the hard circumstances you're facing. And while it may take every bit of energy you have to trust Him, do it. God won't let you fall.

. . . .

Lord, help me appreciate You are God, and I am not.
Help me be grateful for Your mysterious ways.

INFUSED WITH GOD'S STRENGTH

*On the day I needed You, I called, and You
responded and infused my soul with strength.*
PSALM 138:3 VOICE

Take heart! And be secure in the truth that God sees your desires, hears your prayers, and will respond with what you need. While He's not our servant who's available at the snap of our fingers, God is our loving Father who cares deeply for His children. And like any good parent, He will most certainly respond to our cries.

Where do you need His strength today? Is there an upcoming difficult conversation with someone who intimidates you? Do you need to advocate for yourself at work? Are you struggling to hold the line with your kids? Was the pregnancy test negative again? Is your hope of marriage floundering? Do you feel unqualified for the next step? Take each need to God right now and let Him infuse your soul so you can move forward in His strength.

Hopelessness has no place in the life of a believer. With God, you are neither weak nor ineffective. But there are some moments in life that challenge your faith. So, when you find yourself in one, let God be the one who helps you navigate it with strength. Remember that you're strong because He is strong.

....

*Lord, let me be brave and courageous through faith,
knowing You will always give me what I need in the moment.*

SEEN AND KNOWN

*You have surrounded me on every side, behind me and before me,
and You have placed Your hand gently on my shoulder. It is the
most amazing feeling to know how deeply You know me, inside and
out; the realization of it is so great that I cannot comprehend it.*

PSALM 139:5–6 VOICE

As women, one of our greatest desires is to be seen and known. We
want others to not only know us but *want* to know us. We want to be
a destination. We crave having someone who understands who we are,
what we want, and why we do what we do. Our desire is to be wholly
appreciated even in the messy and moody moments.

What a gift to know God meets this need with perfection. You
don't have to hope, because scripture tells us He fills it. Every moment
of every day, you are surrounded by God. No matter what struggles
or challenges you're facing, He is right there to help. He even puts a
holy hand on you for comfort, letting you know He's nearby.

Take heart! God deeply loves you and knows you. He sees who
you are, inside and out. Let that beautiful truth wash over you today,
and be reminded of His all-consuming presence in your life.

. . . .

*Lord, I'm so grateful and humbled
to be seen and known by You!*

THE DESIRE FOR COMMUNITY

Also, if two lie down together, they will keep warm.
But how can one keep warm alone? Though one
may be overpowered, two can defend themselves.
A cord of three strands is not quickly broken.

ECCLESIASTES 4:11–12 NIV

When God made humankind, His master plan was never for us to be alone. You may be an introvert, but that only means your tribe is smaller and times with another person (or two) are further apart. But even then, being together with those you care about is vital.

God's design was for us to find our community of family and friends and live our life as a collective. Because we need people. We need friends to help us stay strong in hard times. We need them to pick up the slack when we're overwhelmed. We need friends to encourage our heart, cover us in prayer, and love us through difficult moments. It may not always feel important to have them around, but it is. And when we choose to embrace others, it will bless us in the most meaningful ways.

So be brave, friend! Embrace your people with fervor. And if you don't have the right community yet, ask the Lord to bring it to you. They are out there, probably looking for their community too.

. . . .

Lord, would You bless me with solid, faith-filled friendships?

BEING TRANSPARENT WITH GOD

Explore me, O God, and know the real me. Dig deeply
and discover who I am. Put me to the test and watch how
I handle the strain. Examine me to see if there is an evil
bone in me, and guide me down Your path forever.

PSALM 139:23–24 VOICE

What if you adopted the attitude of the psalmist in today's reading? It may feel risky, but what an opportunity to grow closer to God. What a powerful way to strengthen your faith and at the same time build up your confidence as a believer.

Owning and implementing today's verses really is an act of surrender. For God already knows the real you. He knows how you'll handle the strain of whatever comes against you. He knows the places where righteous living challenges you. Yet this request is so amazing because it provides for complete transparency and honest assessments. What a beautiful heart is displayed by the psalmist.

Although it may seem scary, opening yourself up like this, asking God to dig deep and examine you, you can be sure you can fully trust Him to be gentle and firm at the right times. This isn't about condemnation because that isn't from the Lord. This is about deepening your trust in Him by revealing and healing whatever may stand between you.

Lord, here I am. I trust You to examine
my heart and restore the broken places.

GOD IS YOUR HELMET

"Eternal One," I said, "You are my one and only God. Hear me,
O Eternal, hear my humble cry for rescue. O Lord, Eternal One,
power of my deliverance, You are my helmet in the day of battle."
PSALM 140:6–7 VOICE

Consider the importance of God being your helmet through battles.
A helmet is solely designed to protect your head, keeping your mind
safe from injury. In doing so, you're able to function. You can weigh
options and make decisions. Your brain allows you to strategize and
be creative in problem-solving. And it enables you to remember to
call on God for help.

The psalmist knew how vital it was for the Lord to protect his
thought life, especially when things got chaotic. Let's grasp the beauty
and power of this truth. Let's choose to be women who trust God to
help guard our minds against the enemy's lies. Through prayer and time
in His Word, we can be confident our convictions will stand strong.
And we'll know with assurance that God is our hope and deliverer.

So today, thank the Lord for being your helmet of protection.
Thank Him for knowing how very important that piece of armor is
for every believer.

Lord, You are my helmet. That truth strengthens my mind
and my heart. You always know exactly what I need to
thrive in life. For that and so much more I love You.

ON THE SIDE OF VICTIMS

I know that you, GOD, are on the side of victims, that you care for
the rights of the poor. And I know that the righteous personally
thank you, that good people are secure in your presence.
PSALM 140:12–13 MSG

The reality of being a victim is that they feel all alone. And so often, it's the victim who usually comes under great scrutiny from others. Rather than feel supported and cared for, they feel even more victimized. For many, it seems to be the gift that keeps giving. It's a terrible situation that leaves one with a profound sense of hopelessness.

If you've been the victim—and who hasn't from time to time—take heart knowing that, based on scripture, God is on your side. No one else may show compassion, but the Lord sees your circumstances and is in your corner. Even more, justice matters to Him. And in His perfect timing, every wrong will be made right.

Never forget that God's presence in your life brings great strength. It brings a security unmatched by anything the world can offer. Your worth to the Father is immeasurable. So, when it feels like the world is against you, cling to the truth that God is *always* for you.

Lord, what a gift to know You promise to stand with me
when I feel knocked down and abandoned by others.

THE BEST IS YET TO COME

Our bodies are buried in brokenness, but they will be
raised in glory. They are buried in weakness, but they will
be raised in strength. They are buried as natural human
bodies, but they will be raised as spiritual bodies.

1 CORINTHIANS 15:43–44 NLT

Let today's verses bring hope to a weary spirit! We may have a profound understanding of just how broken and weak we are, but we can hold tight to the promise that the best is yet to come. We won't be suffering forever. The difficulties we face every day won't follow us into eternity. And while life may feel very overwhelming in the moment, we can find comfort knowing it will pass. There is an expiration date to our earthly struggles.

So, take heart! Choose to stand in victory even while navigating hard times. Let God's strength course through your veins. Be hopeful, knowing these challenging moments won't last much longer.

Your body isn't built for eternity. It's built to handle this life, one day at a time. And when you press into the Lord for help and hope, He will hold you up to walk out today.

. . . .

Lord, what a beautiful gift to know my current body will be replaced
with a new and improved one. Thank You for strengthening the
one I have right now, with a promise of a better one soon!

LOVING OTHERS

*Learn to do right; seek justice. Defend the oppressed. Take up
the cause of the fatherless; plead the case of the widow.*
ISAIAH 1:17 NIV

Because God not only asks but also requires us to love others, it should
be a top priority in our life. Without fail, choosing compassion should
be a daily decision as we try to live righteously and glorify God with
our words and actions. But sometimes it's hard to understand what
that looks like and how to love others well.

A good key to keep in mind is God's heart for the least of these.
While He loves us all, His heart is especially tender toward those
struggling the most. Knowing that, look for opportunities to seek
justice and defend those who are oppressed. Help the orphans and
widows when the chance presents itself. When at all possible, find
ways to make life easier for those who face the bigger challenges.
That's being God's hands and feet. It's showing love.

Every time you choose to help rather than hurt or love rather
than loathe, the Lord sees it. He makes note of your kindness and
obedience. And because scripture confirms it, you can be assured that
when you obey His lead, a blessing will follow.

*Lord, open my eyes to see who needs help, and give me
creative and practical ways to bless them in Your name.*

PAYING IT FORWARD

He comforts us in all our troubles so that we can comfort others.
When they are troubled, we will be able to give them the same
comfort God has given us. For the more we suffer for Christ, the
more God will shower us with his comfort through Christ.

2 CORINTHIANS 1:4–5 NLT

Doesn't God think of everything? In His economy, nothing goes to waste. And there is deep encouragement found in today's verses we can't miss.

First, relish in the truth that God promises to comfort us when we're in need. In those desperate times when we can't make heads or tails of life, He is there to secure our heart. Be it a financial pit, a health scare, a heartbreaking loss, or the end to an important relationship, you can always count on God to be right there, waiting with open arms. Secondly, He will give us opportunities to use the comfort given us to comfort others in pain. Sometimes there's nothing better than talking to someone who has lived through a hardship and come out the other side intact.

Why not change your perspective about each challenge you face? Why not be grateful God will not only be with you through it but also bless you with important moments to pay it forward to another.

Lord, I'm in awe of Your economy and how
You make the world go around. I love You!

ALLOWING GOD TO LEAD

*Teach me how to do Your will, for You are my God.
Allow Your good Spirit to guide me on level
ground, to guide me along Your path.*
PSALM 143:10 VOICE

Let's choose to be women of courage, always asking God to teach us to obey His plans for our life. Doing so will usher in freedom! So at every turn, let's ask for His Spirit to be the one to guide us into righteous living. Let's decide today that before we take the next step forward, we will wait for God's leading so we stay on the path He has chosen. It's not an impossible task, just a deliberate one.

Be confident in knowing your heart will be lighter and your focus stronger when you include the Lord in your journey. Are you contemplating a big career move? Are you starting treatment? Are you newly single? Does parenting overwhelm you? Have you lost someone special? Did your friendship implode? These are often tough paths to navigate well. But keep in mind it's God's presence that will strengthen you along the way, giving hope and encouragement for what life brings.

We need God to show us where to tread. We need His guidance so our lives can be a spotlight of hope for others. And in those times we feel lost and confused, it's God who will straighten the crooked path before us.

Lord, where You lead, I will follow.

DEATH STENCH OR SWEET AROMA?

Our lives are a Christ-like fragrance rising up to God.
But this fragrance is perceived differently by those who are
being saved and by those who are perishing. To those who
are perishing, we are a dreadful smell of death and doom.
But to those who are being saved, we are a life-giving
perfume. And who is adequate for such a task as this?
2 CORINTHIANS 2:15–16 NLT

You either have a death stench or a sweet aroma. It doesn't matter how often you shower or what body spray you use, to God's nose these are the only options available. To Him, what do you smell like?

If you aren't a believer and follower of Christ, don't let another day pass without securing your salvation. There's no good reason to hold off on making the most important decision in this life. By choosing to believe and declaring that Jesus is the Son of God, who came to earth, died on the cross for your redemption, and rose three days later, your eternity in heaven is locked. That simple yet profound decision replaces your dreadful smell with a life-giving perfume.

This journey may not be easy. It may be filled with constant ups and downs. But when your eternal life is settled, there will be a new perspective. You'll understand life is but a breath and be expectant for things to come.

. . . .

Lord, let me be a sweet aroma to You!

OUR LIMITLESS GOD

*The Eternal is great and deserves endless praise; His greatness
knows no limit, recognizes no boundary. No one can
measure or comprehend His magnificence. One generation
after another will celebrate Your great works; they will pass
on the story of Your powerful acts to their children.*
PSALM 145:3–4 VOICE

Take heart knowing you serve a God who has no limits. There are
no boundaries anywhere that have the power to keep Him reined in.
Try as we might, it's impossible to accurately measure His magnificence. The depth of it, we can't even begin to comprehend. God is
uncontainable, incalculable, and unending. And that is good news!

Why? Imagine if you could figure Him out or predict His next
move. What if you could fully define His awesomeness? Or what if
you were able to explain God's will and ways? If so, then He would
be nothing more than ordinary. He would be average, no better than
any of us.

So let the truth of God's magnificence receive your endless praise!
Be encouraged knowing He is all-knowing and all-powerful. And be
diligent to share His mighty acts in your life with others so they will
understand just how glorious and splendid God is!

. . . .

*Lord, thank You for being so wonderful in every way!
What a blessing to be in Your presence every day.*

ONLY GOD

Do not put your trust in the rulers of this world—kings and princes. Do not expect any rescue from mortal men. As soon as their breath leaves them, they return to the earth; on that day, all of them perish—their dreams, their plans, and their memories.

PSALM 146:3–4 VOICE

If your confidence is secured in humankind, you will find yourself deeply disappointed. As much as your friends love you, they are not your savior. Your significant other can't make everything rough run smoothly. Mom and dad may have every good intention, but their best will never be good enough. Neither will promises from politicians, processes, or other people. At every turn, they will fall short.

But take heart because God will never fall short. He won't ever let you down. When you need wisdom, He will impart it. When you need strength, God will deliver it. When you need perspective, it will be revealed in the right way at the right time. When you are in desperate need of rescue, the Lord will send a lifeline to bring you to safety.

Friend, you are loved and covered by the Father. When He created you, God didn't stop there. He always intended to be the one you depended on for every need. You can be confident in that truth!

Lord, remind me to not look at humankind as my savior. You are my Father, and You promise to take care of me.

LIVE BY BELIEVING

*So we are always confident, even though we know that
as long as we live in these bodies we are not at home with
the Lord. For we live by believing and not by seeing.*

2 CORINTHIANS 5:6–7 NLT

Can we agree that living by belief rather than by sight is difficult at best? Yet faith requires it. When we agree to this grand adventure with God, it means we choose to trust even when we can't see the plan. We follow when we can't see the path. And we obey when we can't see the purpose.

You can be confident that God is always working things out for your good and His glory. Each day and in every circumstance, He is preparing us to be with Him. Sometimes it's hard to navigate life here when we long to be in heaven with the Lord. But until that splendid day arrives, we're to cling to our faith and follow His leading. With God's help, we can embrace the time on earth while expectant for eternity.

Where in your life does this challenge you right now? Where are you struggling to have belief over sight? Why not ask God to give you courage to flex your faith today?

. . . .

*Lord, help me make the best use of my time here,
even though I'm longing to be in Your presence.
Give me confidence to trust You every day.*

ETERNAL PERSPECTIVE

We are ignored, even though we are well known. We live close to death, but we are still alive. We have been beaten, but we have not been killed. Our hearts ache, but we always have joy. We are poor, but we give spiritual riches to others. We own nothing, and yet we have everything.

2 CORINTHIANS 6:9–10 NLT

What a great perspective! Paul is focusing on eternal things rather than earthly. He's contrasting the difference between worldly worries and a heavenly understanding of life. And if we adopt this same viewpoint, it will create in us an unshakable hope because we'll see the bigger picture. It will help us keep the right perspective about the struggles and troubles we may face. It will strengthen us for the journey because we'll know without a doubt that God has us.

How do today's verses encourage you in this season? How do they reshape how you're looking at a situation? It takes courage to see life the way Paul does. It takes a great measure of faith to live with this mindset. But when you do, there will be a calm that overtakes any anxious heart. And eternal perspective is a beautiful thing.

Lord, help me see life through the lens of faith.
And help my heart be hopeful because of it.

WONDERFUL THINGS

*Lord, you are my God; I will exalt you and praise
your name, for in perfect faithfulness you have done
wonderful things, things planned long ago.*
ISAIAH 25:1 NIV

Need a boost of hope and encouragement today? Think back to God's
awesome displays of power in the Bible. Remember when He parted
the Red Sea, allowing the Israelites to cross on dry land to escape
Pharaoh? What about when Joseph became number two in Egypt?
Daniel survived the night in the lions' den. God gave Noah building
plans that saved him and his family. Esther found the courage to
expose Haman's plans and save her people. Nehemiah rebuilt the wall
surrounding Jerusalem.

Now, take time to recall the wonderful things God has done in
your life. What has He healed? A relationship. An illness. A financial
free fall. Where has the Lord restored something that felt too far
gone, like your confidence or hope? What else has God done for you?

Let this exercise reignite the truth of God's faithfulness. He
may sometimes feel far away, but He hasn't moved. Have you? Today,
reconnect with your Father who adores you. He is your God, and His
dependability is unshakable.

. . . .

*Lord, help me remember Your goodness every day, especially
when life feels overwhelming. And give me eyes to see Your
wonderful works, because I know they are there. I love You!*

ALWAYS A REASON TO PRAISE

Praise the Eternal! Praise the True God inside His temple.
Praise Him beneath massive skies, under moonlit stars and rising
sun. Praise Him for His powerful acts, redeeming His people. Praise
Him for His greatness that surpasses our time and understanding.
PSALM 150:1–2 VOICE

Notice the psalmist's desire to praise God anywhere and everywhere. He praised the Lord for His wondrous acts as well as His incalculable awesomeness. The writer recognized God's redemption for His people. What a great example for us to follow, because something powerful happens when we embrace the goodness of God and celebrate it.

One of the best ways we can enrich our heart with hope is to remember what makes the Lord magnificent. Every time we recount His hand in our circumstances, it grows our confidence. Speaking out His splendor and majesty encourages us to trust our big God with our big problems.

There is nothing God can't do in our life. He can mend a broken relationship. He can give you strength to persevere. He can bring provision and usher in peace. And He can redirect after a bad choice. So, take heart and hold on for the Lord to move His mighty hand. And then. . .praise Him for it.

. . . .

Lord, hear my praises for Your unmatched
goodness in my life, for Your being all-powerful
and all-knowing. What a privilege to be Your child.

IMPERFECT PARENTS

*So, my son, pay attention to your father's guidance, and do not
ignore what your mother taught you—wear their wisdom as a
badge of honor and maturity, as fine jewelry around your neck.*
PROVERBS 1:8–9 VOICE

Maybe your parents were amazing as you were growing up. Maybe
their love was beautifully evident by the ways they treated you. Maybe
you consistently felt supported, even when you failed. And when you
needed encouragement or advice, it flowed out of their hearts to yours.
But maybe this wasn't your experience at all.

For many, childhood memories are filled with dysfunctional
parents who left deep scars. There may have been pockets of goodness,
but they were overshadowed by tension, and still are today. If this was
your experience, take heart! Our earthly parents are imperfect people,
living in an imperfect world, who raised imperfect children. And no
matter the struggle and strain, God chose them for you.

Ask God to help you see their moments of wisdom and guidance.
Ask Him to help you see them through His eyes so you can appreciate
their effort. And ask for rose-colored glasses so you can have hope
for your future relationship.

* * *

*Lord, thank You for my parents. Even through the tough times,
I know it's important to honor my mom and dad. Whether
by adoption or birth, give me a tender heart toward them,
knowing they are flawed people. . .just like me.*

YOUR RESCUE AT HAND

We've been waiting for you, Eternal One, to come and shower us with grace. In the morning, be our strength; in times of trouble, be what saves us.

Isaiah 33:2 voice

Trust God to show up and rescue you. Expect it, even. Don't you know how much He loves you? Do you understand the value you hold in His heart? God may not follow your time frame or respond in the exact ways you ask, but that doesn't negate the reality that He will never abandon you. And when you're in a rough patch, it's the Lord who is mighty to save.

So, exhale in relief because God sees you. Thanks to His great compassion, you don't have to grin and bear it anymore. You don't have to push through the pain as you try to bandage the situation. Instead, you can lean into the one who gives grace, letting Him straighten the crooked path before you. And while you're waiting for God to intervene, be prayerful. Be honest with Him about your struggles. Unpack your fears and worries. And then continue waiting and trusting God, confident He is working on your behalf and your rescue is at hand.

Lord, I will wait on You to save and strengthen me. You're my knight in shining armor!

GOD'S WISDOM

Turn to me and receive my gentle correction; watch and I will pour out my spirit on you; I will share with you my wise words in order to redirect your lives. You hear, but you have refused to answer my call. My hands reached out, but no one noticed.

PROVERBS 1:23–24 VOICE

You're a smart woman. You've lived a lot of life. Maybe you earned a college degree or maybe you have hard-won wisdom from the school of hard knocks. Regardless, you have insight into the world's way and how to navigate it with ease. But that doesn't compare with the kind of wisdom God imparts to those who love Him.

The truth is our understanding will only take us so far. It's not complete by any stretch of the imagination. And if we rely on ourselves, it won't ever be. But God wants to bless us with His wisdom. With it, He promises to correct and guide us. He says He'll pour out His spirit. Even more, He vows to share His wisdom so we'll know the right next step to take.

So take heart! Where you feel lacking in knowledge, He will give it. Where you have made wrong choices, God will correct it. Be open to the Father and wait for His leading. Watch as He brings fresh revelation, opening doors and closing them appropriately.

. . . .

*Lord, let me lead my life with Your wisdom
so I can live according to Your ways.*

WHEN WEAKNESS IS GOOD

I am at peace and even take pleasure in any weaknesses,
insults, hardships, persecutions, and afflictions for the sake of the
Anointed because when I am at my weakest, He makes me strong.
2 Corinthians 12:10 voice

The choice is easy to see. We can either be strong in ourselves, always striving to be in control and carrying the burden of our circumstances on our shoulders. Or we can embrace our weakness and rest, fully believing God will make up the difference. And while that may be easy to see, it is often hard to walk out.

Think of your weakness as a good thing. When you're persecuted, let it be. At every hardship or affliction, find your peace. This is counterintuitive of the world's ideas, but when you embrace your troubles and trust God, you will find strength through Him to keep you steady. When you get out of the way, the Lord moves in mightily!

Take heart knowing God will fill in every gap left by your humanity. You don't need a superhero cape or spectacular powers to get through life. You just need the Lord.

. . . .

Lord, thank You for covering my weakness with Your
strength. What a relief to understand it's not all up to me!

HOPING IN THE LORD

*Even youths grow tired and weary, and young men stumble
and fall; but those who hope in the LORD will renew their
strength. They will soar on wings like eagles; they will run
and not grow weary, they will walk and not be faint.*

ISAIAH 40:30–31 NIV

There's a difference between earthly hope and biblical hope. The first
feels less secure, like you're crossing fingers and wishing for the best.
It seems like a roll of the dice. There's an uncertainty to it. And since
our humanity limits our ability to make things happen, we are literally
at the mercy of chance. But biblical hope has weight to it.

Biblical hope not only desires a good outcome but expects it.
There is a confident expectation for a positive future driving it. And
when scripture says that hoping in the Lord will renew a believer's
strength, it's because we are anticipating strength from Him. We're
awaiting it with conviction. Our belief is strong. Our assurance is
based on God's perfect track record in our life. It's faith.

Today moving forward, choose to have confident expectation
in the Lord. When you're in need, He sees it. And you can trust He
will meet each of those needs in the right way and at the right time.

....

*Lord, I believe You. I trust You. And in those moments
where my faith falters, remind me to hope in You again.*

WHEN FEAR IS A BIG DEAL

"So do not fear, for I am with you; do not be dismayed,
for I am your God. I will strengthen you and help you;
I will uphold you with my righteous right hand."

ISAIAH 41:10 NIV

If fear is a big deal in your life, then let the promises from today's scripture flood your heart with peace. Let the knowledge of God's constant presence strengthen you so you're able to stand strong in life's trials. Be encouraged because His holy hand is on you, keeping you steady and safe.

There are a million reasons to be afraid. Life has a way of destabilizing and discouraging even the strongest of people. And there are no shortages of worrisome situations to obsess over. But God is the remedy. He is the answer. Just understanding the power of His presence in your life is enough to make you brave and bold to navigate anything. You may still feel your knees knocking from time to time, but fear will lose its power. It won't be able to grip you like before.

Dear one, you don't have to meander through life afraid. There is no reason to be daily dismayed, disappointed, or discouraged. With God, there is hope! So, ask Him to heal that fear reflex that drives your emotions.

. . . .

Lord, increase my faith so I lean on You in fearful
moments. I know You will make everything okay.

IT'S NOT BY WORKS

*But we know that no one is made right with God by meeting
the demands of the law. It is only through the faithfulness of
Jesus the Anointed that salvation is even possible. This is why
we put faith in Jesus the Anointed: so we will be put right with
God. It's His faithfulness—not works prescribed by the law—
that puts us in right standing with God because no one will be
acquitted and declared "right" for doing what the law demands.*

GALATIANS 2:16 VOICE

Today's verse provides the perfect reason to celebrate and praise at the same time! To realize there's nothing we can do to earn our salvation is a beautiful truth that ushers in freedom to our heart. Following "religious" rules doesn't bring us closer to God. Instead, it brings us closer to condemnation because we always fall short. It's a lose-lose situation.

Yet when our faith is activated and we choose to live in a right relationship with God, the weight of the law lifts. Embracing His love rather than working for it removes guilt and shame. And accepting the blood of Jesus as our redemption allows us to walk in the freedom He came to give.

Today, ask God to help you off the treadmill of performance. Let Him remind you there's nothing you can do to earn His love or your salvation.

. . . .

*Lord, thank You for not expecting me
to be good enough for eternity!*

STAY CALM

Stay calm; there is no need to be afraid of a sudden disaster or to worry when calamity strikes the wicked, for the Eternal is always there to protect you. He will safeguard your each and every step.
PROVERBS 3:25–26 VOICE

Maybe you would agree that two of the most annoying words in the English language are *stay calm*. When life is falling apart and we're freaking out, they are the last thing we want to hear. They feel condescending. They feel dismissive. But when we take a step back and consider these words through the lens of faith, they help to refocus us in difficult times. Because when we truly embrace God's promise to protect us, it allows us to stay calm regardless of the chaos swirling around us.

Remember this is a choice. It's a deliberate decision to keep our eyes on the Master rather than on the madness. We press into the Divine and not the disorder. We look to the Creator rather than focusing on the commotion. This is faith over fear, and it changes everything.

So be encouraged! Your every step is safeguarded by God. That means even when the curveball comes or calamity strikes, His protection surrounds you. You don't have to give in to those emotions of doom and gloom. Instead, trust God to bring you through!

*Lord, remind me that You are always with me,
sheltering and shielding me with Your love and protection.*

BEATEN UP AND BEATEN DOWN

*Heavens, raise the roof! Earth, wake the dead! Mountains,
send up cheers! God has comforted his people. He has
tenderly nursed his beaten-up, beaten-down people.*

ISAIAH 49:13 MSG

If you're feeling mentally beat-up today by life, choose to be strong
in faith! If you are feeling like a beaten-down person, be confident in
God's promise to tenderly nurse you back to sound emotional health.
At every turn and in each circumstance, the Lord will comfort those
who love Him. He has the perfect way to soothe an anxious heart and
console a weary spirit. And better than anyone else, God can bring a
sense of calm that reassures He is with us.

Where do you need His comfort today? Are you battling fear
with finances? Are you grieving the loss of a loved one? Is national
news wearing you down? Has an important relationship crumbled?
Are you at your wit's end with a situation? Regardless, God is with
you and ready to ease the anxiousness. Have you asked for His help?

Life is hard and the journey difficult. But you have a wonderful
Father who's ready to encourage and guide you each step of the way.
Lean into Him.

. . . .

*Lord, it brings relief to know You care when I
feel overwhelmed by life. Please comfort me
today because my heart needs it.*

NEVER FORGOTTEN

Is it possible for a mother, however disappointed,
however hurt, to forget her nursing child? Can she feel
nothing for the baby she carried and birthed? Even if she
could, I, God, will never forget you. Look here. I have made
you a part of Me, written you on the palms of My hands.
Your city walls are always on My mind, always My concern.
Isaiah 49:15–16 voice

What an encouragement to understand God will never leave us. No matter how many times we turn our back on Him, we won't be forgotten. When we in anger walk away, He won't follow suit. We can take heart knowing our names are written on the palms of God's hands. We're intimately known by our Creator.

Chances are people have left you before. We all have a painful story of times we were rejected or abandoned by those we cared for. Sometimes we saw it coming, while other times it caught us off guard. But either way, the pain it inflicted on our heart stays with us—and breeds fear it can happen again. Rest assured, it won't ever be at the hands of God.

No matter what, God will never forget you or leave you. It's a promise!

. . . .

Lord, it settles my spirit to know I'm unforgettable in
Your eyes. Thank You for loving me without fail!

REAL AND LASTING

*"Though the mountains be shaken and the hills be removed
. . .my unfailing love for you will not be shaken nor my
covenant of peace be removed," says the LORD.*

ISAIAH 54:10 NIV

While it's hard to imagine mountains crumbling into the sea and hills being removed, the truth is they won't last forever. God's Word tells us that no earthly thing will remain: "The first heaven and the first earth had passed away, and the sea was no more" (Revelation 21:1 ESV). Even the strongest things on earth will be swept away.

So, what's a girl to do? Is there *anything* she can count on? Is there any reason to hope? . . . The answer is yes! We can find comfort and assurance in God's promise—His love won't be shaken, His promise of peace stands. We can *always* trust and hope in the tender, constant love of our heavenly Creator. His love can withstand anything and everything. His love is as eternal as Christ Himself!

So, for now, enjoy those beautiful mountain views. Gaze at the setting sun as it drops below the hilltops. But don't lose sight of what's real and lasting—God's peace and love that will never crumble or be taken away.

* * *

*Lord, thank You for the temporary, earthly pleasures You created
for my enjoyment. I will delight in them for now. But please help
me to keep my true focus on Your real, lasting love and peace.*

YOU BELONG

"Make sure no outsider who now follows GOD ever has occasion to say, 'GOD put me in second-class. I don't really belong.' And make sure no physically mutilated person is ever made to think, 'I'm damaged goods. I don't really belong.'"

ISAIAH 56:3 MSG

Outcast. Unloved. Misfit. Damaged. Less than. We've probably identified with a few—if not all—of these descriptors at some point in our lives. Whether it's because of how we were raised or the by-product of years of negative self-talk, we've experienced the unwelcome feeling of being an outsider.

But God has a message for you, friend: *you belong!* When you stand for Him. . .strive to do what's right. . .and embrace your faith . . .He calls you *His*. And when you're His, He creates a brand-new identity for you. He calls you

- Loved (Zephaniah 3:17)
- Beautiful (Song of Solomon 4:7)
- Forgiven (Luke 7:48)
- Blessed (Psalm 34:8)
- Chosen (John 15:16)

Embrace your identity in Christ. Know your worth. When He says, "You belong," He speaks truth!

Heavenly Father, I am loved. I am beautiful. I am forgiven. I am blessed. I am chosen. Because You say it, I believe it!

BEAUTIFUL HARVEST

You will always harvest what you plant. Those who live only to satisfy their own sinful nature will harvest decay and death. . . . But those who live to please the Spirit will harvest everlasting life from the Spirit. So let's not get tired of doing what is good. . . . We will reap a harvest of blessing if we don't give up.

GALATIANS 6:7–9 NLT

This principle of reaping and sowing is as old as time. It applies to everyone, saints and sinners alike. It can't be avoided, no matter how hard a person might try.

The Bible is overflowing with examples of men and women who "reaped what they sowed"—with outcomes both good and bad—starting with Adam and Eve in the garden of Eden (Genesis 2–3) and continuing into the New Testament with the likes of the woman at the well (John 4) and Saul on the road to Damascus (Acts 9). From their stories, we can clearly see that sowing good seeds produces good crops, and bad seeds, bad crops. In short, do the right thing, and blessings will follow; do the wrong thing, and the consequences can be quite catastrophic.

What about you? . . . Are you living for your own selfish desires? Or are you living to "please the Spirit"? Choose well and you'll reap the blessings of a beautiful life in Christ!

Heavenly Father, I want to reap all the blessings You have in store for me.

EVERLASTING LIGHT

*"No longer will you need the sun to shine by day,
nor the moon to give its light by night, for the
Lord your God will be your everlasting light."*

Isaiah 60:19 NLT

God created the sun and moon to give us light—one by day, the other by night. We tend to take them both for granted. But what if the sun and moon would cease to exist? For starters, we'd lose all sense of time—day and night would become one. This distortion of time would surely affect our rest: our sleeping and awake patterns would become confused. No doubt about it, complete and total darkness, over time, would create a host of issues for us. Certainly no one would willingly sign up for a life devoid of light.

Yet even if the sun and moon would fail to do their jobs, this scripture from the book of Isaiah promises good news: the Lord gives *eternal* light. In fact, we're promised that as Christ-followers, we won't even have a need for the sun or the moon. God provides permanent light in the darkness. So, while we can't depend on the things of earth, we can *always* depend on the Light of the world.

Are you living in darkness? Or are you living in the light? If you haven't already, choose the brilliant light of Christ today!

Light of the world, please illuminate my life. I choose You today, and I will choose You again tomorrow—and forever!

WHAT WE *DON'T* DESERVE

It wasn't so long ago that you were mired in that old stagnant life of sin. You let the world. . .tell you how to live. . . . We all did it. . . . It's a wonder God didn't lose his temper and do away with the whole lot of us. Instead, immense in mercy and with an incredible love, he embraced us. He. . .made us alive in Christ.

EPHESIANS 2:1–5 MSG

We've all had "I deserve this. . ." or "I deserve that. . ." thoughts. We think we deserve *more* or *better* than we currently have. We want something someone else has. What we have isn't quite good enough. . . . That's certainly the message of the world, isn't it?

And yet, we fail to acknowledge—or it fails to register—that we really don't "deserve" a single good thing. But, because of our sin, we *do* deserve to suffer the undesirable consequences.

But. . .God chose us. And in His choosing, He gifted us immense mercy, incredible love, life in Christ, and an eternal spot in our final, heavenly home.

Today, make it a priority to thank the heavenly Creator for choosing you. Thank Him for giving you everything you *don't* deserve. Thank Him for His love. Thank Him for your best, blessed life.

Heavenly Creator, when You could have given me just what my sin-filled soul deserved, You—in Your abundant love—gave me everything I didn't. I am forever grateful.

GUIDING LIGHT

Follow your father's good advice; don't wander off from your mother's teachings. Wrap yourself in them. . .wear them like a scarf around your neck. . . . For sound advice is a beacon, good teaching is a light, moral discipline is a life path.
PROVERBS 6:20–21, 23 MSG

You probably received a plethora of advice from your mother or father as you were growing up. Sometimes the advice was probably well received. Other times, not so much. Sometimes the advice of a parent is repeated so much throughout the years that it becomes nothing but white noise. Children often grow exasperated by the lessons taught by their parents—not fully appreciating the wisdom and guidance until much later in life. *Mom and Dad really did know what they were talking about!* (Sound familiar?)

Proverbs 6 offers words of wisdom about parental godly instruction: We would do well to wrap ourselves up in Mom and Dad's good teaching and sound advice. They'll guide us, guard us, and prepare us for what's next in life.

What's the best advice you ever received from a parent? Just like the Bible offers light to guide the way, the moral teaching and discipline of a godly parent offers light for living as well.

* * *

Father God, I am so thankful for the godly guidance I've received over the years. Please bring to light any advice or lesson I might have ignored in the past that I need to take to heart today.

YES, YOU CAN!

"LORD," I said, "I do not know how to speak; I am too young." But the LORD said to me, "Do not say, 'I am too young.' You must go to everyone I send you to and say whatever I command you. . . . For I am with you."

JEREMIAH 1:6–8 NIV

Has anyone ever accused you of being "too" *something*? Too young. Too old. Too serious. Too silly. Too talkative. Too quiet. Too opinionated. Too indecisive. Perhaps you've used the "too" argument yourself, as an excuse to get out of something you didn't want to do or were afraid of doing.

Here, Jeremiah is doling out excuses to God. You might know the backstory: God had just appointed Jeremiah as a prophet to the nations. And Jeremiah felt that his inability, or inexperience, was sufficient reason for God to let him off the hook. While it was true that Jeremiah was only a young man, God made it clear that his excuse was completely irrelevant. Because, when God calls, we only have one requirement: *obedience*. And God takes it from there.

The next time you feel God nudging you, calling you to do His work (even if you feel ill-equipped), shove the excuses from your mind and say, "Yes, Lord!" Then prepare to be amazed at how He goes with you and helps you fulfill His calling.

. . . .

Lord, I'm sorry for all the times I've given excuses. If You're asking, my answer is yes!

YOUR BEST LIFE

Keep my words and store up my commands. . . . Keep my commands and you will live; guard my teachings as the apple of your eye. Bind them on your fingers; write them on the tablet of your heart. Say to wisdom, "You are my sister," and to insight, "You are my relative."

Proverbs 7:1–4 niv

Keep. Store up. Guard. Bind. Write. Say. Do *all* these things with God's Word, and you will have life—*your best life*, that is. Because God's Word *is* life, and we were created to live by it. When we become intimately familiar with biblical truth, then we have a strong foundation for a truly wonderful life.

When hard times come—*and they will*—a knowledge of God's hope and healing will bring you through.

When temptations come—*and they will*—God's teachings will help you stay on the path of faith and truth.

When enemies attack—*and they will*—God's promise of protection and victory will shelter you.

What are you struggling with today, beautiful soul? Whatever it is, trust God and His Word to carry you through it. His words will bring you strength, comfort, and peace of mind. Open your Bible and see what He has to say. Meditate on the message God has just for you.

Keep. Store up. Guard. Bind. Write. Say. Repeat!

. . . .

God, You are all good things. Help me to live my best life with You and Your Word front and center!

PRAY ALWAYS

Pray in the Spirit at all times and on every occasion. Stay alert and be persistent in your prayers for all believers. . . . And pray for me, too. Ask God to give me the right words so I can boldly explain God's mysterious plan that the Good News is for Jews and Gentiles alike. . . . Pray that I will keep on speaking boldly for him.
EPHESIANS 6:18–20 NLT

Communicating with God, and God communicating with us—both are so important in life! And prayer is how we accomplish our part of the equation. Through prayer, we can talk to God—thanking Him, asking for His help, expressing our needs, asking Him to help others…

Prayer shouldn't be a brief, one-and-done interaction. It should be an ongoing, daily conversation. This doesn't mean we stay home and do nothing but pray; but it does mean that we remain cognizant of the heavenly Father's presence in and around us all day long—and that we stay in *regular* communication with Him. When you make this your daily practice, you'll find that even everyday thoughts turn into prayers. And you'll soon begin talking to God about *all* things—the big, the small, and everything in between. He hears—and He cares! Constant prayer. . .what a great way to grow your relationship with the heavenly Creator!

Father God, please help me make the practice of constant prayer a daily part of my life.

LIVING, BREATHING WISDOM

*Listen to me! . . . Everything I say is right, for I speak the truth.
. . . My advice is wholesome. There is nothing devious or crooked
in it. My words are plain to anyone with understanding, clear
to those with knowledge. . . . Wisdom is far more valuable
than rubies. Nothing you desire can compare with it.*

PROVERBS 8:6–9, 11 NLT

Would you claim to be a wise woman? Here, in Proverbs 8, we get an in-depth look at wisdom. We get to see what wisdom would be like as a living, breathing human being. And she looks mighty attractive:

Her words? They're right and good and easy to understand.

Her honesty? She always speaks the truth.

Her advice? It's wholesome and well-meaning.

Her instruction? It's preferable to silver and gold.

Her wisdom? It's more valuable than precious gems.

The fantastic news about wisdom is that God offers it to all who follow Him (Proverbs 2:6; Ephesians 1:17; Psalm 111:10). Ask Him to immerse your soul in His wisdom today. Ask Him for guidance before you offer words of advice to a friend. Ask Him to help you look at all angles of a situation before choosing the best path forward. He will show you the right and good way—every time!

*Wisdom-giver, when I have a choice to make or
advice to offer, please guide me to make the
best decision and to share the right words.*

FORGET YOU!

If you've gotten anything at all out of following Christ, if his love has made any difference in your life. . .if you have a heart, if you care . . . Agree with each other, love each other, be deep-spirited friends. Don't push your way to the front; don't sweet-talk your way to the top. Put yourself aside. . . . Don't be obsessed with getting your own advantage. Forget yourselves long enough to lend a helping hand.

PHILIPPIANS 2:1–4 MSG

As we grow from childhood to adulthood, somewhere along the way we get the message of the world loud and clear: *It's all about YOU. So, do what makes you happy. Forget about everybody else! If you're successful and have everything you want, that's all that matters.*

But then. . .we become full-fledged adults, and we realize that this kind of thinking only leads to discontent and unhappiness. Why? Because we're missing the love that Christ intended for us—the kind of love that cares deeply for others. It says to others, "You matter. And I am here for you." And when you *really* experience this kind of others-focused, unselfish love, you'll see what you were missing all along! You'll experience true and lasting fulfillment!

So today, forget yourself! Focus on someone else. . .and experience the deep soul-satisfaction that comes from loving others well.

God of love, thank You for showing me the importance of loving others. Who needs my love and care today?

A WELCOME INVITATION

"So, my dear friends, listen carefully; those who embrace these my ways are most blessed. Mark a life of discipline and live wisely; don't squander your precious life. Blessed the man, blessed the woman, who listens to me, awake and ready for me each morning, alert and responsive as I start my day's work. When you find me, you find life, real life, to say nothing of GOD's good pleasure."

PROVERBS 8:32–35 MSG

YOU'RE INVITED TO: A CELEBRATION OF LIFE!
DATE: TODAY, OCTOBER 12.
PLACE: WHEREVER YOU ARE.
RSVP: SEND UP A PRAYER TO GOD, THE WISDOM-GIVER.

This is one of the very best invitations you'll ever receive. When you accept the invite, you'll encounter blessings galore! Why? . . . Because it's an invitation from God Himself. And He's inviting you to live your very best life. You only need to say yes and make the choice to embrace His wisdom.

When we live and love according to God's Word, we choose a life of wisdom. When we make a conscious effort to be disciplined, making good choices and listening for God's instruction, we experience the best life has to offer—complete with overwhelming joy and approval from the Lord.

So what are you waiting for? Send up your RSVP right now!

. . . .

Yes, Lord! Yes! I choose to fully embrace the wisdom You offer me. Thank You for the invitation to live my best life!

INFINITE VALUE

*I once thought these things were valuable, but now I consider
them worthless. . . . Everything else is worthless when compared
with the infinite value of knowing Christ Jesus my Lord.
For his sake I have discarded everything else, counting it all as
garbage, so that I could gain Christ and become one with him.
I no longer count on my own righteousness through obeying
the law; rather, I become righteous through faith in Christ.*
PHILIPPIANS 3:7–9 NLT

There are so many things that we value—most of it "stuff," like our
homes, vehicles, jewelry, techy gadgets. . .to name just a few.

When we place value on things according to the world's standards,
we miss the mark when it comes to those things that have *eternal*
value—what the writer of Philippians 3 calls "infinite value." Of all
the things that matter, there's *one thing* more valuable than anything
else in the world: it's knowing Jesus Christ as our Lord and Savior.
In comparison, everything else is worthless garbage. All the stuff, our
earthly possessions, doesn't matter one iota in the big picture of life.

What do you own that holds the most value to your heart and
soul? Is it your relationship with Jesus? Have you gained Christ "and
become one with him"?

. . . .

*My Savior, my Lord, compared to my relationship with
You, everything else in life is worthless garbage. Help me
keep my Christ-focus steady all the days of my life.*

LIFE-EXTENDER

*Wisdom will multiply your days and add years to your
life. If you become wise, you will be the one to benefit.
If you scorn wisdom, you will be the one to suffer.*

PROVERBS 9:11–12 NLT

What if you stumbled across a link on social media. . .one that promised to reveal the secret to extending your life, not by minutes, days, or months—but *years*? Would you click the link? Would you watch an hour-long video presentation in the hopes of learning the secret for yourself? Would you purchase a pill, lotion, or special potion if there was a money-back guarantee attached to the promise? . . .

While the world doesn't offer a magic life extender, there *is* a way to claim the promise of long life, and that's what Proverbs 9:10–12 is all about. When you have wisdom, your days will be extended.

Sounds good. . .but how do you gain wisdom, you ask?

- You fear the Lord: you have a healthy respect and reverence for Him.

- You have knowledge of Christ: you become well acquainted with Him, and you accept Him into your heart as Lord of your life.

When you have accepted Him as your Savior, you allow Him to take the lead in your life. This is wisdom—and with it, you'll receive the benefit of blessing upon blessing!

. . . .

*Heavenly Father, please take Your place as rightful
leader of my life. I want the wisdom Your Word promises.*

POSITIVITY

We always thank God, the Father of our Lord Jesus Christ, when we pray for you, because we have heard of your faith in Christ Jesus and of the love you have for all God's people— the faith and love that spring from the hope stored up for you in heaven and about which you have already heard in the true message of the gospel that has come to you.
C OLOSSIANS 1:3–6 NIV

Here in Colossians, Paul is offering up a prayer of positivity—a prayer of thanks to God for the church at Colossae. . .for their faith, their love, their hope.

When was the last time you prayed a prayer that was overflowing with thanks and appreciation for your fellow Christians? In our humanness, we tend to focus on the negative. Our prayers are filled with rants and requests that God change the people around us into what *we* would prefer them to be. Our prayers are typically quite selfish, aren't they?

God would surely rather have a conversation with us about the gifts and good qualities we see in others. And all the good is where our heart *should* take notice. Because, if we look for the good, that is exactly what we will find! Ask God to help you look for the positive today—and He surely will!

. . . .

Please give me Your eyes to see the good in others, Lord Jesus. I want to paint the words of my prayers with positivity, gratefulness, and grace.

THE SAME CLAY

So I went to the potter's house, and. . .the potter was there,
working away at his wheel. Whenever the pot the potter
was working on turned out badly, as sometimes happens
when you are working with clay, the potter would simply
start over and use the same clay to make another pot.

JEREMIAH 18:3–4 MSG

The potter is bent over his wheel, working to create a flawless masterpiece. He stops for a minute, takes a critical look at the finished product, and decides it's inadequate. Perhaps the pot is blemished in some way; maybe it isn't shaped quite right for its intended purpose. Either way, the potter decides to start over. But take notice: He doesn't begin his new project with new clay. No! He starts over, using the *very same clay* from the original, imperfect pot.

Just like the potter, God often starts over with us—using the same "clay." He doesn't cast us aside and put someone else, *someone better*, in our place. He uses us, just as we are, and keeps working until He is satisfied—no matter how long it takes. And in His working, His shaping and crafting, He smooths away our imperfections—our stubbornness, our impatience, our selfish streaks—and keeps refining us in the process. God created us for His good purpose, and He won't ever stop molding us into the beautiful women He intends us to be. Praise Him!

Heavenly potter, thank You for working on me and in me.

BASIC TO BETTER!

*Don't shuffle along, eyes to the ground, absorbed with the
things right in front of you. Look up, and be alert to what
is going on around Christ—that's where the action is.*

Colossians 3:2 msg

Imagine doing nothing more than walking around and staring at the
ground all day, every day. You might spot a lost quarter or two, some
rocks, cracked pavement, grass, various insects, weeds, shadows. . .
Basic stuff, right? It's doubtful you'd witness anything super exciting
taking place directly beneath your feet. But if you'd only look up,
what would you see? The way the leaves rustle in the breeze. . .a fiery
sunset in a blue sky. . .the shapes and shifting of the clouds. . . There's
so much to notice if we'd only look!

In the same way, our faith can be limited by what we bother
to see. . . . Instead of only observing a loved one recovering from
an illness, we can *also* see Christ's healing hand at work. Instead of
only noticing the pay raise at work, we can *also* see God's hand in
the blessing.

We can spend our days noticing only what's in front of our faces
. . .the *basic* stuff. Or, we can make the choice to look up and notice the
better stuff! When we choose to see things from Christ's perspective,
that's when life gets exciting—"that's where the action is"!

Father God, today I choose better over basic. Help me be a noticer!

WHO ARE YOU, *REALLY?*

Put on then, as God's chosen ones, holy and beloved, compassionate hearts, kindness, humility, meekness, and patience, bearing with one another and, if one has a complaint against another, forgiving each other; as the Lord has forgiven you. . . . And above all these put on love, which binds everything together in perfect harmony. And let the peace of Christ rule in your hearts. . . . And be thankful.

COLOSSIANS 3:12–15 ESV

"Who are you?" . . . It's a common question, but have you ever really, truly thought about who you are? It isn't as simple as your name; it's not where you come from, not what you do for a living, and not who your parents, brothers, sisters, cousins, friends are. . . . It's something much, much deeper than that.

Who you are involves your character—it's what's in your heart. And when you choose to follow Christ, your faith and your pursuit of Him are what make you who you are. Your life in Him is the most important thing about you, dear one! Because when you say yes to His invitation, you become a brand-new person, a child of God! And others will know you by what's in your heart!

. . . .

Lord Jesus, when others look at me, may they see a heart that beats with love, compassion, wisdom, gratitude, grace, forgiveness, kindness, peace, and patience. I want others to see You in me!

WISDOM AND WORDS

Walk in wisdom toward outsiders, making the best use of the time. Let your speech always be gracious, seasoned with salt, so that you may know how you ought to answer each person.
COLOSSIANS 4:5–6 ESV

Words are powerful. They can hurt. They can comfort and heal. They can encourage. They can instruct. They can influence—for good or bad. The impact of our words is something we should always consider, especially when we interact with people who don't know Jesus.

If we claim to follow Jesus and speak only harsh, hurtful words, we aren't being good representatives of Christ. We won't lead many of our friends, family, and acquaintances toward Jesus if they never hear "seasoned with salt" words coming from our lips. Every time we interact with others, we have an opportunity to share our Jesus—so we must make "the best use of the time" and choose our words wisely.

Consider this: *today* could be the day of salvation for someone who crosses your path. So, ask God to prepare you by giving you the right words to speak. Take these words from Colossians to heart and make the most of the opportunities that come your way today—and every day—to shine your light!

. . . .

God, I don't always have the right words—in fact, I mess things up a lot when it comes to knowing exactly what to say! Please give me wisdom and confidence to share You with the world.

WITHOUT A WORD

Everywhere the report has gone forth of your faith in God [of your leaning of your whole personality on Him in complete trust and confidence in His power, wisdom, and goodness]. So we [find that we] never need to tell people anything [further about it].

1 THESSALONIANS 1:8 AMPC

These men of God "oozed" their faith wherever they went! It was evident in their character, their trust and confidence, their wisdom and goodness.

Imagine being so sold-out for God that every person you met took notice. Everywhere you went—in your neighborhood, at work, running errands—people could see the light of Christ shining through because of your vibe. You radiated kindness and love, care and compassion, wisdom and peace. . . You were noticeably different from the rest of the world.

Wouldn't that be something if you went about your everyday life and never had to bring up the subject of the Christian faith because people noticed something different—something *special*—about you? And they just had to know what it was?

Purpose to be the kind of woman who radiates Christ. When you show others who He is in your actions and character, they will begin to ask questions. . .and doors will open to share Jesus with the world!

. . . .

Father God, thank You for showing me that I don't always need to shout "Jesus!" from the rooftops. I can quietly share You with the world through the person You created me to be.

WELL WISHES

May the Master pour on the love so it fills your lives. . . .
May you be infused with strength and purity, filled
with confidence in the presence of God our Father.
1 THESSALONIANS 3:12–13 MSG

Are you the kind of woman who wishes the best for everyone—friends, family, and acquaintances alike? What about strangers? Does your heart fill with joy when you see others succeed and encounter blessing upon blessing? Or is it difficult for you to be happy with those who are happy—especially if you're in a bad place physically, emotionally, mentally, spiritually?

Truth is, when life gets us down, it's difficult to watch others live on Easy Street day after day. Not that we want bad things for them, really. We *don't* want that. But it sure would make us feel a tad better if others were struggling right alongside us, wouldn't it?

Sister, God wants us to do better—to *be* better. And if life is dealing you a difficult hand right now, let the words of 1 Thessalonians 3 fill your mind and your soul. Pray that you would have the strength and character to wish others all the blessings they can possibly handle. Then take heart! You'll be pleasantly surprised at how this pivot changes your whole outlook on life.

. . . .

God, please pour out Your blessings on others. I trust
You have only the best plans for me. Thank You
for being by my side through it all!

BLOOM AND GROW

"Their lives will be like a well-watered garden, never again left to dry up. Young women will dance and be happy, young men and old men will join in. I'll convert their weeping into laughter."

JEREMIAH 31:12–13 MSG

Imagine a dead, withered flower garden. Brown leaves rustle and scatter in the breeze; full, colorful blooms have faded; a once-lovely floral aroma has been overtaken by the smell of death and decay. This sad, lifeless flower garden bears resemblance to our lives without Christ. Without Him, we have no sunshine, no rain, no pruning—no life! When He's missing, our story is devoid of hope and light.

But *with* Him? . . . When Christ is front and center in our lives, we are like a well-cared-for garden. Lush and bursting with color. . . an aroma sweet and pleasant! We get just enough sunshine, the perfect amount of rain (right down to the last drop!). Our petals stretch out, colorful and full. And Christ continues to work, day by day, pruning and caring for us so that we can bloom and grow into the splendid daughters He meant us to be.

On days when you feel dried up and hopeless, reach out to the master gardener. Allow Him to pluck, prune, and drench your parched soul in His love and compassion. He will bring what's dead to life again.

Master gardener, I invite You to work on the dried-up parts of my soul. Please give me light, hope, and life!

ALWAYS AND IN ALL CIRCUMSTANCES

Rejoice always, pray continually, give thanks in
all circumstances; for this is God's will for you.
1 Thessalonians 5:16–18 niv

Worship is how we honor God. It's how we express our adoration to Him. These verses from 1 Thessalonians give good advice for our personal worship:

1. Rejoice always. Not only should we feel our joy, but others should be able to *see* it. We can rejoice all the time because our joy isn't dependent on our ever-changing circumstances, but it *is* dependent on our unchanging God!

2. Pray always. While this doesn't mean we're always on our knees, hands folded, eyes closed, it *does* mean that we stay in constant conversation with God. It doesn't matter whether you pray aloud or in silence, standing or on your knees, at work or at home, day or night. You are *never* in a place where you can't pray.

3. Give thanks, no matter what. While you won't be thankful *for* every circumstance that comes your way, you can be thankful *in* every circumstance. This is because our loving heavenly Creator has everything under control—nothing is left to chance.

If you read these guidelines and are thinking following them seems impossible, know that because it is "God's will for you," it is, indeed, possible. With God's help, you *can* do it!

. . . .

Lord, show me how to better worship You!

GOD OF RESTORATION

"I will surely gather them from all the lands where I banish them in my. . .great wrath; I will bring them back. . . . They will be my people, and I will be their God. . . . I will make an everlasting covenant with them. . . . I will rejoice in doing them good and will assuredly plant them in this land with all my heart and soul."
JEREMIAH 32:37–38, 40–41 NIV

When we fall short of God's expectations, we experience feelings of shame and regret. Sometimes we get stuck in those feelings. Because . . .surely, God is *still* mad at us. He will *never* forgive us. And, in the middle of our mess, we often feel like the worst humanity has to offer.

And yet. . .our God of judgment is also a God of restoration. He promises *both*—one is as sure as the other! As these verses from Jeremiah 32 remind us. . .those who had been banished, He *will* gather them back together again. He *will* be their God; and they will belong to Him—along with future generations. He *will* bless them and do good to them. He *will* inspire them so they never turn away from Him. And He makes good on these promises!

If you're struggling today, take heart! Invite the God of restoration to draw you back to Him. He will, with all His heart and soul!

Father, thank You for always bringing me back to You.

IN THE "DOWN" SEASONS

*Pray that we'll be rescued from these troublemakers
who are trying to do us in. . . . The Master never lets us
down. He'll stick by you and protect you from evil.*

2 THESSALONIANS 3:2–3 MSG

Our lives are full of ups, downs, and in-betweens. And there seem to be seasons that weigh heavily upon us, with one "down" after another . . .and no relief in sight. During those times, we often struggle to keep hold of our faith. We think, *Where is God? I need His rescue. I need His strength. And He doesn't seem to be hearing my cries for help. Doesn't He care?*

If we'd only take the time to notice, these difficult seasons are often when we can see and feel God the most. We just need to shift our focus from *us* to *Him*. When we do that, we experience a perspective transformation—and we can clearly see His hand in our lives. Caring. Providing. Protecting. Loving.

As Paul noted in 2 Thessalonians 3, "The Master never lets us down." When things were difficult for Paul and his fellow Christ-followers, they trusted God. They knew He would take care of things—and His people. It was true then, and the same is true for us today!

*Lord Jesus, help me to shift my focus—from me to You.
Thank You for always being here, loving me and caring for me
in my "down" seasons. I trust You have everything under control.*

A DIFFERENT PLAN

*Jesus Christ came into the world to save sinners.
I'm proof—Public Sinner Number One—of someone
who could never have made it apart from sheer mercy.
And now he shows me off—evidence of his endless patience—
to those who are right on the edge of trusting him forever.*
1 TIMOTHY 1:15–16 MSG

Saul was the chief of all sinners—the very worst! Blasphemer. Persecutor. Dangerous. Corrupt. He relished the punishment of Christ-followers. Christ-followers literally quaked in their sandals at the mere whisper of Saul's name.

And yet. . .he, *Saul*, was chosen. This worst-among-all-sinners was handpicked by the heavenly Father to share the gospel message. (Read the full story in Acts 9.) Surely, Saul had been deemed "hopeless" and "forever lost" among the Christian community of his day. But God had a different plan. And on the road to Damascus, Saul's heart began to beat for Jesus. Along with his heart change, God gave him a name change too. Saul became Paul—a man on fire for Jesus. If anyone ever doubted God could use even the worst of sinners, Paul was proof to the contrary.

Take Paul's story to heart today. Remember you can *always* count on this: Jesus came into the world to save sinners—and there's living proof in the lives of the people He has transformed!

. . . .

*Precious Savior, I am so thankful that no one is ever beyond
Your reach. May my life be proof of Your wonderful promise!*

NOT ONLY US, BUT EVERYONE!

*He wants not only us but everyone saved, you know,
everyone to get to know the truth we've learned: that there's
one God and only one, and one Priest-Mediator between
God and us—Jesus, who offered himself in exchange for
everyone held captive by sin, to set them all free.*

1 TIMOTHY 2:4–6 MSG

Murderers. Rapists. Thieves. Liars. Hypocrites. When you think of these people, what feelings rise to the surface of your heart? Fear? Anger? Disgust? Anxiety? . . . *Yes?* On the flip side, what about love? Compassion? . . . If we're completely honest, not likely!

While we might think we're better than the "worst" kinds of people, the truth is that Jesus died for all sinners—sinners like you . . .sinners like me. . .sinners of all ages, shapes, and sizes. We're *all* sinners in need of Jesus! And thankfully, our God has beautiful character. He is generous and gracious. And He offers His love and mercy to even the most unsavory characters on the planet. His love is big enough for every single one of us, no matter how "good" or how "bad" we are.

So, when we find ourselves comparing our sin to the "worse" sin of another, our thoughts should instead go first to the Savior— the one we all need in our lives and hearts. And as He loves, so should we!

*Generous, gracious God, thank You for
saving a sinner like me. You are so, so good!*

MIXED MESSAGES

You've been raised on the Message of the faith and have followed sound teaching. Now pass on this counsel to the followers of Jesus there, and you'll be a good servant of Jesus. Stay clear of silly stories that get dressed up as religion. Exercise daily in God. . . . Workouts in the gymnasium are useful, but a disciplined life in God is far more so. . . . Take it to heart.

1 TIMOTHY 4:6–9 MSG

There are so many mixed messages about God, salvation, creation, heaven, and eternity—really, about any topic related to religion and spirituality. Every day, someone new is claiming to be an expert on faith and religion. It's impossible to keep up with the book releases, podcasts, social media posts. . . And it can get a little confusing.

While some messages ring true, others are obviously *way* off base. And those messages are easy to dismiss. But. . .there are messages sprinkled with *a touch of truth*; and even though they're nothing more than silly stories tied up with a pretty bow, they draw you in. Before any confusion sets in, we need to weigh these messages against the trusted authority of God's Word. It will *always* tell you the truth. It will *never* lead you astray. It will show you the way today—and all your days to come.

. . . .

Heavenly Father, no silly stories wrapped in pretty packages for me! Thank You for the truth of Your Word!

WHAT HAVE YOU DONE FOR ME LATELY?

Be an example to all believers in what you say, in the
way you live, in your love, your faith, and your purity.
Until I get there, focus on reading the Scriptures to the
church, encouraging the believers, and teaching them.

1 TIMOTHY 4:12–13 NLT

If you're a regular church attender, what inspired you to choose your church? Does it have a vibrant children's ministry? Are the music choices to your liking? Do the church leaders encourage small groups—and you found one that was a great fit? . . .

We consider so many variables in choosing a church. But sadly, we often overlook the most important thing in our choosing: instead of entering the church with a "how can I help?" attitude, we enter the doors thinking, *What does this church have to offer ME?* And then, when a church fails to meet our needs or expectations in some way, we begin shopping around for the "perfect" church. Or perhaps, when church has failed us one too many times, we stop attending altogether.

Sister, there's never a better time than now to change how we think about church. Spend some quiet time with God and ask Him to show you how you can better serve His people and His church. He will show you the way!

. . . .

I am sorry, Father, for my all-about-me attitude.
How can I help? How can I better serve You and
my fellow Christians? Show me the way!

CERTAIN THINGS

Teach those who are rich. . .not to trust in their money. . . .
Their trust should be in God. . . . Tell them to use their money to do
good. . . . By doing this they will be storing up their treasure as a
good foundation for the future so that they may experience true life.
1 TIMOTHY 6:17–19 NLT

If you've ever had money—or experienced the lack thereof—you know that one thing is certain: it's 100 percent unreliable. Money can be here in an instant and gone the next—especially in an unpredictable world of inflation, unexpected bills, and ever-increasing taxes. Money often disappears as fast as—or faster than!—you can make it.

Our trust would be better served if we placed it in the reliability of God and His beautiful promise of heaven. When we focus our priorities as God would have us do, then our money becomes a tool to be used to further His kingdom rather than a crutch that feeds our greed. When we use our money for good, only then do we begin to truly experience the life God intended: a life rich in blessings and treasures that can't be bought.

. . . .

Father God, so many things in this life are uncertain. I am so
glad I can fully depend on You. Help me to get—and keep!—
my priorities straight. I want to experience a life rich in blessings.

GRATITUDE OVER GRUMBLING

Every time I say your name in prayer—which is practically all the time—I thank God for you, the God I worship with my whole life in the tradition of my ancestors. I miss you a lot, especially when I remember that last tearful good-bye, and I look forward to a joy-packed reunion.

2 TIMOTHY 1:3–4 MSG

These verses are oozing with gratitude and hope. And while it's not uncommon to come across the thoughts and prayers of a thankful heart in the scriptures, what is most extraordinary in this instance is that Paul—the writer of these words—was in prison for sharing the gospel message. The ancient prison where he was held captive was likely dark, damp, dirty, cold, and lonely. . .certainly not an environment conducive to "all the feels."

Yet, in this uncomfortable, unfair, unfortunate situation, Paul clung to joy and hope. He continued to pray and worship. What a wonderful example when we struggle with situations and circumstances beyond our control. Because, like Paul, we too can depend on the Master Creator to give us strength in our weakness, comfort in our pain, joy in our suffering. When we keep an attitude of gratitude front and center in our lives, joy is sure to follow.

When it feels like the world is crashing down, grab God's hand and hold tight. He won't let go!

Giver of hope, comfort, and strength, infuse my heart with Your power. Today, I choose gratitude over grumbling.

FINDING YOUR WAY

My people have become like lost sheep, and their shepherds have led them astray. They wandered so far from My protection— on mountaintops and hills they lost their way, worshiping false gods, forgetting where I was and where they could find rest.
JEREMIAH 50:6 VOICE

When you feel lost, as if you have wandered from God's protection, take a look at where you are and where God would have you be.

Sometimes our leaders—kings, presidents, and civil rulers—get it wrong. They take us down the wrong road or path, turning us away from the love God would have us give to Him and each other. We are drawn away from God and to false idols such as position, power, money, or possessions. We forget about our true Shepherd, the one we *should* be worshipping, following, and finding our rest in.

Today, consider where you may have gone astray. Take your eyes off your human leaders and look to God alone, for it is before Him you will stand alone. Focus on His face, words, and ways. Ask Him where He would have you be, what He would have you do. Forget about following anyone but Him. For only in Him will you find your true rest, path, and king.

. . . .

Lord, I feel as if I've wandered away from You. So here I am, looking to get back into Your fold, under Your protection, walking Your way, worshipping You. For in You alone I find my way.

GOD'S WORD

All Scripture is inspired by God and is useful to teach us what is true and to make us realize what is wrong in our lives. It corrects us when we are wrong and teaches us to do what is right. God uses it to prepare and equip his people to do every good work.

2 TIMOTHY 3:16–17 NLT

The Spirit of God has moved people to write the Old and New Testaments. It's there we find the training we need to find the truth. It's through the reading of God's Word that we come to realize what's wrong in our lives and where we may be falling short.

To find the right way to live and be, we mustn't neglect reading the Old *and* New Testaments. It's in the stories and the proverbs that we find wisdom. It's in the psalms we discover how to express our feelings to God and how to start a dialogue with Him.

Each day cleanse your mind from all the voices you hear out in the world, and hone in on how God would have you thinking, loving, living, and working to spread His message and do His will. Take heart knowing that by soaking your mind in God's Word, you will find the path He wants you to take.

Show me, Lord, in Your Word what You would have me know and do today. In Jesus' name I live and pray, amen.

KEEP BELIEVING

When it was time for my first defense, no one showed up to support me. Everyone abandoned me (may it not be held against them) except the Lord. He stood by me, strengthened me, and backed the truth I proclaimed with power so it may be heard by all the non-Jews. He rescued me, pried open the lion's jaw, and snatched me from its teeth.

2 TIMOTHY 4:16–17 VOICE

In Jeremiah 51:46 (VOICE), God instructs us to "not lose heart or give in to fear and panic" when we hear reports of nations and rulers proclaiming war and other acts of violence against another.

One way to not lose heart is to remember that even if everyone we know, love, and count on deserts us, the Lord will stand with us, strengthening us, rescuing us, saving us. Because He is by our side we will one day be able to say to ourselves, "I have fought the good fight, I have stayed on course and finished the race, and through it all, I have kept believing" (2 Timothy 4:7 VOICE).

No matter how things look, no matter what rumors you hear or headlines you read, keep your faith. Know that the Lord will always stand by you. Say to yourself, "I know the Lord will continue to rescue me from every trip, trap, snare, and pitfall of evil and carry me safely to His heavenly kingdom" (2 Timothy 4:18 VOICE).

. . . .

Thank You, Lord, for always being here for me!

LIVING WITH LESS

It is better to live with less and honor the Eternal than to have riches and carry the burdens that come with them. Better to eat only vegetables served lovingly than a fattened ox served hatefully.
PROVERBS 15:16–17 VOICE

When we look at the lives of the rich and famous, they seem to have it all. Meanwhile, some of us are unable to afford a car, take a vacation, or purchase a new couch for our living room.

When we're focused on what we *don't* have, we feel cheated. But God makes clear that those of us who have Him but live with less don't have to carry all the burdens that come with excessive tastes, desires, and possessions. A simple life is often the best, for we who have learned to live without all the trappings that come with riches have more love and respect for God, more peace and comfort.

So today, look around you. Thank God for all He has given you, not perhaps in possessions but in love, protection, laughter, and peace—those heavenly treasures that are worth so much more than anything you can find on earth!

. . . .

*Lord, I thank You for all You have given me
in this simple life I love and lead! Amen.*

JUST WAIT

Have courage, for the Eternal is all that I will need. My soul boasts, "Hope in God; just wait." It is good. The Eternal One is good to those who expect Him, to those who seek Him wholeheartedly. It is good to wait quietly for the Eternal to make things right again.

LAMENTATIONS 3:24–26 VOICE

Some people put all their hopes in those who are elected to office. But the Word makes clear that all we need is God and we're to place our hopes in Him. Yet to do so takes not just courage but patience.

Although you might want things to change today, God has a bigger and better plan. That means there may be some waiting to endure on your part. And while you wait, He would have you do so with great expectations, knowing He always works good for those who seek Him sincerely and with their whole heart.

Are you truly seeking God? Are you opening up His Word and allowing it to penetrate your inner core? Are you looking to Him and His ways as you plan your days? Are you quietly waiting for Him to right all the wrongs in this world? If not, take today's verses to heart and allow them to change you from the inside out.

Lord, remind me every day that You alone are all I need. Give me the patience to wait for You to right the wrongs and to seek You with my whole heart.

CALL OUT!

Saying Your name, Eternal One, I called to You from the darkness of this pit. . . . So close when I've called out in my distress, You've whispered in my ear, "Do not be afraid." Taking up my cause, Lord, You've been my champion. You've paid the price; You saved my life.

LAMENTATIONS 3:55, 57–58 VOICE

God is way closer than you think.

To get help, relief, love, comfort, and guidance, simply call out to God. No matter how deep in the pit you are, He will hear you and find you. He will bring you all the light you need to find your way out.

As soon as you call out His name—Eternal One, God, Lord, Holy Spirit, Jesus, Protector, Rock, Refuge, Provider, Light, One Who Hears—you will hear the Lord of all creation whisper in your ear, "My beloved, my little one, my precious daughter, don't be afraid. I am with you. I will see you through. Have courage. You are in My arms. You are not alone. Your Champion walks alongside you."

Today, remember who your God is. Call upon Him when you cannot find your way out of the darkness. Reach out to Him when you need His presence, His love, His provision, His protection. And you will be heard! You will be saved!

. . . .

I call out Your name, Lord! Hear me, hold me, love me, save me!

SINK DEEP

*"Let all my words sink deep into your own
heart first. Listen to them carefully for yourself."*
EZEKIEL 3:10 NLT

When we are lost and confused, hurt and abandoned, misused and abused, longing for love and hope, direction and help, the one place we can turn to for wisdom and consolation, for guidance and understanding is God's Word.

The Bible contains a wealth of knowledge. It shapes and forms us, providing us with a road map so that we can live as God would have us live. Within the divinely prompted scriptures, we can discover the next steps we need and want to take. Yet we just can't read one page and shut the book. We need to consult its pages every day, every hour, every minute. We must pray about our plans, ask God for confirmation, and continue to walk in rhythm with His will with every step we take. As Proverbs tells us, "A man's mind plans his way, but the Lord directs his steps and makes them sure" (16:9 AMPC).

Today, before you open God's book, consider where you are and where you think your next steps may take you. Bring your thoughts and plans to God. Then, as you read, let His words sink into your heart. Listen carefully to what He may be telling you. Then ask Him to direct each step along the way.

*Open my mind and heart, Lord, to Your wisdom as I make
my plans. Make my steps sure, in line with Yours. Amen.*

FINDING GOOD

He who deals wisely and heeds [God's] word and counsel
shall find good, and whoever leans on, trusts in, and is
confident in the Lord—happy, blessed, and fortunate is he.
PROVERBS 16:20 AMPC

It's one thing to read and heed God's Word and wisdom. It's quite another thing to lean on Him, to trust that He knows best and will lead you to good things. For then you will find the confidence you need. Nothing will make you fear or despair because you know that God is with you, looking out for and guiding you.

Each day you do your devotions, glean all the good things you can from them. Lean on what you learn in each story, song, and proverb. Trust that even though the Word is thousands of years old, you can still apply its teachings to your life. That God's truths ring out on every page. Then trust in God with every step you take, knowing He lives through the ages and has so much greater insight than you.

As you find yourself trusting more and more in the one who created you and has a plan for your life in this time and place, you'll find the happiness, blessings, and good fortune others long for.

. . . .

Lord, as I read Your Word, highlight the passages You want me
to incorporate into my life today. Then help me have faith in You
as I take Your wisdom and use it to steer me upon my journey.

ONE CRY AWAY

Because He Himself [in His humanity] has suffered in being tempted (tested and tried), He is able [immediately] to run to the cry of (assist, relieve) those who are being tempted and tested and tried [and who therefore are being exposed to suffering].

HEBREWS 2:18 AMPC

When God came to earth, He did so in the form of a helpless human baby. This babe named Jesus experienced every human test and trial, every emotion and physical pain His followers would perhaps later endure. And He did so not only to eliminate the barrier between believers and God but to help them cope as they walk through this life.

So the next time you suffer amid life's trials, tests, and temptations, you can take heart knowing that when you cry out to Jesus for help, He will immediately respond to your pleas. He will run to your side and help you through whatever you may be experiencing. He will relieve whatever physical pain or emotion you're suffering. He will walk with you, work His strength through your weakness, and give you the hope you need to carry on.

So don't be afraid to cry out to Jesus. For no matter where you are or what you're doing, you can count on Him to come running and pour His comfort and compassion upon you.

. . . .

Lord, thank You for being only one cry away and coming on the run to my aid!

THE CIRCLE OF ENCOURAGEMENT

*Pay close attention so you won't develop an evil and unbelieving
heart that causes you to abandon the living God. Encourage
each other every day—for as long as we can still say "today"—
so none of you let the deceitfulness of sin harden your hearts.
For we have become partners with the Anointed One—
if we can just hold on to our confidence until the end.*
HEBREWS 3:12–14 VOICE

Humans have a habit of losing faith when things don't go their way.
But today's verses remind us we're not only to *take* heart in all aspects
of life but to keep a *soft* heart, one that is as much aligned with Jesus'
heart now as it was the first day we met and believed in Him.

One way to keep our hearts soft and believing in God, staying
close to Him, is to encourage each other every day. The beauty of
this idea lies in the fact that if we keep ourselves in the Word, we
ourselves will receive the encouragement with which we can encourage
others! It's amazing how well God provides for us if we would
just open our eyes to what He offers throughout our walk by
His side.

*Lord, encourage me through Your Word today so that I may,
in turn, encourage other believers. Help us keep our faith as
strong and vibrant today as it was when we first came to believe.*

IN RESPONSE TO GOD

*"I will give them singleness of heart and put a
new spirit within them. I will take away their stony,
stubborn heart and give them a tender, responsive heart."* . . .
"Today when you hear his voice, don't harden your hearts."
EZEKIEL 11:19; HEBREWS 4:7 NLT

When you accepted Christ, you not only received a new life but a new heart, one that will respond to Him when it hears His voice. A heart that is tender to His truth.

How has your heart been lately? Are you open to God, not just hearing His voice but responding to Him? Does your heart have a single purpose—to follow His promptings and go in faith, knowing that God's path is best?

Today, open your heart up to God's voice. Listen when He prompts you. Instead of turning the page, focus on the verses in His Word that are calling to your heart. Respond by being sensitive to what God is trying to tell you, where His Spirit may be leading, the way Christ would have you go. Open your heart, knowing God's will is the pathway that will lead you closer and closer to Him.

. . . .

Lord, as I lift my soul up to You today, my heart is open to Your promptings, my spirit to Your voice, my will to Your way. Amen.

THE HEART OF YOUR MATTER

Then some of the leaders of Israel visited me, and while they were sitting with me, this message came to me from the LORD: "Son of man, these leaders have set up idols in their hearts. They have embraced things that will make them fall into sin. Why should I listen to their requests?"

EZEKIEL 14:1–3 NLT

When we, like Lot's wife, long for what God would have us let go of, we have set up an idol in our own hearts. And because we are centered on something other than God, we end up alienating ourselves from His presence, His will, His way. Now separated from the only true source of love and life, we begin to stumble off the path God would have us tread.

Today, perform a heart check. Look deep within and ask God to help you recognize any idol that may be blocking Him out of your life. Consider what things other than God that you might be embracing. And then ask God to help you remove whatever is not of Him from the heart of your matter so that you will not make a misstep into sin but begin to grow ever closer to Him.

Lord, here is my heart. Help me remove what idols may be residing there. For my sole desire is to grow ever closer to You. In Jesus' name I pray, amen.

COMPASSIONATE CONSOLATION

It is only fitting that we should have a High Priest who is devoted to God, blameless, pure, compassionate toward but separate from sinners, and exalted by God to the highest place of honor.
HEBREWS 7:26 VOICE

How wonderful that we have a High Priest, one who is not just holy, blameless, and devoted to God but is compassionate toward us. For there are times that we feel so sullied by our missteps or so overwhelmed by our troubles that we have no compassion for ourselves.

When Jesus saw those mourning for Lazarus, His heart was so soft He could not help but weep (John 11:26). When Jesus ran into a funeral procession and saw a grieving widow had lost her only son, "He had compassion on her and said to her, 'Do not weep'" (Luke 7:13 skjv). He then touched the young man's coffin and told him to rise up. And he did. Jesus then delivered the son to his mother.

When trouble comes knocking at the door of your heart and you need some heavenly compassion, take heart. Know you have Jesus by your side, seeing all that's happening in your life. Tell Him your troubles. Ask Him to come close, to hold you, to cover you with His kindness. He cannot help but respond.

Lord, come near. Console me with
Your kindness, love, and compassion.

AN ALL-POWERFUL GOD

"And all the trees will know that it is I, the LORD, who cuts the tall tree down and makes the short tree grow tall. It is I who makes the green tree wither and gives the dead tree new life. I, the LORD, have spoken, and I will do what I said!"

EZEKIEL 17:24 NLT

When you feel as if the world is falling apart, when hope seems beyond reach, look to God. For *He* is the one with unsurpassed power. Human leaders may assume they have the world at their beck and call, that they control everything within their reach, but nothing could be further from the truth. God alone is all-powerful. He alone has control of the world, maintaining and sustaining the universe, the seen and unseen.

Yet that's not all. You can rest easy knowing that every promise God has made to you He will keep. That means that if you believe in Jesus, you will have eternal life. You have a unique and particular purpose. Your life has meaning, you are loved, you will never be abandoned, and you will never lack—no matter what anyone else says or believes.

So take heart. God will see you through this life—and will be there with you in the one to come!

Thank You, Lord, for Your eternal promises, provision, and presence!

A STRONG TOWER

The name of the Lord is a strong tower; the [consistently]
righteous man [upright and in right standing with God]
runs into it and is safe, high [above evil] and strong.
The rich man's wealth is his strong city, and as a high
protecting wall in his own imagination and conceit.
PROVERBS 18:10–11 AMPC

When you experience trouble that is common to human beings and was also in some form experienced by Jesus, you have two choices: you can run to God for help and protection or you can take cover with whatever money or possessions you think will guard you. The first choice is that of the wise woman, the second that of a fool.

Only God can give you the strength and protection you need in this life. Only He can keep you safe and secure. Only He can give you the power you need to carry on and carry over from one day to the next.

This world's riches, its material treasures, are just a facade. For they are fleeting and unable to give you firm footing, much less any real protection.

So take heart. Your God is the only source of help you will ever need. Run to Him and you will find the strength, power, and safety you seek.

. . . .

I come running to You, Lord. See me through
these days! For with You alone am I safe.

HOLDING TIGHT

Let us hold tightly without wavering to the hope we affirm, for God can be trusted to keep his promise. Let us think of ways to motivate one another to acts of love and good works. And let us not neglect our meeting together, as some people do, but encourage one another.
HEBREWS 10:23–25 NLT

When we're looking for hope, help, and assurance, we're to look not just to God but to each other.

Today's verses tell us to hold on tightly to our hope and faith in God. We're to acknowledge God can indeed be trusted to do what He has said He will do, that He will stick to His Word. Armed and aligned with that hope, we will find no better way to help ourselves than to help someone else! To motivate others to act in love, to perform good works, to do what is within our power to make this world a better place. Yet how can we inspire and encourage each other if we've stopped meeting together, connecting with each other—whether that be physically or virtually, as a group or individually?

To keep yourself inspired and motivated, reach out to someone in your community of faith. Think of a way to connect to encourage them, to give them hope and love, to take heart, and to do good for others. In doing so, you'll be encouraging yourself as well!

. . . .

Who, Lord, would You have me encourage today?

THE GREAT REWARD

So do not throw away this confident trust in the Lord.
Remember the great reward it brings you! Patient endurance
is what you need now, so that you will continue to do God's
will. Then you will receive all that he has promised.
HEBREWS 10:35–36 NLT

Some female followers faint when faced with a battle. Others stay confident, knowing that in the end, they'll see the sure reward of eternal life and all the blessings of His promises because they remained obedient to God.

So when the going gets tough, when the challenges before you seem insurmountable, when you feel as if you don't have the energy to take another step, take heart. Know that God sees you persevering. He'll come to your aid, reminding you of all the other challenges you have faced and surmounted. He'll see exactly what you need. And knowing that you are continuing to trust in Him, He'll provide whatever strength, supernatural power, confidence, and courage you require to see things through.

Today, know that God knows all that's happening in your life. Understand that He sees you as one of those believers who won't shrink back but will step forward wherever He leads. Realize He cheers your efforts as you walk along His way, knowing that at the end you will reap His great reward.

Thank You, Lord, for always being with me, seeing me,
helping me, empowering me. I will go where You lead.

URGED ON

[Urged on] by faith Abraham, when he was called, obeyed and went forth to a place which he was destined to receive as an inheritance; and he went, although he did not know or trouble his mind about where he was to go.

HEBREWS 11:8 AMPC

Imagine God calling you to a place you'd never seen before. And you went, following God blindly into whatever land He had promised you. How would you react?

Abraham had so much faith in God that when the Lord called him to some unknown destination, he went. He obeyed and began walking according to God's directions. And (here's the tough part) he did so without troubling himself about the path he was taking or what he would find at the end of that path.

The same thing happened to the Israelites when being chased by Pharaoh and his chariots. "[Urged on] by faith the people crossed the Red Sea as [though] on dry land," and amazingly enough, "when the Egyptians tried to do the same thing they were swallowed up [by the sea]" (Hebrews 11:29 AMPC).

When you're unsure of the road that lies ahead, when you don't know where you're going to end up, allow your faith in God to urge you on. Allow Him to continually remind you that you're safe in His hands. Just take heart and go. God's got you.

*When fear and doubt rise up within me, Lord,
may I be urged on by my complete trust in You.*

PROMPTED BY FAITH

*Because of faith the walls of Jericho fell down after they
had been encompassed for seven days [by the Israelites].
[Prompted] by faith Rahab the prostitute was not destroyed
along with those who refused to believe and obey, because
she had received the spies in peace [without enmity].*
HEBREWS 11:30–31 AMPC

Rahab had devised a plan for her life. Perhaps it didn't go exactly as
she had hoped. Maybe, amid or because of her circumstances, she had
found the path of least resistance and determined her road to survival
lay in becoming a prostitute. But she, as we often do ourselves, later
discovered that "we humans keep brainstorming options and plans,
but GOD's purpose prevails" (Proverbs 19:21 MSG).

When Rahab met the Israelite spies who had come into her house,
and realized they were followers of the God who had shown so much
power, she hid them from the king's men. This enabled the spies to
complete their mission and God's people to bring down the walls
of Jericho, saving her and her family, her reward for receiving God's
spies in peace. Later, she ended up becoming an ancestor of Jesus!

When you allow your faith in God to prompt you to follow
His pathway, you, like Rahab, will see endless reward, victory after
victory, peace by peace.

*Lord, help me to be open to the promptings of my faith so
that I will find not only You but the peace and place I long for!*

FOCUSED FOLLOWER

Stay focused on Jesus, who designed and perfected our faith. . . .
Consider the life of the One who endured such personal attacks
and hostility from sinners so that you will not grow weary or
lose heart. . . . My child, do not ignore the instruction that comes
from the Lord, or lose heart when He steps in to correct you.

HEBREWS 12:2–3, 5 VOICE

The distractions of the world can block out the instructions God is sending our way, removing us from the pathway He has called us to follow. Even Proverbs warns, "My child, should you stop listening to instruction, you will wander from the voice of knowledge" (19:27 VOICE).

So what's a modern woman to do? Keep her eyes on Jesus, her ears attuned to God's wisdom, and her heart open to the promptings of the Spirit. She can do this by keeping her mind in the Word, listening to the wisdom she finds there, and asking God where He'd have her go, what He'd have her do. And to keep up her courage, she can remind herself of what Jesus endured and how He still managed to triumph in the end!

. . . .

Jesus, help me keep my eyes on You, my ears open to
the wisdom of God, and my heart attuned to the Spirit's
promptings. Help me to not lose heart when You reach
out to correct me. In Your name I pray, amen.

THE PATH OF HONOR

*Work at living in peace with everyone, and work at living
a holy life, for those who are not holy will not see the Lord.
Look after each other so that none of you fails to receive
the grace of God. Watch out that no poisonous root of
bitterness grows up to trouble you, corrupting many.*

HEBREWS 12:14–15 NLT

Instead of picking fights or being contentious with others, we are
advised to work to be at peace with everyone—not just our fellow
believers. Instead of yielding to a spirit of combativeness, seeking
revenge on whoever we deem has wronged us in some way, we're to
aim to be holy. To let that be the great achievement of our life. At the
same time, we're to take special care that no root of bitterness grows
up among us and poisons our body of believers.

Although living at peace, staying holy, and eschewing bitterness
seem like impossibilities in these fractious days, *with God anything is
possible*. So take heart knowing He has freely given us a grace we're
to extend to all we meet. Holding this truth in our minds, hearts,
and spirits, we can, with the Lord at our side, find the path of honor
He would have us take.

*Thank You, Lord, for Your grace. I pray You would give
me the strength to work at living a peaceful and holy life
and to recoil from all bitterness—within and without. Amen.*

NO LACK

Keep your lives free from the love of money, and be content with what you have because He has said, "I will never leave you; I will always be by your side." Because of this promise, we may boldly say, The Lord is my help—I won't be afraid of anything. How can anyone harm me?

HEBREWS 13:5–6 VOICE

Money and possessions cannot give you the confidence you need to live this life. Only God can do that. About Him, David wrote, "The Lord is my Shepherd [to feed, guide, and shield me], I shall not lack" (Psalm 23:1 AMPC). With the Lord by our side we can live our lives content with what we have at hand because our Good Shepherd has promised to never leave us. He has vowed to always be walking by our side, no matter where we are or what we're doing.

And because we have our Creator and Sustainer with us, even when our savings are low and our possessions few we can say in our hearts, "I need not be afraid of anything. God is helping me this very moment. Because of His presence in my life, there's no way anyone or anything can harm me today and tomorrow."

Rest in this assurance. Be content with what you have. And thank God for all.

. . . .

Lord, thank You for always being at my side. Because You are with me, I lack nothing. In You I am content.

SPREADING GOODNESS AND LOVE

Every good gift bestowed, every perfect gift received comes to us from above, courtesy of the Father of lights. He is consistent. He won't change His mind or play tricks in the shadows. We have a special role in His plan. He calls us to life by His message of truth so that we will show the rest of His creatures His goodness and love.

JAMES 1:17–18 VOICE

Every good thing we see, every benevolent act has its origin in the one true God that created us. Called the Father of lights, the one who is the source of all light never changes. He will always be there to hold, help, and hover over us. God won't change His mind, nor will He play tricks on us or renege on His promises.

This good God has called us to be good creatures performing good acts. It's we who have secured a special role in what He is doing and will do. It's we who are to be and act like Him, showing all others His goodness and love.

Today and every day, revel in God's goodness. Soak in His love. Know He will give you not just the power but the opportunity to spread both His goodness and love, making you not only a better person but making this planet a better world.

. . . .

Lord, show me today what You would have me do to spread Your light, goodness, and love in this world.

ALL YOU NEED

I Myself will watch over My sheep and feed My flock. Whenever they are tired, I will lead them to rest on the cool mountain grass. When they are lost, I will seek them and bring back every last stray. I will bind up the injured and strengthen the weak.
EZEKIEL 34:15–16 VOICE

When you need help, whom or what do you seek out for comfort, warmth, strength, and direction? Some women look to their possessions. When they are worried or upset, they may buy something new just to make themselves feel better. But that rush of satisfaction soon fades away and the emptiness inside comes back to hinder and harm them.

When you are at a loss, look to God, your Shepherd. Know that He *is* watching over you. His arms are full of whatever needs and blessings you require. When you are tired, He will not fail to guide you to a place of rest and refreshment. When you are lost, He will actively seek you out and bring you back into the fold, into His arms, into His love and light. If you are injured, your Shepherd will heal you. If you feel weak, He will give you the strength you need to carry on.

During hard times, take heart. God is all you need.

I feel so lost and alone, Lord. Cover me with Your love, fill me with Your strength, lead me to Your peace.

YOUR HOME, HIS HEART

*I will establish a covenant of peace—an everlasting promise—
with them. I will make them strong and numerous in the
land I gave them. My sanctuary will be at the heart of
their community forever. I will make My home with them.
I will be their God, and they will be My people.*
E<small>ZEKIEL</small> 37:26–27 <small>VOICE</small>

God wants to be the center of your life, not an afterthought. He wants to be at the heart of all you do, think, say, and desire. He wants to live within you, not reside on the outskirts, just someone you turn to when your luck has run dry or you've run out of ideas about how to save yourself.

God has made peace with you by offering His Son, Christ the Mediator, the one who has reconciled you with the Lord God. He offers you even more peace and purity through the heavenly wisdom of which you have full access (James 3:17).

God has not left you to struggle through this life alone. He offers you His very self, peace, and strength. He offers you a home that's closer than you may think. To access the Lord, open His Word, call His Spirit, or run into His arms. For only when you make the God of love and peace the center of your life and heart are you truly home.

. . . .

*Lord, I need Your peace. Allow it to envelop
me now as I bask in Your love and light.*

SNUGGLE UP CLOSE

*God gives us more grace when we turn away from our own interests.
. . . So submit yourselves to the one true God and fight against
the devil and his schemes. If you do, he will run away in failure.
Come close to the one true God, and He will draw close to you. . . .
Cleanse your heart, because your mind is split down the middle,
your love for God on one side and selfish pursuits on the other.*
JAMES 4:6–8 VOICE

Through James, God makes clear that when we want something, we don't get it for two reasons: "You don't have what you want because you don't ask God for it. And even when you ask, you don't get it because your motives are all wrong" (James 4:2–3 NLT).

So what's a girl to do? Turn away from your own interests and selfish desires. Then snuggle up close to God. Submit yourself to Him entirely. As you draw close to Him, He'll draw close to you and steer you and your desires in the right direction.

As you prepare to pray each day, consider your thoughts and desires. Separate the selfish from the selfless. Then get close to God and tell Him what's on your mind, what your requests are. And as your will aligns with His, your prayers will be answered.

*Here I am, Lord, snuggling up close to You,
looking to align my will and desires with Yours.*

HEART RIGHT

Confess to one another therefore your faults (your slips, your false steps, your offenses, your sins) and pray [also] for one another, that you may be healed and restored [to a spiritual tone of mind and heart]. The earnest (heartfelt, continued) prayer of a righteous man makes tremendous power available [dynamic in its working].

JAMES 5:16 AMPC

It's hard to admit to ourselves when we've slipped up. Often in those moments we're too embarrassed and ashamed of ourselves to fess up. Yet God would have us come clean not just to ourselves but to others.

So when you've erred, don't just sweep it under the rug. Admit to yourself that you've made a mistake. Then tell a believer you trust where you've gone wrong and ask that person to pray with and for you.

Although confessing your misdeeds sounds like a frightening endeavor, it's exactly what you need to do to heal and restore your mind and heart. It's the remedy you require to get back on your feet mentally, emotionally, and spiritually. For afterward, your prayers, having been rooted in your right standing with God, will take on power.

. . . .

Oh, Lord, I have made a mess of things. Please give me the courage to unburden myself by confessing my missteps to another, then praying for restoration so that my heart may be right with Yours once again.

A GIVING GOD

Blessed is God, the Father of our Lord Jesus, the Anointed One!
Because He has raised Jesus the Anointed from death, through His
great mercy we have been reborn into a living hope—reborn for an
eternal inheritance, held in reserve in heaven, that will never fade
or fail. Through faith, God's power is standing watch, protecting you
for a salvation that you will see completely at the end of things.

1 PETER 1:3–5 VOICE

Today is a day to thank God for all He has done for you. For He not
only created you and gave you the breath of life, but He raised His
Son, Jesus, from the dead so you could be reborn into this new life,
a life of hope.

Because of what God has done for you, you have an eternal home
awaiting you in heaven, a place where you will be able to live with
the Lord forever. This home and the treasures it contains will never
fail, fade, or decay.

Although you may have trouble in this world, because you believe
in Jesus, God is guarding you with His power. He's overflowing you
with His love. He's watching over you as only the most careful of
fathers would do until the end of days. How wonderfully amazing
is that?

Thank You, Lord, for all You've done for me,
with me, and in me. Because You're in my life,
I know all is and will be well, from beginning to end.

THE GUARDIAN LORD

*The eyes of the Lord keep guard over knowledge and him who
has it, but He overthrows the words of the treacherous.*

PROVERBS 22:12 AMPC

Today's world is struggling to know the truth. More than ever before
some people are spurting untruths so easily and so often that it
becomes more and more difficult to know what to believe.

Yet you can take heart. Because God protects those with
knowledge. He will frustrate the words and ruin the plans of those
who are evil. In the end, they who speak falsehoods to stir up trouble
or gain power will be uncovered and embarrassed. All their plans
will come to nothing.

In the meantime, keep your head, heart, and mind in "the Word
of the Lord (divine instruction, the Gospel) [which] endures forever"
(1 Peter 1:25 AMPC). For although some things will one day fade
away, just as flowers droop then die, the Word of God is immortal,
everlasting, and always truthful.

*Lord, help me to always tell the truth. Lead me into Your Word,
which prompts me to follow Your will and way. Help me not
to let falsehoods mislead me. Help me not to get hung up on
those who are telling lies but to rest in Your peace, knowing
that Your Word will endure forever. In Jesus' name, amen.*

LIGHT WALKER

*You are a chosen people. . .God's own; so that you may proclaim
the wondrous acts of the One who called you out of inky darkness
into shimmering light. . . . Once you had not received mercy,
but now you have received it. Beloved, remember you don't
belong in this world. You are resident aliens living in exile,
so resist those desires of the flesh that battle against the soul.*

1 PETER 2:9–11 VOICE

Have you ever felt like a stranger walking upon this earth? That you
just weren't designed—mentally, emotionally, physically—to be a part
of this world?

If so, don't worry. It's only natural that you might feel that way.
Because God has chosen you and brought you out of "inky darkness
into shimmering light." Through His great love and mercy, God has
sacrificed His Son, Jesus, so you could be reconciled to Him.

Thus, if you feel you don't belong here, don't fret. You don't. You're
a resident alien, living in exile in this world. Your stay here is only
temporary. God has a much more wonderful place for you in heaven
when your purpose here on earth is fulfilled.

So keep away from the worldly wiles that want to wage war
against your soul. Instead, keep your head and heart in God and His
Word, following the promptings of the Spirit, until you are called
up yonder to your forever and true home.

Thank You, Lord, for choosing me to walk in Your light!

DO GOOD NO MATTER WHAT

*For God called you to do good, even if it means suffering, just
as Christ suffered for you. He is your example, and you must
follow in his steps. He never sinned, nor ever deceived anyone.*

1 PETER 2:21–22 NLT

If there was a sign-up sheet for suffering, nobody would jump at the
chance to write their name on the list. We plan our lives and schedule
our days trying to avoid difficult times, and rightfully so—none of
us want to add more struggles to an already hard life!

But Peter gives us a reality check in 1 Peter 2:21–22: Our sin-
less Savior, Jesus, suffered greatly while doing good on earth. He
endured ridicule, slander, betrayal, lies, physical beating, bleeding,
crucifixion, and death. And yet, He did good. He did more than
good—He did the ultimate good by laying down His will and dying
to pay for our freedom from sin through His grace.

When we follow Christ's example and live for others, we too
may suffer. Pray for the strength to face hard times as Jesus did—with
patience, peace, and confidence that God is in control and will lead
us to victory no matter what.

. . . .

*Father, I will do good—even if it means suffering. Even if
it means momentary disappointment. Even if it means
losing something to gain more of You. Jesus, thank
You for Your perfect example of sacrificial love.*

SHARING YOUR PERSONAL FAITH

*In your hearts revere Christ as Lord. Always be prepared to give
an answer to everyone who asks you to give the reason for the
hope that you have. But do this with gentleness and respect.*

1 PETER 3:15 NIV

Your faith is deeply personal. It's a relationship with your loving
Father who created you on purpose and with purpose (Ephesians
2:10), who values you and counts every hair on your head (Luke
12:6–7), who cares about you intimately (1 Peter 5:7), who is
always with you (Joshua 1:9), who hears and answers your prayers
(Matthew 7:7).

But God doesn't intend your personal faith to be kept solely to
yourself. Telling others about what God's doing in your life shouldn't
be loud or abrasive, but 1 Peter 3:15 says that we should always be
ready to give an answer—gently and genuinely—when someone
asks about our faith, our hope, our Christian perspective.

Spend time thinking about what your faith means to you so when
others ask about it, you can simply and easily talk about the difference
that Jesus makes in your life. You may plant seeds that bloom into a
deeply rooted faith for someone else in the future.

*Father, thank You for being a personal God. With Your Spirit
alive in my heart, I know I can face anything! Give me confidence
and courage to talk about You. I have real hope because of
You—a hope that the people around me desperately need.*

STRENGTH IN NUMBERS

Stay alert! Watch out for your great enemy, the devil. He prowls around like a roaring lion, looking for someone to devour. Stand firm against him, and be strong in your faith. Remember that your family of believers all over the world is going through the same kind of suffering you are.

1 PETER 5:8–9 NLT

Peter describes the devil as a prowling lion that scopes out young, sick, or straggling animals to attack. Lions choose victims who are alone, inexperienced, or not paying attention. That's why we need to be on our guard from attacks from Satan, especially when we are going through difficult times. When we feel alone, weak, helpless, and cut off from other believers, we may be extra vulnerable to the prowling devil.

So when you're in a difficult season, seek out other Christians for support. Be willing to lay down your pride and admit you need help. There is strength in numbers, as seen in Ecclesiastes 4:12 (NIV) where a group of believers closing ranks around a struggling friend is illustrated: "Though one may be overpowered, two can defend themselves. A cord of three strands is not quickly broken."

Above all, keep your eyes on Jesus, who will help you resist the devil. Then, scripture promises, Satan will flee from you (James 4:7).

Jesus, I will keep my eyes on You at all times. Point out friends who might be struggling and give me the confidence to help strengthen them with Your help and hope.

THE KING'S DREAM

*"Upon hearing this, Daniel (also known as Belteshazzar)
was overcome for a time, frightened by the meaning of the
dream. Then the king said to him, 'Belteshazzar, don't be
alarmed by the dream and what it means.' Belteshazzar
replied, 'I wish the events foreshadowed in this dream would
happen to your enemies, my lord, and not to you!'"*

DANIEL 4:19 NLT

God gave Daniel prophetic understanding of Nebuchadnezzar's
dream, but it still broke Daniel's heart to deliver such bad news to the
Babylonian king. Even though Nebuchadnezzar had been responsible
for the destruction of Daniel's home and nation, Daniel had already
forgiven him. Because of that forgiveness, God was able to use Daniel
in a mighty way.

Often when someone has wronged us, we find it difficult to forget
the past. We may even be glad when that person suffers, but holding
a grudge puts up barriers between us and the person who wronged us
and between us and God. Forgiveness means putting the past behind
us. Can you love someone who has hurt you? Can you serve someone
who mistreated you? Ask God to help you forgive, forget, and love.
God may use you in an extraordinary way in that person's life.

. . . .

*Father, when I am struggling with unforgiveness, help me to realize that
You have forgiven me completely. Tear down any walls in my heart so
that I can forgive and You can use me for Your glory in amazing ways.*

STRENGTH TEST

*If you fall apart during a crisis, then you
weren't very strong to begin with.*
PROVERBS 24:10 VOICE

We all like to think we are strong. But until some trial tests our strength, we don't really know what we can handle. Maybe little daily stresses don't affect you much, but a tidal wave of difficulty knocks you off your feet.

While most of us don't seek out struggles, the truth is that times of trouble can be ultimately helpful. Hard seasons can show us who we really are and what kind of character we have. Enduring through trials can help us grow stronger.

Paul explained it this way to the church in Rome: "We can rejoice. . .when we run into problems and trials, for we know that they help us develop endurance. And endurance develops strength of character, and character strengthens our confident hope of salvation" (Romans 5:3–4 NLT). Find joy in hope, Paul wrote in Romans 12:12, practice patience through a crisis, and pray continually.

God is faithful to stay by our side, even if we fall apart (2 Timothy 2:13), and Jesus promises to be with us "to the very end of the age" (Matthew 28:20 NIV). Take courage in the fact that regardless of our strength or weakness, God will hold us in His strong, capable hands (Psalm 139:10; Isaiah 41:10).

*Lord, I marvel at Your strength and Your promise to be
the strength in my weakness (2 Corinthians 12:9–10).*

AN HONEST ANSWER

An honest answer is like a kiss of friendship.
PROVERBS 24:26 NLT

Have you ever fudged the truth to keep from hurting a friend? Although it's human nature to want to avoid conflict, ignoring an uncomfortable truth can hurt a relationship in the long run, while honesty that is communicated with love will build trust in a friendship.

Real friends gently challenge each other to grow deeper in their faith and closer to each other. Proverbs 27:17 (VOICE) illustrates this by saying, "In the same way that iron sharpens iron, a person sharpens the character of his friend." The words of a true friend can be trusted to have our best interest at heart, and even tough love can feel worthwhile.

Jesus answered His friends honestly, even if the truth was hard to hear. When the disciples argued among themselves about who would be the greatest, Jesus told them the lowliest servant among them would be the greatest (Luke 22:24–30). When Peter was overly confident, saying that he would even die for Jesus, the Lord told him the hard truth: "Before the rooster crows tomorrow morning, you will deny three times that you even know me" (Luke 22:34 NLT).

In all things, even in hard honesty, follow the example of Jesus Christ. Truth in love will set you free.

. . . .

*Jesus, when I'm tempted to bend the truth with a friend,
remind me that stepping out in truth is the best foot
forward in any relationship, including Yours and mine.*

NO DARKNESS TO BE FOUND

This is the message we heard from Jesus and now declare to you: God is light, and there is no darkness in him at all.

1 JOHN 1:5 NLT

Young children inherently know the comfort light brings. When their night-light emits its soft glow, whatever scary, evil creature who lives in the dark (even if only in their imagination) cannot hide. Light and darkness cannot coexist.

God's very nature is light—goodness, purity, holiness, and reliability. Only God and Jesus, His Son, can guide us out of the darkness of sin. Just as darkness can't exist in the presence of light, sin cannot exist in the presence of a holy God. That's where His forgiveness of sin comes into play.

The Bible tells us the benefits of living in God's light every day in 1 John 1:7 (NLT): "If we are living in the light, as God is in the light, then we have fellowship with each other, and the blood of Jesus, his Son, cleanses us from all sin." And as God's children, we are to bring His light into the dark world by doing good (Matthew 5:14–16).

How brightly are you shining today? If you feel the brilliance is fading, step closer to God. Spend time with Him in prayer, and praise Him as you watch the darkness flee.

. . . .

Lord, thank You for making a way for me to walk in Your light now and through all of eternity.

JUST THE RIGHT MOMENT

A well-spoken word at just the right moment
is like golden apples in settings of silver.
PROVERBS 25:11 VOICE

The Bible provides ample warning about the destruction our words can cause. James 3 describes the tongue as a "flame of fire" that "can set your whole life on fire" (verse 3:6 NLT).

Yet for all the devastation the tongue is capable of, it can also encourage and build up. "The tongue of the wise brings healing," Proverbs 12:18 (NIV) says. A heart that is filled with the wisdom of God's Word will offer kind words that Proverbs 16:24 (NLT) says are "like honey—sweet to the soul and healthy for the body."

So how can we know the right words to say at the right moment? Pray and ask the Holy Spirit for opportunities to offer well-spoken truth to the people around you. When you are a source of God's love and encouragement, others will seek out your advice and good words. Then you'll be living out scripture's teaching in Colossians 4:6 (NLT) that says, "Let your conversation be gracious and attractive so that you will have the right response for everyone."

. . . .

Father, purify my heart so that my tongue can be a
source of good, well-spoken love to everyone around me.
When I need encouragement, send a pure-hearted friend
to offer me Your wisdom at just the right moment.

LABELS

*See how very much our Father loves us, for he
calls us his children, and that is what we are!*

1 JOHN 3:1 NLT

Throughout our lives, we define ourselves in different ways. You may be mom, wife, daughter, sister, aunt, student, employee, boss. Maybe you define yourself by the things you do: runner, musician, artist, scrapbooker, influencer. Or maybe difficulties you've experienced have shaped what you call yourself: cancer survivor, recovering addict, widow.

No matter what you call yourself, God calls you His beloved child, and that's where your authentic identity and worth are found. When you first accepted God's gift of grace, you were counted as an integral part of His family and Christ's church. Your status as an heir to the King of kings isn't reserved for heaven—you are His heir *here* and *now* (Romans 8:17). There's amazing freedom in knowing who you are and whose you are.

So on the days when you're feeling limited by the labels you put on yourself and the world puts on you, remember you are loved by a gracious Father, created in His image (Genesis 1:27), redeemed by the blood of Jesus (Hebrews 9:11–14), and forever a sister and friend to Jesus (Hebrews 2:11; John 15:15).

* *

*Father, when I feel I have lost myself, bury me in an avalanche
of Your love. By myself, I am not enough. You make me worthy;
You make me whole. Your Spirit fills me with confidence.*

GREATER IS HE

The Spirit who lives in you is greater
than the spirit who lives in the world.

1 JOHN 4:4 NLT

Some days the problems we face seem overwhelming. The evil that Satan spreads in the world is obviously stronger than we are, so why even attempt to overcome it?

The amazing truth for Christians is that the Holy Spirit is more powerful than any evil that exists—stronger than the devil himself. Even better, the Holy Spirit is a personal, intimate God and He lives inside every person who believes.

Here's some of what God's Word says about the Holy Spirit:

- He was with God from the beginning (Genesis 1:2).

- He will never leave us (John 14:16).

- He helps us (John 14:16).

- He teaches us (John 14:26).

- His power raised Jesus from the dead (Romans 8:11).

Instead of focusing outward on all the impossibly difficult situations in the world, focus inward on the power of the Holy Spirit. He is with you and He is for you. He defeated death once and for all, and He will overcome any obstacle in your way!

I need Your help every day, Holy Spirit. Forgive me when I forget just how powerful and essential You are in my life. I will not stand in Your way. Lead me in the perfect plan the Father has for my life now and into eternity. I will follow You to victory in every way!

PERFECT LOVE

There is no fear in love. But perfect love drives out fear,
because fear has to do with punishment. The one
who fears is not made perfect in love.

1 JOHN 4:18 NIV

God loves you perfectly, wholly, and unconditionally. But while God's love is unchanging, fear has a sneaky way of finding cracks in our insecurities and feeding our worries. So when you fear the future, the unknown, judgment, the things you cannot control, or something else, remember the truths of God's immeasurable love for you:

- Nothing can separate you from God's love
  (Romans 8:37–39).

- He loved you while you were still a sinner (Romans 5:8).

- His love offers peace (Zephaniah 3:17).

- His love is steadfast (Psalm 25:6–7).

- He loves you as His daughter (1 John 3:1).

- God, by His very nature, *is* love (1 John 4:8) .

- When you embrace God's love, fear flees (1 John 4:18).

If you are struggling with fear today, open your Bible and meditate on one or more of these scriptures. Ask God to give you a fuller understanding of His love. Fear will have no home in your heart!

Father, today I'm giving You my fears, and I'm
asking for Your perfect love to cover me with
the confidence of Your mercy and grace.

AVOID THE BITE

*Interfering in someone else's argument
is as foolish as yanking a dog's ears.*
PROVERBS 26:17 NLT

Yank on a dog's ear, and there's a good chance you'll get bitten. Stick your nose into someone else's argument, and there's a good chance the fighters will turn against you. Sometimes it's best to steer clear when it's none of your business.

Yet if you're a peacemaker by nature, you may feel the urge to step into an argument to help smooth it over—especially when the fight is between two people you love. If you decide to act as a mediator, it's wise to wait until the arguers have cooled off a bit. Ask the Holy Spirit to help guide you in love. God's Word has much to say about how to love others in a heated situation. Attitude and tone can be the difference between peace and discord: "A gentle answer deflects anger, but harsh words make tempers flare" (Proverbs 15:1 NLT). And James 1:19 (VOICE) advises, "Listen, open your ears, harness your desire to speak, and don't get worked up into a rage so easily."

With God's help, you may be able to help others mend their differences and restore and strengthen their relationship.

. . . .

*God, give me the wisdom to know when and how to
help in an argument. And if You do not want me to get
involved, give me the peace to know that You are working
in other ways to restore peace in the relationship.*

TOUGH LOVE

*Wounds from a sincere friend are better
than many kisses from an enemy.*
PROVERBS 27:6 NLT

Tough love is a difficult thing to give and receive. But Proverbs 27:6 makes the point that a sincere friend really does have your best interest at heart. Maybe that person is your husband, maybe it's your soul sister, or maybe it's your mom or daughter or cousin or coworker, but no matter who it is, it's someone you trust.

An enemy, on the other hand, may offer sweet words and flattery—good feelings that last for a while—but that person will happily send you down a pathway to consequences and regret.

Do your friends feel comfortable being authentic with you? When someone you trust attempts to speak the truth in love, consider listening without immediately reacting, even when it stings. Sincere friends will weigh their words carefully, and even difficult conversations can strengthen the bond in your relationship. There's no better way to hear hard truth than from a friend who just *gets you*. Proverbs 27:9 (AMPC) puts it this way: "Oil and perfume rejoice the heart; so does the sweetness of a friend's counsel that comes from the heart."

. . . .

*Father, thank You for true friends. Help us to speak
the truth in love, even when it's hard to do so.
Strengthen our bond and shared faith in You.*

LOOK OUT

A prudent person foresees danger and takes precautions.
The simpleton goes blindly on and suffers the consequences.
PROVERBS 27:12 NLT

God didn't create you to be a fearful person, but He did create you to be empowered by the Holy Spirit to make wise decisions (2 Timothy 1:7).

Jesus tells us in John 16:33 that we will encounter trouble in this life, so when we see the storm clouds start to gather, it's a good idea to take precautions. A wise person will set money aside for emergencies because she never knows when a car will need repairing or an appliance replacing. When we feel a rift forming in a relationship, we are wise to mend it before the rift becomes a canyon that is much harder to cross.

Yes, we will have challenges in this life, but God created us with logical, sound minds that can often see danger on the horizon. When we wisely take precautions, we can avoid some lingering consequences.

So keep your eyes on the horizon—not out of fear, but because you know that no matter what, Jesus is with you. He has overcome every trouble, danger, and disappointment the world can put in your path.

. . . .

Lord, I need You every day. Thank You for creating me strong in mind, heart, and spirit. Make me wise in Your Word and secure in Your great love for me. With You in my life, I have nothing to fear.

TREASURE TIME

Be sure you know the condition of your flocks, give careful attention to your herds; for riches do not endure forever, and a crown is not secure for all generations.

PROVERBS 27:23–24 NIV

The life expectancy of a woman in North America is 81 years. That's 972 months; 29,585 days; 710,040 hours; 42,602,400 minutes; 2,556,144,000 seconds. This time is a gift, and what we choose to do with it is important to God.

Proverbs 27:23–24 teaches us that some of that time should be spent giving responsible attention to our homes, our families, and our careers. Thinking ahead is a duty, not an option, for God's people.

Yet spending time on these duties is not the utmost pursuit for Christians. Jesus tells us in Matthew 6:19 that the things the world values are fleeting and can be stolen away. But when we spend time building eternal treasures—things like a generous spirit (Mark 10:21), a servant's heart (Mark 10:45), love and care for others (John 13:34–35)—then we are creating a legacy that will continue forever in heaven (Matthew 6:20–21).

True wisdom means using our time wisely and always for the glory of God. Ask Him to guide your decisions about how to use your time to grow His kingdom here on earth and forever in heaven.

Father, thank You for the gift it is to live for You. You made me with a purpose. May my life be a living sacrifice to You.

AS BOLDLY AS LIONS

The wicked run away even when no one is chasing them;
the right-living, however, stand their ground as boldly as lions.
PROVERBS 28:1 VOICE

When people are doing the right thing—living with integrity and making upright choices—they have little reason to be paranoid. They don't have to look over their shoulder; they don't have to wonder who will catch up to them or when they will be found out. There's peace in knowing no justified blame can come their way.

People who hold themselves to a high standard of right have a self-assurance that's grounded in their choices. Isaiah 33:15 describes these people as honest and fair, people who stay away from bribes and who refuse to be tempted by evil. Those who choose righteous good are ethically and morally sound; they make the same choices when others are watching and when they can't be seen.

Do you want to live a bold, sure-footed life? Your faith in Jesus Christ gives you the confidence to ask God for guidance in all you do (Ephesians 3:12). Look forward as you follow Him in righteousness, and then you can proclaim, "The LORD is my helper, so I will have no fear" (Hebrews 13:6 NLT).

. . . .

Father, I want more of the kind of confidence that comes
with Your righteousness. I choose a life of right living
because I know it pleases You. May every choice I make
be one that glorifies You and helps others to find You.

UNIQUELY GIFTED

*"I am coming soon. Hold on to what you have,
so that no one will take your crown."*

REVELATION 3:11 NIV

The promised Messiah, Jesus, fulfilled Old Testament prophecy by coming to the earth as a baby more than two thousand years ago. Because of His life, death, and resurrection we can be confident in Jesus' promise to return to earth again.

As Christians, while we wait for Christ's return, we are to love God and love others (Matthew 22:37–39) and to share the good news of Jesus with the world (Matthew 28:16–20). God has given us unique gifts to help us follow these instructions—we each have different passions, abilities, experience, and maturity. And as we wait for Jesus' second coming, He tells us to "hold on" to what we have by persevering and growing stronger and more mature in our faith.

You may be a new believer and feel that your faith and spiritual strength are still growing. Or maybe you've been a Christian for years and you've lost some excitement for using your talents for the Lord. Today, ask the Holy Spirit to show you every opportunity to use your gifts to live for Christ, and God will use it for your good and His glory.

. . . .

*Father, thank You for the talents and passions You have
placed inside me. Show me the best, most effective ways
to use my gifts to live out Your plan for my life.*

WORTHY OF OUR PRAISE

*"You are worthy, O Lord our God, to receive glory
and honor and power. For you created all things,
and they exist because you created what you pleased."*
REVELATION 4:11 NLT

There are lots of reasons that God is worthy of your praise today. Praise Him for the beauty of the sun dawning over the horizon. Thank Him for the unexpected blessing that came your way yesterday. Give Him glory for His faithfulness in every situation—for providing exactly what you need when you need it.

The point of Revelation chapter 4 is summed up in verse 11. All of creation will praise God because He is the Creator of all and He sustains everything. You exist today because He lovingly designed and formed you. He thought of you before you had a form, and by His amazing artistry, He created your soul, mind, body, and heart. He made you unique and purposeful and with the same powerful hands that created the vast cosmos and the smallest atom. Into you He poured the care of a loving Father who gives good things.

God is great and He is good. His care for you didn't end after He created you. In Him we can become new creations, striving every day to be more like His Son, Jesus. He is a personal God who is worthy of our personal praise.

*Father, I praise You for who You are.
I thank You, honor You, and give You glory.*

YOUR MIGHTY DEFENDER

*"Because of the violence against your brother Jacob, you will
be covered with shame; you will be destroyed forever.
On the day you stood aloof while strangers carried off
his wealth and foreigners entered his gates and cast
lots for Jerusalem, you were like one of them."*

OBADIAH 10–11 NIV

As descendants of Jacob's brother, Esau, the Edomites were blood
relatives of Israel (Genesis 25:19–27:45). Of all people, the Edomites
should have rushed to the aid of their relatives, the nation of Israel.
Instead, the Edomites gloated over Israel's problems, captured
and delivered fugitives to the enemy, and even looted Israel's land.
Obadiah 10–11 shows God's punishment for anyone who would
harm His children.

Today, God's holy nation is His church—those who accept
Christ as their Savior and live to serve Him. As Christians, we are
God's adopted children, and we can be sure God will defend us as
mightily as He fought for Israel. As you read Obadiah, find hope in
the reality of what it means to be God's child, loved and protected by
Him. See how the heavenly Father responds to anyone—including
the devil—who would attack those He loves.

* * *

*Lord, You are my powerful shield, and I trust You to come to
my defense when I need help. I know You stand in my corner,
and no one can defeat You. Because of this, I choose to live without
fear. I choose to live in hope of Your powerful love for me.*

THE REMEDY FOR FOOLS

*Mockers can get a whole town agitated,
but the wise will calm anger.*

PROVERBS 29:8 NLT

Few things can escalate a tense situation more than a fool spouting off. Mockers belittle. They patronize. They are spiteful and cutting with no regard to the feelings of others.

Satan revels in the divisiveness that exists in the world today. Face-to-face, in a public setting, or online, mockers find their way to wreak havoc wherever they can. Proverbs warns against such foolishness—encouraging us both to not engage in mockery and to avoid fools:

- "Anyone who rebukes a mocker will get an insult in return. Anyone who corrects the wicked will get hurt. So don't bother correcting mockers; they will only hate you." (Proverbs 9:7–8 NLT).

- "Don't answer the foolish arguments of fools, or you will become as foolish as they are" (Proverbs 26:4 NLT).

The truth is that we are not at the mercy of mockers. The wisdom of calmer heads will always win out in the end. Ask God for insight and understanding in your communication with others. Speak the truth in love, and to the best of your ability, live in peace and harmony with everyone (Romans 12:16–18).

Father, make me an instrument of Your peace. When others stir up strife, help me be a soothing agent of truth, understanding, and love. Fill my heart with the peace that comes with knowing Jesus Christ.

A PROMISE FULFILLED

But you, O Bethlehem Ephrathah, are only a small village among all the people of Judah. Yet a ruler of Israel, whose origins are in the distant past, will come from you on my behalf.

MICAH 5:2 NLT

The prophet Micah predicted the Messiah's birthplace hundreds of years before Jesus was born. Although Christ has no beginning and no end, He entered our human history as the man named Jesus of Nazareth.

When God reveals the future, His purpose is much bigger than to satisfy our curiosity about what is to come. God's fulfilled promises—like the one in Micah 5:2—give us hope for His many other promises that are yet to come true. We know Jesus will come again (Luke 21:25–28), and this should affect our choices today. As Christians, our forever begins now; and a glimpse of God's plan for us should motivate us to obey and serve Him, no matter what the rest of the world is doing.

This Christmas, thank God for His many promises. Celebrate the greatest gift of Jesus, see what God is doing today, and look forward to the fulfillment of God's promises for the future and all of eternity.

Father, thank You for being a God who keeps His promises. What You say I can believe. I praise You for being the God of my past, present, and future. I cherish Your promises, and I want my heart and my actions to align with Your plan.

A LOWLY MANGER FOR AN HONORABLE KING

Pride brings a person low, but the lowly in spirit gain honor.
PROVERBS 29:23 NIV

Jesus' list of titles is long and impressive: Son of God, member of the Trinity, High Priest, Teacher, Leader, Savior of humankind, just to name a few. Yet instead of bragging about His position, Jesus chose humility instead. Philippians 2:7 (NIV) says Jesus "made himself nothing by taking the very nature of a servant, being made in human likeness."

Jesus could've come to earth in a miraculous spectacle—in a way that no one could deny that He was God on earth. But instead, He chose to come as a helpless baby, born to an unwed mother and an earthly father of modest means. He came first to the poor—the shepherds on the hillside (Luke 2:8–18)—and He continued throughout His life in servanthood to others—healing the sick, raising the dead, paying attention to the people no one else wanted. He humbled Himself in obedience to His heavenly Father and died on a cross. But His story didn't end there.

"God elevated him to the place of highest honor," Philippians 2:9–11 (NLT) explains, "and gave him the name above all other names, that at the name of Jesus every knee should bow. . .and every tongue declare that Jesus Christ is Lord, to the glory of God the Father."

God, help me have the same attitude as Jesus. I am Your humble servant.

THE REMEDY FOR SOCIAL ANXIETY

Fearing people is a dangerous trap,
but trusting the LORD means safety.

PROVERBS 29:25 NLT

Christmastime means spending time with people. Lots of people. From intimate family gatherings to large-scale events that draw crowds of hundreds, the extroverts among us live their best lives in December. But introverts and those who are anxious around people may have a difficult time in this season.

If your calendar includes social events that you dread, give your fears to God. He cares about your struggles (1 Peter 5:7) and is faithful to go before you into any situation (Joshua 1:9). If you know someone who struggles with social anxiety, pray for them, and when you can, kindly help them navigate tough situations.

God created us to be with others. From the companionship provided for Adam in the form of Eve to the words of Ecclesiastes 4:9–10 (NLT)—"Two people are better off than one, for they can help each other succeed. If one person falls, the other can reach out and help"—it's clear we were never meant to do life alone. Find freedom today in trusting God, and your heart will sing, "The LORD is my strength and my shield; my heart trusts in him, and he helps me" (Psalm 28:7 NIV).

Father, when people intimidate me, remind me that Your Holy Spirit living inside me is not fearful—He is courageous, loving, and strong (2 Timothy 1:7). He is with me and will help me through any situation.

GOD WITH US

The LORD, the King of Israel, is with you;
never again will you fear any harm.
ZEPHANIAH 3:15 NIV

The tiny infant born in a manger in Bethlehem was *Immanuel*, a name that in Hebrew means "God with us." He lived on earth, fully human and fully divine—with us. And when He returned to heaven, He sent His Holy Spirit to remain—with us.

Today God is with you in the celebrations of Jesus' birth. He is with you in the get-togethers, special meals, gift exchanges, and holy moments of Christmas. Yes, He is with you in the joyful celebrations, but your Father God is also with you if you are missing a loved one this year. He is "close to the brokenhearted and saves those who are crushed in spirit" (Psalm 34:18 NIV). Your sorrow doesn't go unnoticed by God. "You have collected all my tears in your bottle," Psalm 56:8 (NLT) says. "You have recorded each one in your book."

Today, as you look forward to the holiday tomorrow, spend a quiet moment enjoying the all-loving presence of Immanuel, and rest in the fact that He was there in your past, is present in your now, and will be with you in your future and for eternity.

. . . .

Jesus, thank You for being here. . .with me. I praise You
as Immanuel—my God who willingly came to earth as
a baby and lived as a man. From my beginning to end,
I know You understand me and love me well.

WILLING HANDS

"'But now be strong, Zerubbabel,' declares the LORD. 'Be strong, Joshua son of Jozadak, the high priest. Be strong, all you people of the land,' declares the LORD, 'and work. For I am with you,' declares the LORD Almighty. 'This is what I covenanted with you when you came out of Egypt. And my Spirit remains among you. Do not fear.'"

HAGGAI 2:4–5 NIV

God wants to change the world through you.

When you became a Christian, God started preparing you for big things. And when you feel a nudge from the Holy Spirit, it's time to get to work.

Your Father has given you work to do in the church, in your career, and at home. . .roles that are uniquely suited to you and your talents. When you work to build God's kingdom, your efforts will make a difference. "My dear brothers and sisters," Paul wrote in 1 Corinthians 15:58 (VOICE), "stay firmly planted—be unshakable—do many good works in the name of God, and know that all your labor is not for nothing when it is for God."

No matter what difficulties you face or how frustrating your work may be, God's Spirit is with you. He is faithful to help you through anything—for His glory!

. . . .

God, thank You for creating me with a purpose and with work to do for You. Align my talents and my passions with the needs in my church, at my job, and at home. I find joy in working willingly for You!

REFLECTION

*"Great and marvelous are your deeds, Lord God
Almighty. Just and true are your ways, King of the nations.
Who will not fear you, Lord, and bring glory to your name?
For you alone are holy. All nations will come and worship
before you, for your righteous acts have been revealed."*

REVELATION 15:3–4 NIV

End-of-the-year retrospectives fill the news cycle as December ends. What happened in 2024? What were the hottest trends, most popular movies, bestselling books? It's a good time for reflection, and that can be true of your own faith journey too. What has God done this year? What prayers did He answer? How did He transform your heart, attitude, and perspective? In what ways have you become more like Jesus?

Revelation 15:3–4 includes a song to the Lamb that celebrates the ultimate deliverance of God's people from the power of Satan. This song sounds a bit like the song of Moses in Exodus 15 that the people sang after God parted the Red Sea and they escaped from Pharaoh's army on dry ground.

The escape of the Israelites was amazing, but how much more miraculous is our salvation from sin and death? Reflect on the marvelous deeds of the Lord God Almighty today and sing a song of praise to the Savior who has saved you for all of eternity.

Jesus, You are worthy of my praise—for all You have done and for all You have yet to do. Thank You for all You have accomplished this year.

A LONG PROCESS

"Just as you, Judah and Israel, have been a curse among
the nations, so I will save you, and you will be a blessing.
Do not be afraid, but let your hands be strong."
ZECHARIAH 8:13 NIV

For more than fifteen years, God and prophets like Zechariah had been urging the Jews to build the temple. A decade and a half is a long time for any building project, and it was one that the people struggled to keep going. Here in Zechariah 8:13, God gave them visions of the future that helped them persevere.

Doing God's work often takes endurance on our part. And when we don't see change or see how our effort makes any difference, we may be tempted to slow down. But don't give up! Paul reminds us of the eternal importance of our work in Colossians 3:23–24 (VOICE), where he writes, "So no matter what your task is, work hard. Always do your best as the Lord's servant, not as man's, because you know your reward is the Lord's inheritance."

Let God's promised future—eternity in His presence—encourage you now. He knows what the results of your work will be. Ask Him to give you the perspective that will keep your hands strong for Him today.

Father, when I am tempted to give less than my
best to You, remind me of what is to come.
My effort in Your kingdom is worth it!

WHAT WE NEED

"From Judah will come the cornerstone, from him the tent peg, from him the battle bow, from him every ruler."
ZECHARIAH 10:4 NIV

When life is especially hard, we aren't always sure what we need to make it through the day. But if we took the time to make a list of our needs, it would likely include things like *strength*, *stability*, *hope*, and *confidence*.

But even on our best days, by ourselves it's a challenge to be strong, to be stable, and to live in hopeful confidence that things will get better. The good news is that we don't have to be all those things . . .that's where Jesus comes in.

This prophecy in Zechariah 10:4 came five hundred years before Jesus arrived on earth as a baby. In it, Christ is called the cornerstone (see also Isaiah 28:16), a tent peg that serves as a strong support (see also Isaiah 22:23), a bow that wins the battle, and a ruler who was a man of action (see also Genesis 29:10; Micah 5:2). The coming Messiah would be strong, stable, victorious, and trustworthy, and Jesus has fulfilled every promise to be those things to all people.

When times are tough, Jesus is the remedy for every need—whether we can pinpoint those needs or not. If you are struggling or feel like you've got everything under control today, find your strength, stability, hope, and confidence in Jesus Christ.

Jesus, thank You for being everything that I need.

FIRE

"I will bring that group through the fire and make them pure.
I will refine them like silver and purify them like gold.
They will call on my name, and I will answer them. I will say,
'These are my people,' and they will say, 'The LORD is our God.'"

ZECHARIAH 13:9 NLT

The Bible uses the imagery of fire to describe both a time of trial as well as a method of purifying precious metals. Gold that is thrust into fire hotter than 1,948 degrees Fahrenheit will melt, allowing impurities to be removed. This process makes the gold stronger and more valuable.

So when the Bible tells us that God will bring us through the fire (Zechariah 13:9) and that He will be with us and protect us through the fire (Isaiah 42:3), we can be confident that God will use trials to remove anything that gets in the way of our complete trust in Him. Then, 1 Peter 1:7 (NLT) says, "when your faith remains strong through many trials, it will bring you much praise and glory and honor on the day when Jesus Christ is revealed to the whole world."

When tough times come, realize that God wants to use them to refine your faith and purify your heart. On the other side of the fire, you will be more like Jesus.

God, I will not fear times of trial, because I
know You are using them to make me stronger.

THE ROLE OF THE PROVERBS 31 WOMAN

Who can find a truly excellent woman? One who is superior in all that she is and all that she does? Her worth far exceeds that of rubies and expensive jewelry.
PROVERBS 31:10 VOICE

Some people say that the Proverbs 31 woman has no place in the twenty-first century—that she is backward, submissive to the point of absurdity, and a slave in her domesticity. But this is simply not true! This amazing woman is an excellent wife and mother. She is also a manufacturer, importer, manager, real estate agent, farmer, seamstress, upholsterer, and merchant. Superwoman has nothing on her!

But her worth does not come from her impressive résumé. It is a result of her faith in God and the wisdom she gleans from His Word. In today's world where physical beauty counts for so much, it's surprising that her appearance is never mentioned. Her attractiveness comes entirely from her character and heart.

We aren't each meant to be clones of the Proverbs 31 woman; we don't have enough hours in the day to do everything she does. Instead, let her inspire you to be all you can be as you walk confidently along the path God has prepared for you.

Lord, I admit that I often feel inadequate when I read Proverbs 31. But You tell me that You aren't finished with me yet, and I am confident that You will continue to do Your good work in me until Jesus comes again.

PRACTICAL INSTRUCTIONS

She is clothed with strength and dignity, and she laughs without fear of the future. When she speaks, her words are wise, and she gives instructions with kindness. . . . Charm is deceptive, and beauty does not last; but a woman who fears the LORD will be greatly praised.

PROVERBS 31:25–26, 30 NLT

Proverbs opens by telling us that the fear of the Lord is the foundation of true knowledge (1:7) and ends with the picture of a virtuous woman who lives out this truth. The qualities she displays and the disciplines she practices are mentioned throughout Proverbs—including hard work, respect for her spouse, foresight, encouragement, peacemaking, care for others, concern for the poor, wisdom in financial matters, and more. These qualities, when coupled with a living faith in God, lead to joy, success, honor, and confidence.

Do you want to be a woman who "laughs without fear of the future," who speaks wisdom, makes good decisions, and loves well? Proverbs offers the practical instructions you need to get closer to this ideal. Ask God to show you how to become more like the Proverbs 31 woman, and in becoming more like her, you will find lasting rewards as you become more like Jesus Christ.

. . . .

Father, as this year closes and another dawns, continue to do Your good work in me. Go before me into 2025 and light my way forward so that I may become more like Jesus every day.

CONTRIBUTORS

Donna K. Maltese is a freelance writer, editor, and writing coach. Mother of two children, grandmother of one very active grandchild, and caretaker of two rescue animals, she resides in Bucks County, Pennsylvania, with her husband. When not reading or writing, Donna, an avid knitter and crocheter, can be found frequently wrestling yarn from her cat. You can check out her website at donnakmaltese.com. Donna's devotions appear in the months of March, July, and November.

Kelly McIntosh is a wife, twin mom, writer, and editor from Ohio. She loves books, the beach, and everything about autumn (but mostly pumpkin spice lattes). Kelly's devotions appear in the months of February, June, and October.

Carey Scott is an author, speaker, and certified Biblical Life Coach. With authenticity and humor, she challenges women to be real, not perfect, and reminds them to trust God as their Source above all else. Carey is a single mom with two kids in college and lives in Colorado. You can find her at CareyScott.org. Carey's devotions appear in January, May, and September.

Annie Tipton made up her first story at the ripe old age of two when she asked her mom to write it down for her. Since then she has read and written many words as a student, newspaper reporter, author, and editor. She has a passion for making God's Word come to life for readers through devotions and Bible study. Annie loves snow (which is a good thing because she lives in Ohio), wearing scarves, eating sushi, playing Scrabble, and spending time with friends and family. Annie's devotions appear in April, August, and December.

READ THROUGH THE BIBLE
IN A YEAR PLAN

1-Jan	Gen. 1-2	Matt. 1	Ps. 1
2-Jan	Gen. 3-4	Matt. 2	Ps. 2
3-Jan	Gen. 5-7	Matt. 3	Ps. 3
4-Jan	Gen. 8-10	Matt. 4	Ps. 4
5-Jan	Gen. 11-13	Matt. 5:1-20	Ps. 5
6-Jan	Gen. 14-16	Matt. 5:21-48	Ps. 6
7-Jan	Gen. 17-18	Matt. 6:1-18	Ps. 7
8-Jan	Gen. 19-20	Matt. 6:19-34	Ps. 8
9-Jan	Gen. 21-23	Matt. 7:1-11	Ps. 9:1-8
10-Jan	Gen. 24	Matt. 7:12-29	Ps. 9:9-20
11-Jan	Gen. 25-26	Matt. 8:1-17	Ps. 10:1-11
12-Jan	Gen. 27:1-28:9	Matt. 8:18-34	Ps. 10:12-18
13-Jan	Gen. 28:10-29:35	Matt. 9	Ps. 11
14-Jan	Gen. 30:1-31:21	Matt. 10:1-15	Ps. 12
15-Jan	Gen. 31:22-32:21	Matt. 10:16-36	Ps. 13
16-Jan	Gen. 32:22-34:31	Matt. 10:37-11:6	Ps. 14
17-Jan	Gen. 35-36	Matt. 11:7-24	Ps. 15
18-Jan	Gen. 37-38	Matt. 11:25-30	Ps. 16
19-Jan	Gen. 39-40	Matt. 12:1-29	Ps. 17
20-Jan	Gen. 41	Matt. 12:30-50	Ps. 18:1-15
21-Jan	Gen. 42-43	Matt. 13:1-9	Ps. 18:16-29
22-Jan	Gen. 44-45	Matt. 13:10-23	Ps. 18:30-50
23-Jan	Gen. 46:1-47:26	Matt. 13:24-43	Ps. 19
24-Jan	Gen. 47:27-49:28	Matt. 13:44-58	Ps. 20
25-Jan	Gen. 49:29-Exod. 1:22	Matt. 14	Ps. 21
26-Jan	Exod. 2-3	Matt. 15:1-28	Ps. 22:1-21
27-Jan	Exod. 4:1-5:21	Matt. 15:29-16:12	Ps. 22:22-31
28-Jan	Exod. 5:22-7:24	Matt. 16:13-28	Ps. 23
29-Jan	Exod. 7:25-9:35	Matt. 17:1-9	Ps. 24
30-Jan	Exod. 10-11	Matt. 17:10-27	Ps. 25
31-Jan	Exod. 12	Matt. 18:1-20	Ps. 26
1-Feb	Exod. 13-14	Matt. 18:21-35	Ps. 27
2-Feb	Exod. 15-16	Matt. 19:1-15	Ps. 28
3-Feb	Exod. 17-19	Matt. 19:16-30	Ps. 29
4-Feb	Exod. 20-21	Matt. 20:1-19	Ps. 30
5-Feb	Exod. 22-23	Matt. 20:20-34	Ps. 31:1-8
6-Feb	Exod. 24-25	Matt. 21:1-27	Ps. 31:9-18
7-Feb	Exod 26-27	Matt. 21:28-46	Ps. 31:19-24
8-Feb	Exod. 28	Matt. 22	Ps. 32
9-Feb	Exod. 29	Matt. 23:1-36	Ps. 33:1-12
10-Feb	Exod. 30-31	Matt. 23:37-24:28	Ps. 33:13-22
11-Feb	Exod. 32-33	Matt. 24:29-51	Ps. 34:1-7
12-Feb	Exod. 34:1-35:29	Matt. 25:1-13	Ps. 34:8-22
13-Feb	Exod. 35:30-37:29	Matt. 25:14-30	Ps. 35:1-8
14-Feb	Exod. 38-39	Matt. 25:31-46	Ps. 35:9-17
15-Feb	Exod. 40	Matt. 26:1-35	Ps. 35:18-28
16-Feb	Lev. 1-3	Matt. 26:36-68	Ps. 36:1-6
17-Feb	Lev. 4:1-5:13	Matt. 26:69-27:26	Ps. 36:7-12
18-Feb	Lev. 5:14 -7:21	Matt. 27:27-50	Ps. 37:1-6
19-Feb	Lev. 7:22-8:36	Matt. 27:51-66	Ps. 37:7-26
20-Feb	Lev. 9-10	Matt. 28	Ps. 37:27-40
21-Feb	Lev. 11-12	Mark 1:1-28	Ps. 38
22-Feb	Lev. 13	Mark 1:29-39	Ps. 39
23-Feb	Lev. 14	Mark 1:40-2:12	Ps. 40:1-8
24-Feb	Lev. 15	Mark 2:13-3:35	Ps. 40:9-17
25-Feb	Lev. 16-17	Mark 4:1-20	Ps. 41:1-4
26-Feb	Lev. 18-19	Mark 4:21-41	Ps. 41:5-13
27-Feb	Lev. 20	Mark 5	Ps. 42-43

28-Feb	Lev. 21-22	Mark 6:1-13	Ps. 44
1-Mar	Lev. 23-24	Mark 6:14-29	Ps. 45:1-5
2-Mar	Lev. 25	Mark 6:30-56	Ps. 45:6-12
3-Mar	Lev. 26	Mark 7	Ps. 45:13-17
4-Mar	Lev. 27	Mark 8	Ps. 46
5-Mar	Num. 1-2	Mark 9:1-13	Ps. 47
6-Mar	Num. 3	Mark 9:14-50	Ps. 48:1-8
7-Mar	Num. 4	Mark 10:1-34	Ps. 48:9-14
8-Mar	Num. 5:1-6:21	Mark 10:35-52	Ps. 49:1-9
9-Mar	Num. 6:22-7:47	Mark 11	Ps. 49:10-20
10-Mar	Num. 7:48-8:4	Mark 12:1-27	Ps. 50:1-15
11-Mar	Num. 8:5-9:23	Mark 12:28-44	Ps. 50:16-23
12-Mar	Num. 10-11	Mark 13:1-8	Ps. 51:1-9
13-Mar	Num. 12-13	Mark 13:9-37	Ps. 51:10-19
14-Mar	Num. 14	Mark 14:1-31	Ps. 52
15-Mar	Num. 15	Mark 14:32-72	Ps. 53
16-Mar	Num. 16	Mark 15:1-32	Ps. 54
17-Mar	Num. 17-18	Mark 15:33-47	Ps. 55
18-Mar	Num. 19-20	Mark 16	Ps. 56:1-7
19-Mar	Num. 21:1-22:20	Luke 1:1-25	Ps. 56:8-13
20-Mar	Num. 22:21-23:30	Luke 1:26-56	Ps. 57
21-Mar	Num. 24-25	Luke 1:57-2:20	Ps. 58
22-Mar	Num. 26:1-27:11	Luke 2:21-38	Ps. 59:1-8
23-Mar	Num. 27:12-29:11	Luke 2:39-52	Ps. 59:9-17
24-Mar	Num. 29:12-30:16	Luke 3	Ps. 60:1-5
25-Mar	Num. 31	Luke 4	Ps. 60:6-12
26-Mar	Num. 32-33	Luke 5:1-16	Ps. 61
27-Mar	Num. 34-36	Luke 5:17-32	Ps. 62:1-6
28-Mar	Deut. 1:1-2:25	Luke 5:33-6:11	Ps. 62:7-12
29-Mar	Deut. 2:26-4:14	Luke 6:12-35	Ps. 63:1-5
30-Mar	Deut. 4:15-5:22	Luke 6:36-49	Ps. 63:6-11
31-Mar	Deut. 5:23-7:26	Luke 7:1-17	Ps. 64:1-5
1-Apr	Deut. 8-9	Luke 7:18-35	Ps. 64:6-10
2-Apr	Deut. 10-11	Luke 7:36-8:3	Ps. 65:1-8
3-Apr	Deut. 12-13	Luke 8:4-21	Ps. 65:9-13
4-Apr	Deut. 14:1-16:8	Luke 8:22-39	Ps. 66:1-7
5-Apr	Deut. 16:9-18:22	Luke 8:40-56	Ps. 66:8-15
6-Apr	Deut. 19:1-21:9	Luke 9:1-22	Ps. 66:16-20
7-Apr	Deut. 21:10-23:8	Luke 9:23-42	Ps. 67
8-Apr	Deut. 23:9-25:19	Luke 9:43-62	Ps. 68:1-6
9-Apr	Deut. 26:1-28:14	Luke 10:1-20	Ps. 68:7-14
10-Apr	Deut. 28:15-68	Luke 10:21-37	Ps. 68:15-19
11-Apr	Deut. 29-30	Luke 10:38-11:23	Ps. 68:20-27
12-Apr	Deut. 31:1-32:22	Luke 11:24-36	Ps. 68:28-35
13-Apr	Deut. 32:23-33:29	Luke 11:37-54	Ps. 69:1-9
14-Apr	Deut. 34-Josh. 2	Luke 12:1-15	Ps. 69:10-17
15-Apr	Josh. 3:1-5:12	Luke 12:16-40	Ps. 69:18-28
16-Apr	Josh. 5:13-7:26	Luke 12:41-48	Ps. 69:29-36
17-Apr	Josh. 8-9	Luke 12:49-59	Ps. 70
18-Apr	Josh. 10:1-11:15	Luke 13:1-21	Ps. 71:1-6
19-Apr	Josh. 11:16-13:33	Luke 13:22-35	Ps. 71:7-16
20-Apr	Josh. 14-16	Luke 14:1-15	Ps. 71:17-21
21-Apr	Josh. 17:1-19:16	Luke 14:16-35	Ps. 71:22-24
22-Apr	Josh. 19:17-21:42	Luke 15:1-10	Ps. 72:1-11
23-Apr	Josh. 21:43-22:34	Luke 15:11-32	Ps. 72:12-20
24-Apr	Josh. 23-24	Luke 16:1-18	Ps. 73:1-9
25-Apr	Judg. 1-2	Luke 16:19-17:10	Ps. 73:10-20
26-Apr	Judg. 3-4	Luke 17:11-37	Ps. 73:21-28
27-Apr	Judg. 5:1-6:24	Luke 18:1-17	Ps. 74:1-3
28-Apr	Judg. 6:25-7:25	Luke 18:18-43	Ps. 74:4-11
29-Apr	Judg. 8:1-9:23	Luke 19:1-28	Ps. 74:12-17
30-Apr	Judg. 9:24-10:18	Luke 19:29-48	Ps. 74:18-23

1-May	Judg. 11:1-12:7	Luke 20:1-26	Ps. 75:1-7
2-May	Judg. 12:8-14:20	Luke 20:27-47	Ps. 75:8-10
3-May	Judg. 15-16	Luke 21:1-19	Ps. 76:1-7
4-May	Judg. 17-18	Luke 21:20-22:6	Ps. 76:8-12
5-May	Judg. 19:1-20:23	Luke 22:7-30	Ps. 77:1-11
6-May	Judg. 20:24-21:25	Luke 22:31-54	Ps. 77:12-20
7-May	Ruth 1-2	Luke 22:55-23:25	Ps. 78:1-4
8-May	Ruth 3-4	Luke 23:26-24:12	Ps. 78:5-8
9-May	1 Sam. 1:1-2:21	Luke 24:13-53	Ps. 78:9-16
10-May	1 Sam. 2:22-4:22	John 1:1-28	Ps. 78:17-24
11-May	1 Sam. 5-7	John 1:29-51	Ps. 78:25-33
12-May	1 Sam. 8:1-9:26	John 2	Ps. 78:34-41
13-May	1 Sam. 9:27-11:15	John 3:1-22	Ps. 78:42-55
14-May	1 Sam. 12-13	John 3:23-4:10	Ps. 78:56-66
15-May	1 Sam. 14	John 4:11-38	Ps. 78:67-72
16-May	1 Sam. 15-16	John 4:39-54	Ps. 79:1-7
17-May	1 Sam. 17	John 5:1-24	Ps. 79:8-13
18-May	1 Sam. 18-19	John 5:25-47	Ps. 80:1-7
19-May	1 Sam. 20-21	John 6:1-21	Ps. 80:8-19
20-May	1 Sam. 22-23	John 6:22-42	Ps. 81:1-10
21-May	1 Sam. 24:1-25:31	John 6:43-71	Ps. 81:11-16
22-May	1 Sam. 25:32-27:12	John 7:1-24	Ps. 82
23-May	1 Sam. 28-29	John 7:25-8:11	Ps. 83
24-May	1 Sam. 30-31	John 8:12-47	Ps. 84:1-4
25-May	2 Sam. 1-2	John 8:48-9:12	Ps. 84:5-12
26-May	2 Sam. 3-4	John 9:13-34	Ps. 85:1-7
27-May	2 Sam. 5:1-7:17	John 9:35-10:10	Ps. 85:8-13
28-May	2 Sam. 7:18-10:19	John 10:11-30	Ps. 86:1-10
29-May	2 Sam. 11:1-12:25	John 10:31-11:16	Ps. 86:11-17
30-May	2 Sam. 12:26-13:39	John 11:17-54	Ps. 87
31-May	2 Sam. 14:1-15:12	John 11:55-12:19	Ps. 88:1-9
1-Jun	2 Sam. 15:13-16:23	John 12:20-43	Ps. 88:10-18
2-Jun	2 Sam. 17:1-18:18	John 12:44-13:20	Ps. 89:1-6
3-Jun	2 Sam. 18:19-19:39	John 13:21-38	Ps. 89:7-13
4-Jun	2 Sam. 19:40-21:22	John 14:1-17	Ps. 89:14-18
5-Jun	2 Sam. 22:1-23:7	John 14:18-15:27	Ps. 89:19-29
6-Jun	2 Sam. 23:8-24:25	John 16:1-22	Ps. 89:30-37
7-Jun	1 Kings 1	John 16:23-17:5	Ps. 89:38-52
8-Jun	1 Kings 2	John 17:6-26	Ps. 90:1-12
9-Jun	1 Kings 3-4	John 18:1-27	Ps. 90:13-17
10-Jun	1 Kings 5-6	John 18:28-19:5	Ps. 91:1-10
11-Jun	1 Kings 7	John 19:6-25a	Ps. 91:11-16
12-Jun	1 Kings 8:1-53	John 19:25b-42	Ps. 92:1-9
13-Jun	1 Kings 8:54-10:13	John 20:1-18	Ps. 92:10-15
14-Jun	1 Kings 10:14-11:43	John 20:19-31	Ps. 93
15-Jun	1 Kings 12:1-13:10	John 21	Ps. 94:1-11
16-Jun	1 Kings 13:11-14:31	Acts 1:1-11	Ps. 94:12-23
17-Jun	1 Kings 15:1-16:20	Acts 1:12-26	Ps. 95
18-Jun	1 Kings 16:21-18:19	Acts 2:1-21	Ps. 96:1-8
19-Jun	1 Kings 18:20-19:21	Acts2:22-41	Ps. 96:9-13
20-Jun	1 Kings 20	Acts 2:42-3:26	Ps. 97:1-6
21-Jun	1 Kings 21:1-22:28	Acts 4:1-22	Ps. 97:7-12
22-Jun	1 Kings 22:29- 2 Kings 1:18	Acts 4:23-5:11	Ps. 98
23-Jun	2 Kings 2-3	Acts 5:12-28	Ps. 99
24-Jun	2 Kings 4	Acts 5:29-6:15	Ps. 100
25-Jun	2 Kings 5:1-6:23	Acts 7:1-16	Ps. 101
26-Jun	2 Kings 6:24-8:15	Acts 7:17-36	Ps. 102:1-7
27-Jun	2 Kings 8:16-9:37	Acts 7:37-53	Ps. 102:8-17
28-Jun	2 Kings 10-11	Acts 7:54-8:8	Ps. 102:18-28
29-Jun	2 Kings 12-13	Acts 8:9-40	Ps. 103:1-9
30-Jun	2 Kings 14-15	Acts 9:1-16	Ps. 103:10-14

1-Jul	2 Kings 16-17	Acts 9:17-31	Ps. 103:15-22
2-Jul	2 Kings 18:1-19:7	Acts 9:32-10:16	Ps. 104:1-9
3-Jul	2 Kings 19:8-20:21	Acts 10:17-33	Ps. 104:10-23
4-Jul	2 Kings 21:1-22:20	Acts 10:34-11:18	Ps. 104: 24-30
5-Jul	2 Kings 23	Acts 11:19-12:17	Ps. 104:31-35
6-Jul	2 Kings 24-25	Acts 12:18-13:13	Ps. 105:1-7
7-Jul	1 Chron. 1-2	Acts 13:14-43	Ps. 105:8-15
8-Jul	1 Chron. 3:1-5:10	Acts 13:44-14:10	Ps. 105:16-28
9-Jul	1 Chron. 5:11-6:81	Acts 14:11-28	Ps. 105:29-36
10-Jul	1 Chron. 7:1-9:9	Acts 15:1-18	Ps. 105:37-45
11-Jul	1 Chron. 9:10-11:9	Acts 15:19-41	Ps. 106:1-12
12-Jul	1 Chron. 11:10-12:40	Acts 16:1-15	Ps. 106:13-27
13-Jul	1 Chron. 13-15	Acts 16:16-40	Ps. 106:28-33
14-Jul	1 Chron. 16-17	Acts 17:1-14	Ps. 106:34-43
15-Jul	1 Chron. 18-20	Acts 17:15-34	Ps. 106:44-48
16-Jul	1 Chron. 21-22	Acts 18:1-23	Ps. 107:1-9
17-Jul	1 Chron. 23-25	Acts 18:24-19:10	Ps. 107:10-16
18-Jul	1 Chron. 26-27	Acts 19:11-22	Ps. 107:17-32
19-Jul	1 Chron. 28-29	Acts 19:23-41	Ps. 107:33-38
20-Jul	2 Chron. 1-3	Acts 20:1-16	Ps. 107:39-43
21-Jul	2 Chron. 4:1-6:11	Acts 20:17-38	Ps. 108
22-Jul	2 Chron. 6:12-7:10	Acts 21:1-14	Ps. 109:1-20
23-Jul	2 Chron. 7:11-9:28	Acts 21:15-32	Ps. 109:21-31
24-Jul	2 Chron. 9:29-12:16	Acts 21:33-22:16	Ps. 110:1-3
25-Jul	2 Chron. 13-15	Acts 22:17-23:11	Ps. 110:4-7
26-Jul	2 Chron. 16-17	Acts 23:12-24:21	Ps. 111
27-Jul	2 Chron. 18-19	Acts 24:22-25:12	Ps. 112
28-Jul	2 Chron. 20-21	Acts 25:13-27	Ps. 113
29-Jul	2 Chron. 22-23	Acts 26	Ps. 114
30-Jul	2 Chron. 24:1-25:16	Acts 27:1-20	Ps. 115:1-10
31-Jul	2 Chron. 25:17-27:9	Acts 27:21-28:6	Ps. 115:11-18
1-Aug	2 Chron. 28:1-29:19	Acts 28:7-31	Ps. 116:1-5
2-Aug	2 Chron. 29:20-30:27	Rom. 1:1-17	Ps. 116:6-19
3-Aug	2 Chron. 31-32	Rom. 1:18-32	Ps. 117
4-Aug	2 Chron. 33:1-34:7	Rom. 2	Ps. 118:1-18
5-Aug	2 Chron. 34:8-35:19	Rom. 3:1-26	Ps. 118:19-23
6-Aug	2 Chron. 35:20-36:23	Rom. 3:27-4:25	Ps. 118:24-29
7-Aug	Ezra 1-3	Rom. 5	Ps. 119:1-8
8-Aug	Ezra 4-5	Rom. 6:1-7:6	Ps. 119:9-16
9-Aug	Ezra 6:1-7:26	Rom. 7:7-25	Ps. 119:17-32
10-Aug	Ezra 7:27-9:4	Rom. 8:1-27	Ps. 119:33-40
11-Aug	Ezra 9:5-10:44	Rom. 8:28-39	Ps. 119:41-64
12-Aug	Neh. 1:1-3:16	Rom. 9:1-18	Ps. 119:65-72
13-Aug	Neh. 3:17-5:13	Rom. 9:19-33	Ps. 119:73-80
14-Aug	Neh. 5:14-7:73	Rom. 10:1-13	Ps. 119:81-88
15-Aug	Neh. 8:1-9:5	Rom. 10:14-11:24	Ps. 119:89-104
16-Aug	Neh. 9:6-10:27	Rom. 11:25-12:8	Ps. 119:105-120
17-Aug	Neh. 10:28-12:26	Rom. 12:9-13:7	Ps. 119:121-128
18-Aug	Neh. 12:27-13:31	Rom. 13:8-14:12	Ps. 119:129-136
19-Aug	Esther 1:1-2:18	Rom. 14:13-15:13	Ps. 119:137-152
20-Aug	Esther 2:19-5:14	Rom. 15:14-21	Ps. 119:153-168
21-Aug	Esther. 6-8	Rom. 15:22-33	Ps. 119:169-176
22-Aug	Esther 9-10	Rom. 16	Ps. 120-122
23-Aug	Job 1-3	1 Cor. 1:1-25	Ps. 123
24-Aug	Job 4-6	1 Cor. 1:26-2:16	Ps. 124-125
25-Aug	Job 7-9	1 Cor. 3	Ps. 126-127
26-Aug	Job 10-13	1 Cor. 4:1-13	Ps. 128-129
27-Aug	Job 14-16	1 Cor. 4:14-5:13	Ps. 130
28-Aug	Job 17-20	1 Cor. 6	Ps. 131
29-Aug	Job 21-23	1 Cor. 7:1-16	Ps. 132
30-Aug	Job 24-27	1 Cor. 7:17-40	Ps. 133-134
31-Aug	Job 28-30	1 Cor. 8	Ps. 135

1-Sep	Job 31-33	1 Cor. 9:1-18	Ps. 136:1-9
2-Sep	Job 34-36	1 Cor. 9:19-10:13	Ps. 136:10-26
3-Sep	Job 37-39	1 Cor. 10:14-11:1	Ps. 137
4-Sep	Job 40-42	1 Cor. 11:2-34	Ps. 138
5-Sep	Eccles. 1:1-3:15	1 Cor. 12:1-26	Ps. 139:1-6
6-Sep	Eccles. 3:16-6:12	1 Cor. 12:27-13:13	Ps. 139:7-18
7-Sep	Eccles. 7:1-9:12	1 Cor. 14:1-22	Ps. 139:19-24
8-Sep	Eccles. 9:13-12:14	1 Cor. 14:23-15:11	Ps. 140:1-8
9-Sep	SS 1-4	1 Cor. 15:12-34	Ps. 140:9-13
10-Sep	SS 5-8	1 Cor. 15:35-58	Ps. 141
11-Sep	Isa. 1-2	1 Cor. 16	Ps. 142
12-Sep	Isa. 3-5	2 Cor. 1:1-11	Ps. 143:1-6
13-Sep	Isa. 6-8	2 Cor. 1:12-2:4	Ps. 143:7-12
14-Sep	Isa. 9-10	2 Cor. 2:5-17	Ps. 144
15-Sep	Isa. 11-13	2 Cor. 3	Ps. 145
16-Sep	Isa. 14-16	2 Cor. 4	Ps. 146
17-Sep	Isa. 17-19	2 Cor. 5	Ps. 147:1-11
18-Sep	Isa. 20-23	2 Cor. 6	Ps. 147:12-20
19-Sep	Isa. 24:1-26:19	2 Cor. 7	Ps. 148
20-Sep	Isa. 26:20-28:29	2 Cor. 8	Ps. 149-150
21-Sep	Isa. 29-30	2 Cor. 9	Prov. 1:1-9
22-Sep	Isa. 31-33	2 Cor. 10	Prov. 1:10-22
23-Sep	Isa. 34-36	2 Cor. 11	Prov. 1:23-26
24-Sep	Isa. 37-38	2 Cor. 12:1-10	Prov. 1:27-33
25-Sep	Isa. 39-40	2 Cor. 12:11-13:14	Prov. 2:1-15
26-Sep	Isa. 41-42	Gal. 1	Prov. 2:16-22
27-Sep	Isa. 43:1-44:20	Gal. 2	Prov. 3:1-12
28-Sep	Isa. 44:21-46:13	Gal. 3:1-18	Prov. 3:13-26
29-Sep	Isa. 47:1-49:13	Gal 3:19-29	Prov. 3:27-35
30-Sep	Isa. 49:14-51:23	Gal 4:1-11	Prov. 4:1-19
1-Oct	Isa. 52-54	Gal. 4:12-31	Prov. 4:20-27
2-Oct	Isa. 55-57	Gal. 5	Prov. 5:1-14
3-Oct	Isa. 58-59	Gal. 6	Prov. 5:15-23
4-Oct	Isa. 60-62	Eph. 1	Prov. 6:1-5
5-Oct	Isa. 63:1-65:16	Eph. 2	Prov. 6:6-19
6-Oct	Isa. 65:17-66:24	Eph. 3:1-4:16	Prov. 6:20-26
7-Oct	Jer. 1-2	Eph. 4:17-32	Prov. 6:27-35
8-Oct	Jer. 3:1-4:22	Eph. 5	Prov. 7:1-5
9-Oct	Jer. 4:23-5:31	Eph. 6	Prov. 7:6-27
10-Oct	Jer. 6:1-7:26	Phil. 1:1-26	Prov. 8:1-11
11-Oct	Jer. 7:26-9:16	Phil. 1:27-2:18	Prov. 8:12-21
12-Oct	Jer. 9:17-11:17	Phil 2:19-30	Prov. 8:22-36
13-Oct	Jer. 11:18-13:27	Phil. 3	Prov. 9:1-6
14-Oct	Jer. 14-15	Phil. 4	Prov. 9:7-18
15-Oct	Jer. 16-17	Col. 1:1-23	Prov. 10:1-5
16-Oct	Jer. 18:1-20:6	Col. 1:24-2:15	Prov. 10:6-14
17-Oct	Jer. 20:7-22:19	Col. 2:16-3:4	Prov. 10:15-26
18-Oct	Jer. 22:20-23:40	Col. 3:5-4:1	Prov. 10:27-32
19-Oct	Jer. 24-25	Col. 4:2-18	Prov. 11:1-11
20-Oct	Jer. 26-27	1 Thes. 1:1-2:8	Prov. 11:12-21
21-Oct	Jer. 28-29	1 Thes. 2:9-3:13	Prov. 11:22-26
22-Oct	Jer. 30:1-31:22	1 Thes. 4:1-5:11	Prov. 11:27-31
23-Oct	Jer. 31:23-32:35	1 Thes. 5:12-28	Prov. 12:1-14
24-Oct	Jer. 32:36-34:7	2 Thes. 1-2	Prov. 12:15-20
25-Oct	Jer. 34:8-36:10	2 Thes. 3	Prov. 12:21-28
26-Oct	Jer. 36:11-38:13	1 Tim. 1:1-17	Prov. 13:1-4
27-Oct	Jer. 38:14-40:6	1 Tim. 1:18-3:13	Prov. 13:5-13
28-Oct	Jer. 40:7-42:22	1 Tim. 3:14-4:10	Prov. 13:14-21
29-Oct	Jer. 43-44	1 Tim. 4:11-5:16	Prov. 13:22-25
30-Oct	Jer. 45-47	1 Tim. 5:17-6:21	Prov. 14:1-6
31-Oct	Jer. 48:1-49:6	2 Tim. 1	Prov. 14:7-22
1-Nov	Jer. 49:7-50:16	2 Tim. 2	Prov. 14:23-27

2-Nov	Jer. 50:17-51:14	2 Tim. 3	Prov. 14:28-35
3-Nov	Jer. 51:15-64	2 Tim. 4	Prov. 15:1-9
4-Nov	Jer. 52-Lam. 1	Ti. 1:1-9	Prov. 15:10-17
5-Nov	Lam. 2:1-3:38	Ti. 1:10-2:15	Prov. 15:18-26
6-Nov	Lam. 3:39-5:22	Ti. 3	Prov. 15:27-33
7-Nov	Ezek. 1:1-3:21	Philemon 1	Prov. 16:1-9
8-Nov	Ezek. 3:22-5:17	Heb. 1:1-2:4	Prov. 16:10-21
9-Nov	Ezek. 6-7	Heb. 2:5-18	Prov. 16:22-33
10-Nov	Ezek. 8-10	Heb. 3:1-4:3	Prov. 17:1-5
11-Nov	Ezek. 11-12	Heb. 4:4-5:10	Prov. 17:6-12
12-Nov	Ezek. 13-14	Heb. 5:11-6:20	Prov. 17:13-22
13-Nov	Ezek. 15:1-16:43	Heb. 7:1-28	Prov. 17:23-28
14-Nov	Ezek. 16:44-17:24	Heb. 8:1-9:10	Prov. 18:1-7
15-Nov	Ezek. 18-19	Heb. 9:11-28	Prov. 18:8-17
16-Nov	Ezek. 20	Heb. 10:1-25	Prov. 18:18-24
17-Nov	Ezek. 21-22	Heb. 10:26-39	Prov. 19:1-8
18-Nov	Ezek. 23	Heb. 11:1-31	Prov. 19:9-14
19-Nov	Ezek. 24-26	Heb. 11:32-40	Prov. 19:15-21
20-Nov	Ezek. 27-28	Heb. 12:1-13	Prov. 19:22-29
21-Nov	Ezek. 29-30	Heb. 12:14-29	Prov. 20:1-18
22-Nov	Ezek. 31-32	Heb. 13	Prov. 20:19-24
23-Nov	Ezek. 33:1-34:10	Jas. 1	Prov. 20:25-30
24-Nov	Ezek. 34:11-36:15	Jas. 2	Prov. 21:1-8
25-Nov	Ezek. 36:16-37:28	Jas. 3	Prov. 21:9-18
26-Nov	Ezek. 38-39	Jas. 4:1-5:6	Prov. 21:19-24
27-Nov	Ezek. 40	Jas. 5:7-20	Prov. 21:25-31
28-Nov	Ezek. 41:1-43:12	1 Pet. 1:1-12	Prov. 22:1-9
29-Nov	Ezek. 43:13-44:31	1 Pet. 1:13-2:3	Prov. 22:10-23
30-Nov	Ezek. 45-46	1 Pet. 2:4-17	Prov. 22:24-29
1-Dec	Ezek. 47-48	1 Pet. 2:18-3:7	Prov. 23:1-9
2-Dec	Dan. 1:1-2:23	1 Pet. 3:8-4:19	Prov. 23:10-16
3-Dec	Dan. 2:24-3:30	1 Pet. 5	Prov. 23:17-25
4-Dec	Dan. 4	2 Pet. 1	Prov. 23:26-35
5-Dec	Dan. 5	2 Pet. 2	Prov. 24:1-18
6-Dec	Dan. 6:1-7:14	2 Pet. 3	Prov. 24:19-27
7-Dec	Dan. 7:15-8:27	1 John 1:1-2:17	Prov. 24:28-34
8-Dec	Dan. 9-10	1 John 2:18-29	Prov. 25:1-12
9-Dec	Dan. 11-12	1 John 3:1-12	Prov. 25:13-17
10-Dec	Hos. 1-3	1 John 3:13-4:16	Prov. 25:18-28
11-Dec	Hos. 4-6	1 John 4:17-5:21	Prov. 26:1-16
12-Dec	Hos. 7-10	2 John	Prov. 26:17-21
13-Dec	Hos. 11-14	3 John	Prov. 26:22-27:9
14-Dec	Joel 1:1-2:17	Jude	Prov. 27:10-17
15-Dec	Joel 2:18-3:21	Rev. 1:1-2:11	Prov. 27:18-27
16-Dec	Amos 1:1-4:5	Rev. 2:12-29	Prov. 28:1-8
17-Dec	Amos 4:6-6:14	Rev. 3	Prov. 28:9-16
18-Dec	Amos 7-9	Rev. 4:1-5:5	Prov. 28:17-24
19-Dec	Obad-Jonah	Rev. 5:6-14	Prov. 28:25-28
20-Dec	Mic. 1:1-4:5	Rev. 6:1-7:8	Prov. 29:1-8
21-Dec	Mic. 4:6-7:20	Rev. 7:9-8:13	Prov. 29:9-14
22-Dec	Nah. 1-3	Rev. 9-10	Prov. 29:15-23
23-Dec	Hab. 1-3	Rev. 11	Prov. 29:24-27
24-Dec	Zeph. 1-3	Rev. 12	Prov. 30:1-6
25-Dec	Hag. 1-2	Rev. 13:1-14:13	Prov. 30:7-16
26-Dec	Zech. 1-4	Rev. 14:14-16:3	Prov. 30:17-20
27-Dec	Zech. 5-8	Rev. 16:4-21	Prov. 30:21-28
28-Dec	Zech. 9-11	Rev. 17:1-18:8	Prov. 30:29-33
29-Dec	Zech. 12-14	Rev. 18:9-24	Prov. 31:1-9
30-Dec	Mal. 1-2	Rev. 19-20	Prov. 31:10-17
31-Dec	Mal. 3-4	Rev. 21-22	Prov. 31:18-31

SCRIPTURE INDEX

OLD TESTAMENT

NEW TESTAMENT